*interrogating* TEXTS

General Editors
PATRICIA WAUGH AND LYNNE PEARCE

Titles in the INTERROGATING TEXTS series

Already published:

**Practising Postmodernism/Reading Modernism**
Patricia Waugh

**Reading Dialogics**
Lynne Pearce

**Critical Desire**
*Psychoanalysis and the Literary Subject*
Linda R. Williams

**Cunning Passages**
*New Historicism, Cultural Materialism, and Marxism in the Contemporary Literary Debate*
Jeremy Hawthorn

**Theorising the Fantastic**
Lucie Armitt

Forthcoming:

**Essentially Plural**
*Feminist Literary Theory*
Marion Wynne-Davies

# THEORISING THE FANTASTIC

Lucie Armitt
Lecturer in English,
University of Wales, Bangor

A member of the Hodder Headline Group
LONDON • NEW YORK • SYDNEY • AUCKLAND

First published in Great Britain 1996 by
Arnold, a member of the Hodder Headline Group,
338 Euston Road, London NW1 3BH
175 Fifth Avenue, New York, NY 10010

Distributed exclusively in the USA by
St Martin's Press, Inc.
175 Fifth Avenue, New York, NY 10010



*British Library Cataloguing in Publication Data*
A catalogue record for this book is available from the British Library

*Library of Congress Cataloging-in-Publication Data*
Armitt, Lucie, 1962–
Theorising the fantastic/Lucie Armitt
p. cm. – (Interrogating texts)
Includes bibliographical references and index.
ISBN 0–340–67726–0 (hardbound). – ISBN 0–340–60587–1 (pbk.)
1. Fantastic literature–History and criticism. 2. Fantastic. The (Aesthetics), in literature. I. Title. II. Series.
PN56.F34A74 1996
809.3'8766–dc20 96–21671
CIP

ISBN 0 340 67726 0 (hb)
ISBN 0 340 60587 1 (pb)

Typeset in 10 on 12pt Palatino by
Phoenix Photosetting, Chatham, Kent
Printed and bound in Great Britain by
J. W. Arrowsmith Ltd, Bristol

# Contents

# General Editors' Preface

*Interrogating Texts* is a series which aims to take literary theory – its key proponents, debates, and textual practices – towards the next century.

As editors we believe that despite the much vaunted 'retreat from theory', there is so far little material evidence of this supposed backlash. Publishers' catalogues reveal 'theory' (be it literary, cultural, philosophical or psychoanalytic) to be an expanding rather than a contracting market, and courses in literary theory and textual practice have now been established in most institutions of higher education throughout Europe and North America.

Despite significant improvements to high school syllabuses in recent years, however, most students still arrive at university or college ill-prepared for the 'revolution' that has shaken English studies in the past twenty years. Amid the welter of increasingly sophisticated and specialized critical works that now fills our libraries and bookshops, there is a pressing need for volumes like those represented by this series: volumes that will summarize, contextualize and *interrogate* the key debates informing contemporary literary theory and, most importantly, assess and demonstrate the *effectiveness* of the different approaches in the reading of literary texts.

It is, indeed, in its 'conceptual' approach to theory, and its 'interrogation' of theory *through* textual practice, that the series claims to be most strikingly new and distinctive. Instead of presenting literary theory as a series of 'approaches' (eg., Structuralism, Marxism, Feminism) that can be mechanistically 'applied' to any text, each volume will begin by examining the epistemological and conceptual frameworks of the theoretical discourse in question and examine the way in which its philosophical and political premises compare and contrast with those of other contemporary discourses. (The volumes on *Postmodernism* and *Dialogics* both consider their epistemological relation to the other, for example.) Each volume, too, will provide an historical overview of the key proponents, texts, and debates represented by the theory, as well as an evaluative survey of the different ways in which the theory has been appropriated and deployed by literary critics. Alongside this informative and evaluative contextualization of the theory, each volume will perform readings of a selection of literary texts. The aim of these readings, as indicated earlier, is not simplistically to demonstrate the way in which the theory in question can be 'applied' to a text, but to question the suitability of certain aspects of the theory *vis-à-vis* certain texts, and ultimately to use the texts to *interrogate the theory itself*: to reveal its own inadequacies, limitations and blindspots.

Two of the most suggestive theoretical keywords of the 1980s were *dialogue* and *difference*. The *Interrogating Texts* series aims to (re)activate both terms in its attempt to map the great shifts and developments (the 'continental drift'?!) of literary theory over the past twenty years and into the twenty-first century: the differences both within and between the various theoretical discourses, and the dialogues that inhere and connect them.

Eschewing the mechanical association between theory and practice, it should also be pointed out that the individual volumes belonging to the series do not conform to any organizational template. Each author has been allowed to negotiate the relationship between theory and text as he or she thinks best, and in recognition of the fact that some of our theoretical categories will require a very different presentation to others.

Although both the substance and the critical evolution of the theoretical discourses represented by this series are often extremely complex, we hope that the perspectives and interrogations offered by our authors will make them readily accessible to a new generation of readers. The 'beginnings' of literary theory as a revolutionary threat and disruption to the Academy are fast receding into history, but their challenge – what they offer each of us in our relentless interrogation of literary texts – lives on.

Lynne Pearce
Patricia Waugh
1996

# Acknowledgements

Special thanks are due to a number of people who, during the course of this project, have provided personal and professional help and support. My first acknowledgement must go to Lynne Pearce and Pat Waugh, both of whom and in differing ways have been deeply influential to my career. As always Jean, Eric and Judith Armitt have given their unquestioning support and that is especially appreciated. I also wish to thank my colleagues at the University of Wales, Bangor and my former colleagues at Bolton Institute for help ranging from general support to the more tangible loaning of books and video material. Among these, particular thanks go to Tom Corns, Jon Glover, Peter Kitson, Janet Lewison, Jill Marsden, John Peacocke, Steve Price, David Rudd and Martin Thomasson. David Punter and Paulina Palmer were early readers of some of the ideas discussed here and much gratitude goes out to them for believing these worthy of further development. Thanks also go to Christopher Wheeler of Arnold. Three people, in particular, have my total admiration. The first of these is Linda Jones, for her unquestioning help and patience and her significant computing expertise. The second is Susan Bassnett, whose loyalty, interest and unstinting encouragement continue to make her the very best possible mentor. The third is Scott Brewster for – well everything really.

**Dedicated to the memory of**
**Kathryn Emma Mason**
**1966–1995**

# Introduction: Situating Fantasy and the Fantastic

'Fantastic', like its partner 'fabulous', carries unequivocally positive (if imprecise) connotations in common speech. But place it in a literary context and suddenly we have a problem. Suddenly it is something dubious, embarrassing (because presumed extra-canonical). Suddenly we need to justify our interest in it. What we overlook when situating fantasy on the margins of literary creativity is that fantasy (or at least 'phantasy') is central to all fictional work. As psychoanalysis tells us, phantasy is that intangible source of unconscious fears and desires which fuels our dreams, our phobias and therefore our narrative fictions. It is this understanding of the related word fantasy that we tend to draw upon in everyday parlance. The reason for fantasy's conventionally marginal stance in literary terms is that we deliberately forget this aspect of its impact and prioritize certain specifically content-led groupings which celebrate reader gratification at the expense of the 'literary'. Thus, while the word 'fantasy' can and often does mean different things to different readers, its presumed association with the formulaic inevitably attracts two negative constants: escapism and pulp fiction. Once we have introduced these, it takes only a small step not just to connect fantasy with 'popular' rather than 'serious' literature, but actually to presume that the terms fantasy fiction and formula fiction are simple synonyms for each other.

For reasons not unconnected with this, it is traditional for the first page of an academic study of literary fantasy to gesture the reader in with a (direct or indirect) apology. Irving Massey's excellent study of the metamorphic, for example, opens with a rather self-deprecating reference to its own morbidity, while Kathryn Hume sets up her own reading of fantasy by situating it in relation to the rather more 'acceptable' mimesis.[1] Literary fantasy and the fantastic have always fascinated many committed and well-informed critics, most of whom have self-consciously set up their work from a standpoint of canonical marginalization, some explicitly using their research on the fantastic as a pleasurable (even recreational) diversion from what they perceive to be more 'weighty' publications. It is not saying anything new to claim that those literary modes which are anti-realist and pro-fantastic have often been considered more frivolous than the mimetic. The history of the novel is generally read as a history of mimesis and, in more general terms, we only need to look at the work of Coleridge to see how the slur of the 'fanciful' has traditionally helped to conspire against any sustained and serious appreciation of this field.[2] This can have its advantages, for it certainly helps to perpetuate the productive association of fantasy and the fantastic with the world of the anti-conventional. But is it always and intrinsically productive to document fantasy in these terms? As Kathryn Hume recognizes, '[All m]odern literature is in its way a literature of quest, a literature . . . in search of its proper form rather than already possessed of that form'[3] and in that sense it shares much of fantasy's commitment to innovation. Indeed, many of contemporary literature's most interesting trends have been inherited from fantasy forms. Hume's use of the word 'quest' here infers this, drawing upon a typical fantasy trope as the impetus for a whole literary projection beyond the limitations of the known, the familiar (indeed the well-worn). Fantasy, even when projecting backwards into the past, foregrounds a trajectory into an unknown that, in textual terms, is always new and therefore always pointing forwards into the future (even in the sense of the new territory of the next page). Nor should we overlook Hume's utilization of the phrase 'proper form' here. Just as the individual form of the metamorphic body stands at the centre of the transforming dimensions of fantasy fictions, so here the whole of literature emerges as a collectively shapeshifting body of work. As we will see, this ultimately conspires against reducing the innovations of the fantastic to the formal fixities of genre theory.

That the body has a collective as much as an individual significance reminds us of its aptitude for the literary exploration of socio-political subversions. The important work of Rosemary Jackson highlights this when, utilizing the discourse of psychoanalysis as the foundation for her approach to fantasy, she argues that the relationship fantasy narratives have with 'the unsaid and the unseen . . . that which has been silenced, made invisible, covered over and made "absent"' render them particularly well-suited as a mode for such representations.[4] Certainly feminist writers and critics have capitalized on this, developing a substantial corpus of work which utilizes genre fantasy to reconceive gender relations in so-called 'other' cultural spaces as a means of interrogating our own ideological and narrative structures.[5] Rather more reactionary critics have taken very different advantage of Jackson's reading however, using fantasy's existence as a subversive medium as an excuse for *refusing* to engage with at least one of the more disruptive of recent critical innovations: the fabulous world of critical theory. If, such critics argue, fantasy is at its most subversive when located on the margins of the canon, then surely there is much to be said for it being likewise located on the margins of theory. It is by no means unusual for theory to be shunned as a high-brow tool of the intellectual establishment, and it is argued to be anomalous, in these terms, to try and relate it to what are often perceived to be anti-elitist fantasy forms.

But is it any longer true that fantasy fictions are 'popular' in the way that tradition implies? The very subversiveness that Jackson perceives to be at work in the fantastic has meant that recent developments in general fiction have led to it paying more and more heed to fantastic tropes while actively resisting generic reductionism. The benefit of this is that it is becoming increasingly possible to challenge the assumption that we need understand the position or indeed the identity of fantasy in terms of unimaginative either/or choices (marvellous or fabulous, space opera or sword and sorcery, fable or myth). Now we can look at the fantastic as a form of writing which is about opening up subversive spaces within the mainstream rather than ghettoizing fantasy by encasing it within genres. In the process it also retains its important subversive properties without capitulating to classification. Any reader who makes even the most tentative of inroads into the vast body of critical material on fantasy literature will discover that, at least historically, by far the majority of this work concerns itself solely with issues of classification and categorization and the manner in which the generic limits which define and confine texts can be continually tightened and made ever more absolute. So Kingsley Amis, asserting that 'There are usually good reasons for the existence of barriers', regrets the increasing tendency for speculative fictions to place as much importance upon style as content and integrate into their narrative structures 'tricks with typography, one-line chapters, strained metaphors, obscurities, obscenities, drugs, Oriental religions and left-wing politics'.[6] Few approaches could render more explicit the connection between ideological and literary conservativism.

Inevitably, Amis tells us less about the state of contemporary fantasy fictions and more about the way in which traditional science-fiction criticism operates. Genre is simply a convenient label that points us in the direction of a particular type of writing. It is neither a positive nor a negative determinant of quality. Approaches such as his will never do anything to legitimize the position of fantasy as a 'literary' critical discourse. Fantasy (at least in its most creative of guises) is, like all other literary modes, fluid, constantly overspilling the very forms it adopts, always looking, not so much for escapism but certainly to escape the constraints that critics like this always and inevitably impose upon it. As Tzvetan Todorov acknowledges: 'Genre represents . . . a configuration of literary properties, an inventory of options. But a work's inclusion within a genre still teaches us nothing as to its meaning.'[7] If we perceive genre as a category that 'contains' (being entirely content-led), then the fact that the fantastic concerns itself with the world of the 'beyond' (beyond the galaxy, beyond the known, beyond the accepted, beyond belief) should immediately alert us to the attendant difficulties it has coping with limits and limitations. How strange that its traditional critics should have worked so hard to lock it up within a conceptual cage.

## Textual Play and its Spatial Dimensions

Whether one feels positively or negatively about fantasy and the fantastic, it is the concept of game-playing that structures our assumptions about its pleasures. This can conspire against its success for, in texts such as Lewis Carroll's *Alice in Wonderland* (1871) and *Through the Looking Glass* (1865), it is precisely these playful tropes that have historically projected them beyond the realms of serious study except insofar as they appeal to child readers. But one of the best 'traditional' studies of fantasy fictions, W.R. Irwin's *The Game of the Impossible*, brands such conceptual play through the very title of the text. In his terms, such dynamics must accompany these textual violations and their attendant contraventions of the rules of the 'real'.[8] Play is perceived to be synonymous with pleasure, both sharing an etymological connection. Play also appears to be inherently carnivalesque for, as Roger Abrahams asserts, it 'invokes the power of license or excuse just at the point where society would begin to impinge with its "but seriously . . ." rules'.[9] What we realize at this point, however, is that precisely because play is determined by an implied prohibition that says it may only take place within certain temporal and spatial constraints (between but not within lessons, and within the playground not the classroom), it is often analogous with the pleasures of all texts. For they too are 'bound' and the narratives they contain 'framed' by textual devices that cut them off from the outside world. Indeed, according to Roland Barthes, the play of the text is far more carnivalesque than the playing about that takes place beyond its covers. So, in *Mythologies*, he bemoans the fact that children's toys seem increasingly to replicate adult reality for, as a result, 'the child can only identify himself as owner, as user, never as creator'. Freud on the other hand always insists that the relationship between play and phantasy is an intrinsically creative one: 'Might we not say that every child at play behaves like a creative writer, in that he creates a world of his own, or, rather, rearranges the things of his world in a new way which pleases him?'[10]

On one level, we might argue that historical markers determine the distinctions intrinsic to these contradictory readings. Barthes places his essay in a specific cultural and temporal location (1950s France), while Freud seems to be talking in ahistoric terms. He speaks as if the world of child's play is both timeless and somehow always distinct from, if parallel to, that of adulthood. In this context play fails to replicate the chronological determinants and shifts of 'reality'. But both have relevance in differing ways to our understanding of the world of the fantastic. As James R. Kincaid reminds us, adults often prefer the idea (the fantasy) of child's play to the reality of its rather monotonous repetitions[11] and, if we apply this to the reading rather than the writing of fantasy texts, we see its significance in literary terms. Instead of Massey's metamorphic morbidities, what we find are the spurious consolations of a formulaic melancholia as we endlessly return to generic repetition.[12] Barthes's words imply that adults are driven by the search for a lost realm of pleasure that must always and inevitably evade our grasp (even as applied to the world of the child), whereas Freud suggests that fantasy's segregation from linear chronology seems positively to *invite* such futile regressions. In some cases temporality itself becomes obsolete, insofar as forms like the fairy tale or the utopia contextualize narrative chronology in terms of what are effectively two competing spatial dimensions. Thus, 'within the outer frame of timelessness, we have an inner frame of sequentially structured time that relies on the day as the basic unit of reference'.[13] That toys and child's play are frequently foregrounded images in both child and adult fantasy fictions is clear from narratives as different as *The Magic Toyshop* (1967) and *Peter Pan* (1904). But what both of these otherwise very distinct texts show, is that their spatial disruptions are predominantly driven by an awareness of maturity (sexual or otherwise) as loss. This feeds into Barthes's reading of the creative dynamic, whereby the writer likewise becomes a plaything of the text, toyed with by loss, 'since the language that constitutes him (writing) is always outside-of-place . . . he is the joker of the pack . . . the dummy in the bridge game'.[14]

This determining sense of the 'outside-of-place' confirms what we already suspect: it is the spatial that determines the realm of textual dynamics, particularly in the context of fantasy forms. As Mary Bittner Wiseman acknowledges, the very language of the text reflects this in being 'an ordered space, a horizon implying a boundary and a perspective, a frontier . . . a limit beyond which lies all that the writer could not say'. The irony of this is that while Barthes's world of child's play is a reductive world threaded through with mimeses and tautology, the world within the text is set free to become a genuine space of creative free- and fore-play. So Barthes associates the functioning of the text with 'trickery and imposture, decoys and baffles, cheatings and leadings astray'.[15] This is not the redundant discourse of genre fiction, it is the narrative equivalent of flirtation, masquerade and sleight of hand. In narrative terms, then, these fictions position their readers as creatures of fore-pleasure, playing upon our own sense of adulthood as bereavement, endlessly anticipating the arrival of a bliss that can never be fulfilled 'in reality'.

But neither play nor space, in and of themselves, necessarily resist reductive and over-protective enclosures. As the very terms 'playground' and 'play-pen' demonstrate, what masquerades as licence is actually a prohibitive structure held in place by firm, territorial demarcations. So Freud, perhaps the first theorist to apply spatial concepts to literary texts, draws an analogy between the writer as game-player and the text as the space within which that play takes place. As he goes to great pains to emphasize, the dimensions and locations of the spatial dynamic are never seriously called into question: 'In spite of all the emotion with which he cathects his world of play, the child distinguishes it quite well from reality . . . The creative writer does the same . . . He creates a world of phantasy . . . while separating it sharply from reality'[16]. Of course we remember that, for Freud, no differentiation exists in these terms between literary fantasy and literary realism. Nevertheless, the analogy holds. If we take his spatial dynamic as a model to apply to the differentation, not between phantasying and reality, but between literary fantasy and literary realism, we discover that this poses a problem for our reading of fantasy purely and simply in terms of genre. W.R. Irwin is keen to differentiate between modes of fantasy determined by their contents and fantastic impulses which drive texts in terms of rather more interrogative strategies. Although Irwin does not explicitly use this to interrogate genre, this is clearly the logical next step. This is also what separates Barthes' work from the Freudian play(ing)-pen, which encloses the play to keep (generic) horizons clearly and carefully discrete from the amorphous outside world of (grown-up) general fiction. Unlike Freud's text, this space struggles to enclose and inscribe the 'free-play' of the signifier that always plays on and around the limitations of the beyond: just like the fantastic itself. Another way of putting this is expressed by Irwin when he perceives the zone of the fantastic to be one in which there 'is a competition for credence in which an assertive "anti-real" plays against an established "real"'.[17]

Chapter 1 of this text explores to the full the emerging dialectic which thrives upon this spatial tension between the static and the dynamic. No theory of the fantastic has more productively utilized this than the groundbreaking work of Todorov, whose impact upon current and recent developments in our reading of fantasy and the fantastic is often not sufficiently valued. Although couched within and seemingly belonging to that form of structuralism that gives birth to the compartmentalization approach to fantasy, Todorov ultimately moves on beyond this. In my view it is only through his crucial differentiation between fantasy as genre fiction and the fantastic as a far more resistant, anti-generic mode that the real potential of this field has been fully opened up to the challenge of critical theory. With this in mind I have adopted his differentiation between 'fantasy' and 'the fantastic' in my usage of terminology throughout this book. But in addition, subsequent developments in theory have now enabled Todorov to be read in a rather more radical and innovative way. By reading him through the filter of Michel Foucault and Georges Bataille, the fantastic is not only opened up to Jackson's socio-political implications, but also to an even fuller theorisation of the workings of the fantastic as the discourse of the limit and what we will see to be its attendant interrogative potential for textual readings.

In many ways it is the gothic, of all fantasy modes, that forms the closest parallel with Todorovian readings of the fantastic. Structured around the discourse of the uncanny, unlike the defamiliarizations of science fiction this world has invaded our own space to fracture and disrupt the reassuring presence of inner worlds. Like metamorphosis, it takes the everyday and forces it into a grotesque relationship with the body – here the body of the house. Gaston Bachelard's key study of the spatial as a site of human intimacy and desire replicates this common dynamic. Taking the location of the house as a starting-point for our relationship with the universe, he points to the dialectical basis of the inner and the outer. Few concepts could more closely align themselves with the fantasy form of gothic fictions than Bachelard's belief that 'the old house is "inured" by its trials'. So, even as we 'feel calmer and more confident when in the old home, in the house we are born in', we nevertheless use it as a site of imagination. Sitting alone while the storm rages, we personify the outside as an antagonist determined to break down the doors and the universe as an invader of our innermost space.[18] In line with this, Chapter 2, dealing with the work of psychoanalytic theory, opens with an evaluation of Freud's work on literary texts as rather static, 'day-dreaming' spaces. His approach results in precisely the type of consolatory mechanisms which fantasy read purely as genre must offer. Only later in his career, when he comes to address the literary implications of the night-dream world of 'The "Uncanny"',[19] can his work provide subsequent links with Todorov and more recent theorists such as Hélène Cixous and Julia Kristeva, opening up new and exciting conceptual terrain.

We are unlikely to be surprised by the fantastic's spatial concerns. 'Space opera', 'outer space' and even 'inner space' are terms with which we have had close textual encounters for as long as we have been reading and watching popular fantasy narratives. But, as my references to Bachelard already imply, space has increasingly become a central metaphor for a number of competing literary (and) theoretical terms in a manner that inevitably evokes the fantastic, even when informing other conceptual paradigms. In line with this, when we read the title of Madeleine Davis and David Wallbridge's book *Boundary and Space*,[20] we might expect it to be less a study of the work of the object-relations theorist D.W. Winnicott, and more a work on outer- or inner-space fiction. It is precisely such shared vocabulary as this that has helped to alert us to the productive links existing between the fantastic and literary theory.

## Alien Territory and Border Crossings

References to borders and frontiers have always been the staple discourse of outer-space fiction. If fantasy is about being absent from home (the abandoned child or assertive voyager of the fairy tale, the science-fiction traveller or pioneer, and the inhabitant of the gothic mansion who finds her space invaded from within by the presence of the uncanny), then the inhabitant of the fantastic is always the stranger. What more recent innovations in fantasy studies have demonstrated is the significance this has for the workings of our inner cultural spaces. Looking at Kristeva's *Strangers to Ourselves*, we find her addressing the issue of the alien without in terms of the alien within. But the term 'without' here does not simply operate as a synonym for 'outside'; in psychoanalytic terms it also functions to indicate the unconscious presence of lack as it encodes itself within the maternal.[21] I have already suggested that one explanation for the particular pleasures offered by the literary fantastic derives from a prevalent awareness of loss. This frequently articulates itself in relation to the mother. So, Bachelard tells us, the human-like qualities of the house of our birth are also the qualities of the space of our birth: 'The house clung to me, like a she-wolf, and at times, I could smell her odor penetrating maternally to my very heart. That night she really was my mother.'[22] In this sense all fantastic fictions of otherness become projections of the uncanny derived from that primary site of boundary negotiation which marks us all as aliens and exiles. This also feeds into Kristevan readings of the abject, which take that same image of the maternal body as a crucial determinant of the way in which we, as a society, perceive the Other as alien. The maternal, as our first site of licence and prohibition, takes on territorial identity. Simultaneously familiar and unknowable, it is our primary metaphor for the defamiliarized explorations into home territory that we project outwards as speculative fictions. Small wonder then that Kristeva frequently utilizes the border negotiations between realism and fantasy as an illustration of the workings of abjection: 'On the edge of non-existence and hallucination, of a reality that, if I acknowledge it, annihilates me. There, abject and abjection are my safeguards.'[23]

If the body is a crucial space of signification whose precarious limits wrestle with themselves, genre is analogous to this in a number of ways. So are the structures of textual desire. After all, if Bachelard is right to argue that 'The space we love is unwilling to remain permanently enclosed. It deploys and appears to move elsewhere without difficulty; into other times, and on different planes of dream and memory',[24] then this must be as true of the generic enclosures of fantasy fictions as it is of anything else. As already noted, for Massey, negotiations between limitations and excesses always take the form of the metamorphic. This is a device which lies at the centre of all fantasy texts, not simply in terms of the symbolism used, but also in the transformative impulses it employs.

As Chapter 3 argues, this articulates the relationship existing between fantastic readings of the body and the language that expresses these corporeal redefinitions. As a process of exchange, the body of the text is also the body within the text and the language is embodied by the forms it inscribes. To appreciate this fully, we perhaps also need to remember that psychoanalytic theorists see all textual representations as linguistic metamorphoses that give visual form to intangible phantasy. Thus literary texts transform the unknowable and the unfathomable through figurative means to produce a form that has verifiable shape and tangibility. In the context of fantastic fictions, phantasy becomes a fantasy enacted with corporeal definition. Or, as Massey puts it, 'Metamorphosis is a process of change essentially unaccompanied by language.'[25] But as with all shape-shifting forms, such fantasies are simply another way of enacting the two-way intersections of border crossings. The final image which adds to this traffic is the truly transformative motif of the cyborg.

This is undoubtedly the most important recent concept to have entered the critical discourse of the fantastic, not least because it uses an *sf* (science/speculative fiction) motif to explore the philosophical, and therefore paves the way for the fantastic to become a means of interrogating texts of all kinds. Despite Jackson's very important psychoanalytic survey in the early 1980s, it has not really been until the explosion of literary postmodernism that fantasy studies have been thrown into a spin. Postmodernism is strewn with the discourse of *sf*, for of course technological advances have ensured that we are, more than ever, at a moment in history when the fantastic surrounds us on all cultural levels. Now space is neither 'out there' nor 'the final frontier'. In its impatience it has come to greet us. So we live in the world of the 'hyperreal', citizens of a giant computer game. The cyborg emerges from Baudrillard's work on machine culture in which, unlike the automaton, the machine exists as a simulacrum of the human form and refuses to ascribe any originary status to its flesh-and-blood equivalent.[26] In this relationship of 'equivalence' lies the key to its impact. So, we discover, the machine annexes the human as much as it is in our pay, the cyborg becoming a game-player who participates, rather than one who spectates or mimetically mimics.

But it is in the work of Donna Haraway that the cyborg is most fully developed, not only as a simulacrum, but as a model for human relations, ideologies and even philosophies. In this way the cyborg embodies its challenge to binary oppositions, being a creation whose hybridity represents the fusion and confusion of pre-existing dichotomies, including those surrounding race, gender, sexuality and class. But the most significant issue of relevance to us once again concerns the implications this has for originary mythologies. As Haraway argues: 'Cyborg writing must not be about the Fall, the imagination of a once-upon-a-time wholeness before language, before writing, before Man.'[27] As we will see later, this marks both the strengths and the weaknesses of this approach for our understanding of fictional writing and/as the fantastic. I have already implied that, for Barthes, storytelling itself is a search for origins[28] and fantasy, in its tracing and retracing of multiple quests, seems to reflect, even as it subverts, our cultural obsession with them. Nevertheless, strategies such as Haraway's have not only enabled us to explore new ways in which fantasy and the fantastic lie at the forefront of our fictional explorations of gender, space and the figure of the stranger/alien. They have also taken great strides towards showing us how fantasy fictions have provided a whole new vocabulary for conceptualizing the real (and by extension the realist). So, as a global culture that seems always to be searching the horizons for utopia while continuing to speed up the coming apocalypse, figures such as the cyborg reflect the fact that we remain locked into a form of escapism that refuses to face the world of everyday. Setting up Bakhtin's overspill image of the grotesque body against Haraway's clinical closures of the cyborg, Chapter 3 demonstrates that these inhabitants of the competing worlds of carnival excess and the realm of the hyperreal are precariously resituated within a troubled and even a troubling space.

All types of literary theory, however innovative and however exciting, are only useful to literary studies insofar as they open up new and exciting readings of texts. This is the function of Part Two of this book. Covering the period from 1865 to 1986, six narratives collectively comprise a wide-ranging spectrum of fantasy fictions, none of which is easily assimilable under the auspices of genre. As my reading of Doris Lessing's *Briefing for A Descent into Hell* (1971) and Iain Banks's *The Bridge* (1986) in Chapter 4 demonstrates, this is at times deliberately foregrounded by the texts themselves. Here the implications of a Todorovian reading of the fantastic manifest themselves in terms of a sustained prevarication between two competing readings. For Todorov, this hesitancy revolves around the world of the supernatural and the psychological, something that leads to critics typically pressing Todorov into service only when dealing with the realm of the uncanny. Yet both of these texts operate as a challenge to this by sharing a preoccupation with the quest for identity (be it psychological or science fictional) by using the motif, not of the unconscious, but of a lapse into unconsciousness. This is not to dismiss psychoanalysis altogether. Where unconsciousness does come into contact with the unconscious is through the discourse of archeology. Utilizing Freud's essay on *Gradiva* in conjunction with Samuel H. Vasbinder's anthropological reading of quest myths, interesting connections start to emerge.[29] Here we find a reworking of the 'lost civilization' motif that digs deep into this unconscious state to unearth what ultimately emerges as the lost realm of the mother's body as ultimate forbidden territory. In Banks's novel, however, this immersion into the depths sends archeology into full reverse thrust by projecting us into a dystopian timelessness which replaces archeology with architectural technology. In the process the discourse of the geological fuels a topography that is textual as well as fantastic as the structural*ist* paradigms of language and wordplay encode themselves within the structur*al* iconography of *The Bridge*. In this respect the various strata set up above-ground are placed in a one-to-one correspondence with the layering of the protagonist's psyche, so the novel appears self-reflexive. Yet conspiring against this is an increasing sense of disorientation that fractures this prevailing symmetry in order to cast the reader adrift in the nebulous wastes of the irreconcilable. For, as the protagonist returns to 'surface' reality, both he and the reader find themselves engaged in a series of destabilizing border dialogues between the machine technology that pervades his unconscious and the speaking subject that is his 'self'.

In Chapter 5 such liminal disruptions are primarily situated in terms of object relations and the implications these have for two gothic texts. Like science/speculative fictions, the gothic focuses upon the figure of the alien, but unlike *sf* it foregrounds the presence of this unspecified monstrous 'other' as something emanating from within: within the unconscious, the house, society at large. This provides the impetus for my reading of R.L. Stevenson's *The Strange Case of Dr Jekyll and Mr Hyde* (1886) and Charlotte Perkins Gilman's *The Yellow Wallpaper* (1892). The unconscious fuelling of fears, desires, and textual trickery in these texts is explored through the boundary demarcations which the works of Norman Holland and Winnicott address. Functioning in terms of spatial and metamorphic transactions, we begin with an exploration of the gothic mansion as 'space between', before moving on to an analysis of the working of the 'in here' and the 'out there' in terms of anal and oral drives and their implications for the construction of fantastic characters who embody the bodily contamination and gothic *dis-ease* of Victorian society as a whole. It is of course in the fantasy motif of the double that these two texts cohere. Gothic texts, in particular, situate themselves within an intertextual 'family narrative' that functions as a fantastic genealogical inheritance. In both of these cases, however, we also (and seemingly conspiring against this) find homoerotic implications within this mirroring dynamic that project desire outwards only in order to keep the inner secrets of the house/body 'safe'. So *The Yellow Wallpaper* uses the device of the palimpsest in order to explore a tension (between true and false selves) couched only in terms of mother/child relations in order to mask a narcissistic relation with the clandestine 'other'. Walling up the 'other woman' behind these patriarchal textual interrelations, Perkins Gilman encodes into her ghostly room a silenced spectre who, like Barthes's writer, plays with the body of the mother. However, rather than taking this, as he does, 'to the limit of what can be known about [that] body', she uses it to paper over those cracks of what are otherwise silenced libidinous urges.[30]

But if the shifting and sinister parameters of the individual and social self interleave themselves within the pages of these gothic texts, such issues are far more playfully explored in the *Alice*s and Angela Carter's *The Passion of New Eve* (1977). Despite being written a century apart, here we find a shared quest which openly seeks out the power of the metamorphic as an exploration into fantastic new forms of identity. In the process this also enables the debate set up between Bakhtin and Baudrillard in Chapter 3 to be brought into a more exacting focus by comparative reading. So we begin by situating the *Alice* texts in terms of ideological game playing and the carnivalesque, critiquing the way in which critics have determined to depoliticize Carroll's usage of body imagery. Later, using the discourses of the postmodern, we also become aware of the narrative explorations of originary mythologies which lie at the heart of both these fictions. In these terms the protagonists stand in for a series of metanarratives (the psychoanalytic, the biblical, the Darwinian) which cohere in an awareness of a knowledge acquired at the expense of irredeemable exile from the utopian garden. In Carter's novel this is also inscribed into the text through the excision of originary organs. Situated at the (literal) cutting edge of the gender 'game', Carter plays dangerously with ideologies to effect (like Baudrillard) a dystopian narrative which takes us to the point of no return. Simultaneously quest myth and a travelogue into future landscapes of death and desire, Carter's novel defamiliarizes the world of our screen fantasies by projecting them hugely upon the giant screen of the desert. Ending with a circular journey into the self, her narrative is a perfect textual encoding of the cybernetic, written into a remythologized world without gender. This is, in itself, a postmodern exploration into the alternative worlds of futurism and cyberspace. As a result, what once cosily existed as the consolations of fantasy has become an all-too-disturbing vision of 'virtual' reality.

## Notes

1 Irving Massey, *The Gaping Pig: Literature and Metamorphosis* (London: University of California Press, 1976) and Kathryn Hume, *Fantasy and Mimesis: Responses to Reality in Western Literature* (New York: Methuen, 1984).

2 'Fancy ... has no other counters to play with but fixities and definites ...'. Samuel Coleridge, *Biographia Literaria* (London: Oxford University Press, 1907), I, p. 202. Cited in W.R. Irwin, 'From Fancy to Fantasy: Coleridge and Beyond', in Roger C. Schlobin (ed.), *The Aesthetics of Fantasy Literature and Art* (Brighton: Harvester, 1982), pp. 36–55 (p. 37).

3 Hume, *Fantasy and Mimesis*, p. 43.

4 Rosemary Jackson, *Fantasy: The Literature of Subversion* (London: Methuen, 1981), p. 4.

5 Perhaps because of the utopian impulse surrounding these ideas, one of the most developed genres for such revisions clusters around speculative fiction. See, for example, Lucie Armitt (ed.), *Where No Man Has Gone Before: Women and Science Fiction* (London: Routledge, 1991); Angelika Bammer, *Partial Visions: Feminism and Utopianism in the 1970s* (New York: Routledge, 1991); Sarah Lefanu, *In The Chinks of the World Machine: Feminism and Science Fiction* (London: The Women's Press, 1988); Natalie M. Rosinsky, *Feminist Futures: Contemporary Women's Speculative Fiction* (Ann Arbor: University of Michigan

Press, 1984); Jenny Wolmark, *Aliens and Others: Science Fiction, Feminism and Postmodernism* (Hemel Hempstead: Harvester, 1993).

6 Kingsley Amis, *The Golden Age of Science Fiction* (London: Hutchinson, 1981) pp. 16 and 12 respectively.

7 Tzvetan Todorov, *The Fantastic: A Structural Approach to a Literary Genre*, trans. Richard Howard (Ithaca, NY: Cornell University Press, 1975), p. 141.

8 W.R. Irwin, *The Game of the Impossible: A Rhetoric of Fantasy* (Urbana: University of Illinois Press, 1976).

9 Roger Abrahams, 'Play', in Venetia J. Newall (ed.), *Folklore Studies in the Twentieth Century: Proceedings of the Centenary Conference of the Folklore Society* (Woodbridge: D.S. Brewer, 1980), pp. 120–5 (p. 122).

10 Roland Barthes, *Mythologies*, trans. Annette Lavers (London: Paladin, 1973) p. 60 and Sigmund Freud, 'Creative Writers and Day-Dreaming', trans. I.F. Grant, in Albert Dickson (ed.), *The Penguin Freud Library, Vol. 14, Art and Literature* (Harmondsworth: Penguin, 1990), pp. 129–41 (p. 132).

11 James R. Kincaid, *Child-Loving: The Erotic Child and Victorian Culture* (New York: Routledge, 1992), p. 79.

12 Melancholia is that state which Julia Kristeva perceives as 'an unsuccessful separation from the mother' resulting in 'mourning for a partial loss which cannot be symbolized'. John Lechte perceives this to be the basic impulse behind artistic creativity. Thus the artist as melancholic 'act[s] out what needs to be elaborated in signs and symbols formed in response to the loss of the object (mother)'. 'Art, Love, and Melancholy in the Work of Julia Kristeva', in John Fletcher and Andrew Benjamin (eds), *Abjection, Melancholia and Love: The Work of Julia Kristeva* (London: Routledge, 1990), pp. 24–41 (pp. 34–5).

13 As argued by W.F.H. Nicolaisen, 'Time in Folklore Narrative', in Newall (ed.), *Folklore Studies in the Twentieth Century*, pp. 314–17 (p. 317).

14 Roland Barthes, *The Pleasure of the Text*, trans. Richard Miller (Oxford: Basil Blackwell, 1990), pp. 34–5.

15 Mary Bittner Wiseman, *The Ecstasies of Roland Barthes* (London: Routledge, 1989), pp. 24 and 39.

16 Freud, 'Creative Writers', p. 132.

17 Irwin, *Game*, p. 8 – my emphasis.

18 Gaston Bachelard, *The Poetics of Space*, trans. Maria Jolas (Boston: Beacon Press, 1994), p. 43.

19 Sigmund Freud, 'The "Uncanny"' in Dickson (ed.), *The Penguin Freud Library, Vol. 14, Art and Literature* , pp. 335–76.

20 Madeleine Davis and David Wallbridge, *Boundary and Space: An Introduction to the Work of D.W. Winnicott* (New York: Brunner/Mazel, 1987).

21 For a fuller discussion of these ideas see Julia Kristeva, *Strangers To Ourselves*, trans. Leon S. Roudiez (Hemel Hempstead: Harvester Wheatsheaf, 1991).

22 Bachelard, *Poetics*, p. 45.

23 For a fuller discussion of this see Julia Kristeva, *Powers of Horror: An Essay in Abjection*, trans. Leon S. Roudiez (New York: Columbia University Press, 1982). This quotation is taken from p. 2.

24 Bachelard, *Poetics*, p. 53.

25 Massey, *Gaping*, p. 51.

26 See Jean Baudrillard, *Simulations* (New York: Semiotext(e), 1983).

27 Donna Haraway, *Simians, Cyborgs, and Women: The Re-Invention of Nature* (London: Free Association Books, 1991), p. 175.

28 Interestingly, this is something Barthes connects with the death of God the father, this having clear implications for our rethinking of authorship and author/ity: 'If there is no longer a Father, why tell stories? Doesn't every narrative lead back to Oedipus?' Barthes, *Pleasure*, p. 47.

29 Sigmund Freud, 'Dreams and Delusions in Jensen's *Gradiva*', trans. James Strachey, in

Dickson (ed.), *The Penguin Freud Library, Vol. 14, Art and Literature*, pp. 27–118 and Samuel H. Vasbinder, 'Aspects of Fantasy in Literary Myths About Lost Civilizations', in C. Schlobin (ed.), *The Aesthetics of Fantasy Literature and Art*, pp. 192–210.

30 'The writer is someone who plays with his mother's body . . . in order to glorify it, to embellish it, or in order to dismember it, to take it to the limit of what can be known about the body . . .'. Barthes, *Pleasure*, p. 37.

# Part One

# READING THEORY

# 1

# Structuralism, Genre and (the) Beyond . . .

Despite the fact that conventional fantasy critics have often been reluctant to address the precepts of contemporary theory in their discussions of fictional works, what we have seen, in the Introduction, to be a central preoccupation with classificatory systems illustrates an affinity with early structuralist critical readings. This is by no means a pejorative comparison. Structuralism, irrespective of its flaws, irrevocably changed the face of literary studies. Suddenly, rather than prioritizing somewhat vague and impressionistic readings of texts, their workings as linguistic systems of signification started to be unravelled for the uninitiated reader. As we know, for the structuralist a text is believed to function akin to a language, being composed of an interrelational series of signs which are, in themselves, arbitrarily connected by socially accepted but by no means logically bound signifiers and signifieds. This self-validating structure, which places its own internal rulings before all external verification, is perfectly positioned as a model for fantasy.

The relationship between fantasy fictions and language systems raises interesting issues about the nature of the relationship between texts and reality. If, as G.W. Grace argues, 'reality construction is probably . . . the primary function of human language',[1] where does this leave the world of the fantastic? Robert Branham, taking up the challenge, turns the terms of this upside down. For him, it is not that language reduces the fantastic to the world of the real, but rather that fantasy is always signalling an overspill beyond language that renders such narratives at least partially ineffable: 'Language is a conventional system for the expression and understanding of conventional experiences. Fantasy fiction, while presented in language, is characterized by its unabashed presentation of imaginary and impossible worlds, phenomena, and cultures.'[2] But while there is an element of truth in this, he is actually misrepresenting an important issue. It is not simply that fantasy fictions are 'presented' as language: they *are* language. The world of the literary fantastic, just like that of classical realism, only exists as a linguistic construct. Literature, more than any other aesthetic medium, reminds us that we understand, create and experience not only the world around us but also the world of our dreams, desires and fears, in terms of the very language we learn to articulate. Fantasy fictions simply bring this to the fore.

The precepts of structuralism as they impinge upon fantasy have enabled this paradigm to be taken a step further. And this is because of the issue of genre. Genre fiction is perceived to be rooted within a socially accepted formula, agreed upon by writer, publisher and reader. In that sense it becomes, in itself, a self-referential sign system. We have expectations of the ghost story, science-fiction narrative and fairy tale that we presume will be fulfilled internally. We anticipate the presence of certain signifiers, such as spectres, time travel, witches, defamiliarization techniques. Indignation or disconcertion is aroused if these expectations are denied. But just as structuralism has been by and large discredited as a 'clackety . . . meaning-making machine' of limited use to narrative theory (being considered too systematic, too self-referential, lacking in fluidity, flexibility and literary evaluation),[3] so the same can be said for much conventional 'structuralist' fantasy criticism. It is not so much that our generically bound expectations are in any way erroneous. After all, genre is one of the founding principles of fantasy forms. What does, nevertheless, remain problematic about so much fantasy criticism is its complete inability to see beyond these parameters. An attendant preoccupation with the 'uncover[ing of] . . . detailed observational analysis and [the mapping of] it out under extended explicatory grids'[4] has been traditionally and almost unilaterally adopted by such critics. Obsessed with classifying and categorizing, differentiating and counter-differentiating between fantasy, science fiction, space opera; or between faery, fantasy and fable, they continue to make redundant distinctions. Few genuinely enable readers to relate better to the narratives with which they engage, because by and large texts are referred to simply as data which fulfil or contradict such pointless differentiations.

One typical example of this critical redundancy is offered by Dieter Petzold, who, despite his own recognition of the pre-existing number and scope of such contradictory accounts, remains determined to add to the heap. So he details what he sees as the 'definitive' (the pun is intentional) critique of the term 'fantasy fiction'. His discourse seems to situate him within a structuralist framework: 'It is clear . . . that ff [fantasy fiction] cannot be defined in isolation but only in relation to other, similar genres'. In other words 'ff' is simply one sign, deriving its meaning from its differential relationship with a whole series of signs (including, presumably, science fiction, sword and sorcery, the fable and others). About this he is completely correct. But what he seems determined to overlook is the fact that, despite his own qualms, the rest of us can easily see why 'one author asserts that as a genre "fantasy" has existed only since the 1960s ... another claims that it flowered between 1880 and 1957 ... and yet another categorically denies fantasy the status of a genre.'[5] It is not that these critics are all wrong and Petzold right in his counter-definition. It is not even that Petzold is wrong in his counter-definition. It is simply that such terms are defined as they suit each individual critic. In and of themselves (as structuralists would tell us) they have no correct and absolute meaning. Far more useful, then, is an approach that accepts genre as a necessary evil: a problem to negotiate, a limit to surpass and a structure to overreach. Beginning here with an analysis of some of the more useful structuralist readings of fantasy texts, we will see how apparent limitation can be significantly transformed into a promising entry-point for theories of the fantastic. One such study is Vladimir Propp's *Morphology of the Folktale*, first published as early as 1928 although not translated into English until 1958. Outside folklore studies Propp's work has, in recent years, been disparaged or dismissed as a limited piece of statistical and formulaic writing. Nevertheless, situating this work within the larger subsequent corpus of material on the fairy tale and folktale proves to be useful in a number of ways.

As Propp makes clear from the beginning, his aim lies with precisely the type of exactitude, accuracy and classifiable data that I have discouraged above. But repositioning his study at the forefront of theoretical developments has the advantage of reminding us that he was genuinely forging new territory, where critics such as Petzold obsessively reiterate old (rather over-grown) ground. It should also be recognized that Propp genuinely acknowledged his own project to be a mere stepping-stone towards a greater understanding of the workings of genre as 'a quite particular structure which is immediately felt and which determines [a] category, even though we may not be aware of it'.[6] What he achieves is a precise awareness of one of the ways in which readers do 'feel' this structure to exist. In order to explore and develop this argument, Propp turns the folktale into a Saussurian *langue* and, as part of that process, occupies himself with it as a syntactic analogy, rather than a lexicon of individual signifiers.[7] In other words, he pays no heed to cataloguing the differentiating features of individual characters or scenes. Instead he interests himself only in those aspects of the tales which seem to be shared by the body as a whole. These he discovers to be a series of archetypal 'functions', the nature of which we will examine in greater detail below.

The issue with which readers remain uneasy is not so much the findings of Propp's exploration (which are convincing enough), but rather the alien manner in which his methodology is devised. Setting himself the task of 'scientifically' analysing criteria which we usually associate with intuition and insight, he privileges the mathematical at the expense of the literary. But what is perhaps more incongruous than anything else is the way in which, having recognised the generic existence of the fairy tale as a discrete entity, Propp then goes on to offer a number of descriptive definitions of its shared qualities which seem entirely unhelpful to the reader of literature. For example, early on in his work he asserts that: 'By "fairy tales" are meant at present those tales classified by Aarne under numbers 300 to 749'.[8] Leaving aside for a moment the fact that a reader needs to be already versed in Aarne's work for this to mean anything, it hardly constitutes a 'literary' definition. Even having developed his own ideas and analysis at greater length, Propp can only offer the following qualification: 'a fairy tale is a story built upon the proper alternation of the above-cited functions in various forms, with some of them absent from each story and with others repeated.'[9] From a purely structuralist perspective, this is as precise and workable a definition of genre fiction as one is likely to find anywhere. But even Propp recognizes the limitations of his approach for general readers: 'Fairy tales could be called tales subordinated to a seven-personage scheme. This term is highly exact but very awkward.'[10]

The truth is, that it is not so much the term as the texts that are 'awkward'. And yet it is precisely this resistance to homogeneity that makes them pleasurable for us to read. Propp's survey has a number of strengths, but an unsuspecting reader looking to him for guidance as to the reading of fairy tales will probably emerge disappointed and frustrated. Although Louis A. Wagner claims otherwise,[11] Propp's study is far more useful to theorists of genre in general than it is to readers of the fairy tale in particular. Albeit accidentally, this also illustrates an earlier point. To reiterate: while certain fantasy forms (including the fairy tale) are basically genre-led, and while critics such as Propp can admirably and convincingly show us that this is the case, our actual interest in them as texts has more to do with the complex way in which an individual tale simultaneously flirts with while overreaching this limiting straitjacket that we know as genre. As Propp has shown, even the generic resists over-exact classification. Bearing this in mind, it is a sorry state of affairs when critics such as Petzold are walking the same critical treadmill almost 60 years later.

That the fairy tale itself follows this flirtatious dynamic becomes abundantly clear when we think of its own resistance to appropriative and author/itarian possession. Where else could one go to find textual authority (in the sense of specified originary authorship) more clearly undermined by its own intergeneric and intertextual playfulness than in the fairy tale? In this respect it is entirely analogous with the development of child's play in which, as Iona and Peter Opie remark, 'the make-up of the individual games may change, even though their names remain the same ... Thus a game which is in the ascendency, which every child wants to play as much as possible, tends to draw parts of other games into it.'[12] From an adult perspective, it is the fairy tale's oral historical roots and its frequent use of embedded and multiple storytellers that attributes it with the pleasurable 'game-playing' dimensions of gossip, rumour and legendary hearsay. For what is frequently overlooked is that Propp's *Morphology of the Folktale* is primarily a study in literary intertextuality. As he acknowledges: 'like any living thing, the [fairy] tale can generate only forms that resemble itself. If any cell of a tale organism becomes a small tale within a larger one, it is built . . . according to the same rules as any fairy tale.'[13] In essence, perhaps it is this lack of any one originary version of a particular fairy story that makes this sub-genre not only intrinsically intertextual, but also interactive with so many other cultural forms. Thus, despite Alan Dundes's disappointment at what he perceives to be Propp's reluctance 'to relate the paradigm(s) he "finds" in myth to the world at large . . .', he nevertheless acknowledges that the results of Propp's work have greatly helped to open up an understanding of any number of cultural and aesthetic forms, including 'comic strips, motion-picture and television plots'. Angela Carter apparently agrees: 'The now defunct US soap opera "Dynasty" . . . utilized a cast list derived with almost contemptuous transparency from that of the Brothers Grimm – the wicked stepmother, the put-upon bride, the ever-obtuse husband and father. "Dynasty's" proliferating subplots featured abandoned children, arbitrary voyages, random misadventure – all characteristic of the genre.'[14]

Such cultural fluidity reinforces Propp's importance, despite his work partly succeeding because of its own slippery relationship with the language that defines it. For it is not simply that Propp, using the term 'folktale', allows for this to encompass the related term 'fairy tale' (a commonsense decision that saves pointless arguments about generic, sub-generic or intergeneric distinctions between the two). It is also, and more problematically, that his all-encompassing terminology hides a difficult linguistic mismatch. Folktales may well be tales about folk, but fairy tales are rarely tales about fairies. Nevertheless, his amalgamation is entirely defensible. We *do* know/sense/feel/intuit precisely what we mean when we use the term 'fairy tale'. After all, we usually fail to perceive any such slippage. Only when we start to articulate a full linguistic definition does this intuitive knowledge seem open to doubt. And there are few equally satisfactory alternatives. Even were we wise enough to select a broad definition such as 'a traditional children's story', we might well be reminded by any number of scholars that many fairy stories are far too erotic, violent, or occult in orientation to render them suitable for a child reader. Nor is it any longer true to say that the fairy story is an oral tale handed down by word of mouth from generation to generation and collectively owned by a particular culture rather than attributed to the work of a single writer. As Mary Ellen Lewis reminds us, oral and written forms 'are not mutually exclusive: the oral does not cease when one learns to read and write; in fact, the two exist simultaneously, sometimes shared by the same individual, sometimes not.'[15] Perhaps, indeed, the purely oral medium of the fairy-tale form has been supplanted by another equally 'popular' mode: 'if defined as orally transmitted narrative with a relaxed attitude to the reality principle and plots constantly refurbished in the retelling, [the fairy tale] has survived . . . in its most vigorous form as the dirty joke.'[16] Unlike most jokes (dirty or otherwise), fairy tales are now written, printed and sold as books, read off the page, attributed to specific editors, collectors or authors. They have even been canonized by the literary tradition, thanks to Charles Perrault, the Brothers Grimm and Hans Christian Andersen. From this point of view, although it is perfectly possible to criticize Propp for his complete evasion of the genre's oral roots, we find that a Proppian analysis is far more useful as a defining approach than many alternative means of definition. Able to come to terms with this cultural slippage, Propp's functions hold good irrespective of readership and irrespective of the market. In that sense Carter may be more correct than she realizes in referring to the term 'fairy tale' as 'a figure of speech',[17] not because of its oral history, but due to its analogous relationship with language as sign system.

This is not to let Propp entirely off the hook. Even he seems frustrated, on occasions, by the inevitable limitations of his own work. Indeed, when he asks: 'if all fairy tales are so similar in form, does this not mean that they all originate from a single source?', he almost belies a betrayal of structuralist principles. For of course in structuralist terms they share *precisely* the same source: that Saussurian *langue* of which they are a mere instance of *parole*.[18] Even to hint of a source outside language is to hint at the shortcomings of structuralist aims. For this reason when we come to consider the relevance of Propp to a contemporary reading of fantasy forms it becomes necessary to move beyond 'pure' structuralism in drawing a distinction between the surface manifestations of a syntagmatic analysis and the latent content underlying this linear sequencing. Once we have differentiated between these two layers, we can begin to open up Propp to new possibilities through the intervention of certain psychoanalytic perspectives.

## Lack, Desire and the Fairy-Tale Form

It is by no means atypical for certain aspects of Propp's work to prove interesting because they demonstrate what Propp ignores, rather than what he exposes. One such aspect derives from the tremendous centrality that Propp ascribes to the concept of lack as it functions within the fairy/folktale, without in any way recognizing the interesting Freudian implications of this concept. So, out of the 151 functions which comprise Propp's schematic analysis of the tale, the function of lack explicitly dominates functions 46–51 (concerned with villainy and avarice), functions

98–101 (concerning the appearance of the princess as object of quest) and functions 114–19 (concerning the fulfilment/resolution of this perceived lack). But in addition, lack implicitly resides in many of the other listed functions, including functions 3–5 concerning childlessness and, more specifically, 'Prayer for the birth of a *son*'. It should be noted that Propp observes, in the main body of his text, that it is through the recognition of lack that the hero is introduced into the tale. For what he is unwittingly arguing is that the fairy tale is an exploration of those dynamics of lack and desire that Freud attributes to his studies on sexuality and his work on Oedipal structures and the family unit.[19] And so, although the full relevance of Freud's work to the fantastic will be analysed in greater depth in the following chapter, it seems important to address this aspect here. Freud, of course, defines woman as *embodiment* of lack, a definition determined by her fantasized existence as castrated other. The only way in which woman can frustrate this awareness of her own negative state is by having a child (the phallic substitute) and/or by temporarily 'borrowing' the phallus through intercourse. What is intriguing about this otherwise dubious and damaging theory is that it clearly replicates itself in these fairy-tale structures.

The hero, as Propp's own functions imply, is the phallic means of assuaging this prevailing sense of lack, not only as far as the heroine is concerned, but also from the perspective of the mere heroine's parents; those poor unfortunates 'lacking' any access to that son who provides 'the most perfect, the most free from ambivalence of all human relationships'.[20] In this respect, the two main types of hero that Propp acknowledges (seekers and victims) are also most fully comprehended when read in Freudian terms. The victimized hero, feminized through being kidnapped or punished in a manner traditionally associated with the fairy-tale heroine, exists as the threatening presence of the castrated male. Lacking the power of the phallus, only by wrenching it back from larger male oppressors can he once again function as fully formed hero. In contrast to this is the seeker, whose role is to fill the lack existing in others. His quest is to find, not only the object which is lacking (conventionally the princess), but also the source of the lack itself. Both of course conjoin in the figure/function of the princess, for she is, as we have seen, both lacking and lack. But how can the acquisition of lack grant anything more than increased lack? What Propp's analysis shows (albeit by inference) is something that readings of fairy tales often overlook. The princess, far from being the ultimate prize, is actually no more than a narrative decoy. After all, in order for the prince to fill the lack, the princess must provide it in the first place through her paradoxical presence as absence. Only then can the prince stave off the threat of castration posed by the victimized hero; becoming child to the mother and suitor to the other in one fell swoop.

Fairy tales are, of course, obsessed with Oedipal structures and this is one of the many characteristics that they share with gothic narratives. In both the emphasis falls upon the nuclear family as a wounded or displaced unit: children are kidnapped, parents die to be replaced by bad substitutes, siblings are separated. Growth of one 'member', it seems, is always at the expense of (or even paid for by) the castration/death or desertion of another. At this stage a further aspect of the morphology comes to light. Dundes, referring to the significance of Propp's final function 'Wedding', asks: 'does not th[is] . . . indicate that Russian fairy-tale structure has something to do with marriage?',[21] a point perhaps expected from a critic whose interest resides in anthropological readings of texts such as these. But Dundes's rather self-evident observation actually misses the point. This issue has far less to do with the significance of marriage as a cultural phenomenon in Russia than with the textual and psychoanalytic function of marriage as a universal narrative device. From the aforementioned psychoanalytic perspective, resolution derives from the fact that marriage brings together, in a socially acceptable manner, sexual fulfilment (hence the phallic resolution of lack) with the forging of new non-Oedipal kinship relations (thus fulfilling the lack of a son).[22] From a generic perspective, marriage is therefore the archetypal closure device; the means by which narrative consolation is effected and loose ends tied up. In this respect it is actually only subordinately part of the plot, a point that may seem surprising. But marriage as a fairy-tale ending is far less part of the plot and far more a crucial part of the generic frame constructed around and within the boundaries of the two linguistic fixtures which begin with Propp's function 'temporal-spatial determination' (the apocryphal 'once upon a time') and end with the equally expected 'happily ever after'. Few readers would argue that the function of the 'Once Upon a Time' resides in plot rather than in structure. Rather, as Angela Carter puts it: 'When we hear the formula "Once upon a time" . . . we know in advance that what we are about to hear isn't going to pretend to be true. Mother Goose may tell lies, but she isn't going to deceive you in *that* way . . .'[23]

But it is perhaps with the work of Jacques Lacan that we find the closest psychoanalytic analogy with Propp. For, as with the structuralists, it is Lacan's presiding emphasis on the function of language that motivates his awareness of the significance of structures; in his terms the structures of desire and the unconscious.[24] On the basis of the analysis of functions expounded by Propp, one need only give it the most cursory of looks to acknowedge that the dynamic between lack and desire is undoubtedly the most substantive thematic patterning of the fairy tale's narrative structure. Small wonder, then, that Propp should single this out as the genre for his survey, despite my aforementioned reservations about the specificity of his approach. According to Lacan the articulation of words is, in itself, an unfulfillable attempt to satisfy a presiding lack at the centre, as the free-floating signifier looses itself from its referent and sets off, like a castrated hero, in search for a signified that will inevitably and endlessly evade him. That Lacan perceives the phallus to be the transcendental signifier renders this analogy between castration and futile heroic searches more than a wilful piece of play. Propp, on the other hand, perceives nothing of the kind at the heart of the folktale. Instead, as he acknowledges: 'Just as the object of seizure does not determine the structure of the tale, neither does the object which is lacking'.[25] Rather than the decoy princess being supplanted by the phallus as symbol of lack, therefore, the function of this 'object' for Propp is far less clear (indeed far less clear-*cut*).

## The Secondary World as Site of Subversion

By examining J.R.R. Tolkien's theoretical perspective on the fairy tale, we begin to see a way of connecting it with other fantasy forms. One of the interesting aspects of Tolkien's approach is that he attributes to fairy tales the same type of wonder and strangeness that we more commonly associate with the mythical dimensions of the traveller's tale: 'Most good "fairy-stories" are about the aventures [sic] of men in the Perilous Realm or upon its shadowy marches. Naturally so . . . elves are not primarily concerned with us, nor we with them . . . Even upon the borders of Faerie we encounter them only at some chance crossing of the ways.'[26] This perennial strangeness and preoccupation with boundaries is not unusual in itself, for defamiliarization techniques are the presiding characteristic of all fantasy forms. But the type of strangeness noted here is not one of former ignorance which can be transformed into knowledge. Here we are dealing with the always/already unknown and the unknowable, the world of alien beings who will always be 'other': in other words the world of speculative fiction. Not surprisingly, then, Tolkien is equally interested in detailing the workings of spatio-temporality: 'Such stories . . . open a door on Other Time, and if we pass through, though only for a moment, we stand outside our own time, outside Time itself, maybe.'[27] Again, it is not unusual for the temporal dimensions of the fantasy text to be understood in terms of otherness. Rather less usual is Tolkien's recognition of such structures in what could only be referred to as a *Lacanian* reading of Otherness. This is indeed the realm of the Imaginary; a point that profoundly challenges the belief that 'fairy tales do *not* . . . open up space without/outside cultural order'.[28] This is a state of loss which is, in truth, far less a statement about temporality and far more one of spatiality (it being another place far more than another time that we are dealing with here). In this sense the introductory 'once upon a time' is just as misleading as the term 'fairy tale', implying a past temporal setting which situates the narrative within the linear chronology of the symbolic order. Indeed, fairy tales are temporally defined primarily in negative terms, in that they deal with a 'never-never' place, a complex understanding of time that defines it primarily in spatial terms, the two combining to form a state (in both senses of the term) situated outside the realms of the dominant discourse and thus beyond its coherent articulation. Perhaps it is for this reason, above all, that the introductory cliché is treated by child and adult readers alike as nothing more than the narrative equivalent of clearing one's throat before commencing the tale.

Indeed, for Tolkien as much as for more conventionally theorised critics such as Bruno Bettelheim, the 'magic of Faerie' is not an end in itself, but primarily a means of exploring desire, 'One of these desires [being] to survey the depths of space and time'. In fact Tolkien's essay 'On Fairy Stories' plots a progression substantively parallel to the work of psychoanalysis, despite never acknowledging this connection. So Tolkien's belief that 'behind the fantasy real wills and powers exist, independent of the minds and purposes of men', evidently connects with the workings of the unconscious. But more interesting than this is the perceptible relationship existing between Tolkien's theory of *secondary worlds* and psychoanalytic readings of the workings of *secondary elaboration* as they impinge upon the construction of fictional narratives. In order to explain this, we need to examine Tolkien's ideas more fully: 'the story-maker proves a successful "sub-creator". He makes a secondary world which your mind can enter. Inside it, what he relates is "true": it accords with the laws of that world . . . [But t]he moment disbelief arises, the spell is broken . . . You are then out in the Primary World again, looking at the little abortive Secondary World from outside.'[29] It takes relatively little in the way of cognitive leaping to recognize this as a parallel for what we will see in the next chapter to be a Freudian theorising of the interrelationship between creative writers and the day-dreaming process. But the emphasis for Tolkien lies with the reader, not the writer, and the parallels that exist here are not so much to do with the day-dream as, in Freudian terms, the night-dream. For surely the breaking of 'the spell' is analogous with the workings of the dream-censor, which reawakens us into the cognitive reality of Tolkien's primary world. Subsequently, Tolkien's reference to looking back at an 'abortive' secondary world becomes his way of articulating that retrospective, falsely analytical, knowing but unknowing process of secondary elaboration whereby we 'make sense' of the insensible dream world that emanates from our unconscious. And yet, as if to put a stop to such *phantastic* implications, Tolkien indignantly criticizes those who 'stupidly and even maliciously confound Fantasy with Dreaming'.[30] From his perspective, it is analogies such as this that result in fantastic literature becoming associated with a sense of passive escapism and mass sopor.

This is something of particular interest to the work of Jack Zipes. Zipes deals frequently and to some extent centrally with the uncanny qualities of the fairy-tale formula and the implications of this for socio-political readings. Indeed, he is primarily motivated by the manner in which fantasy texts 'reflect upon the cultural boundaries within which the reader measures and validates his or her own identity'. Unlike Rosemary Jackson, who rather dismisses the fairy tale as pure narrative consolation, Zipes refers to the existence of a 'dark side' to this genre which seems wilfully to ignore the impact of 'the possible harm of harmlessness' upon subsequent generations of child readers. His approach to this is theoretically intriguing, for although he adopts the discourse of psychoanalysis, he does so only in order to replace the unconscious with a political consciousness: 'Using and modifying Freud's category . . . I want to argue that *the very act of reading a fairy tale is an uncanny experience in that it separates the reader from the restrictions of reality from the onset and makes the repressed unfamiliar familiar once again.*'[31] Perhaps in these terms Zipes's word 'repression' should be replaced by 'suppression' or even 'oppression', for the 'repressed unfamiliar' is its political subversiveness, its ability to threaten the dominant order. For Zipes, the fairy tale is primarily connected with a sense of home, even when its difficulties for this rootless, rather vagrant generic mode render it a place entrenched with ambivalence. Just as Freud perceives us to be simultaneously fascinated and repulsed by the presence of the uncanny, so Zipes's reading of the fairy tale as home relates both to that which we have come to scorn as childish and simplistic and that which we have left behind. Nevertheless, in psychoanalytic terms, home remains a place to which we have never been fully admitted, a point Zipes applies to the history of fairy/folktales.

From a socio-political perspective this homelessness derives from historical censorship, a process which severed these narratives from their subversive roots. The residual consolations of these 'marvellous' tales are largely the result of nineteenth-century changes, when fairy tales underwent a sanitization process in order to render them 'suitable' for child readers of privileged families. As Zipes himself acknowledges, 'there is no such thing as chance or coincidence in a folk tale' and, far from being an unforeseen side-effect, this 'sanitization' process had deep and obvious political ends. Fairy tales were at their most subversive during the seventeenth and eighteeenth centuries, when literacy first started to become widespread in Britain and Europe. Not only did the texts themselves offer a challenge to the established social hierarchy, the very advantages afforded by the ability to read were mirrored by the deeds of the ordinary protagonists, who seem to offer a belief in 'concrete utopias waiting to be realized once the authoritarian rule of the Nome King is overcome'.[32] Ultimately, then, Zipes's political application of the term uncanny derives from a belief that underlying the conformist facade of both generic structure and narrative content there lies an uncanny sense of disruption which threatens to destabilize this acceptable facade.

Above all other perspectives motivated by this issue, it is Jackson's reading of fantasy as subversion that has become predominant. Her work has also enabled a number of politically engaged critics to offer increasingly radical readings of both individual fantasy texts and subgenres as a whole. The fairy tale itself has been substantially targeted in this respect for, as feminists argue, one can reduce the role played by women here to 'Mother, witch, or princess: bad, mad or invisible'.[33] We have seen that the fairy tale is now conventionally structured through consolatory means; means that render it akin to romantic fictions. It is this that enrages the feminist critic. For, as noted above, the only way 'out' for the female protagonist is by winning her prince and embracing the enclosures of the 'happily ever after'. The political dangers of this are that if we are seduced into believing the fairy-tale world to be one of order and harmony, we may end up following the rules of these stories ourselves (this teaching element being traditional to both fable and allegory). And yet as Zipes reminds us, we do not have to be bound by such consolations. Instead we might choose to interrogate such closure by rethinking the possibilities open to us. In their radical writings and rewritings of numerous fantasy modes, feminists have shown what happens when women begin to 'stat[e] their right to have bodies, feelings, action and a language with which to describe themselves in their own value system'.[34] As my reading of Tolkien already implies, another generic mode shares the fairy tale's preoccupation with the defamiliarization of space and place, the encounter with alien territory and its strange inhabitants, and its recent rethinking of consolatory mechanisms. This is the world of science/speculative fiction, and one of the most interesting of this mode's recent developments also results from its feminist re-readings.

That science fiction is a particularly attractive genre for feminist writers and critics is by no means surprising, considering its ability to challenge received notions of contemporary reality. In part this takes an allegorical form, for, as Lee Cullen Khana observes, utopia 'is not, finally, any one place or time, but the capacity to see afresh – an enlarged, even transformed vision'.[35] Furthermore, where fairy tales 'teach women a lesson' by walling them up in towers or employing 'pricks' which/who will send them to sleep, feminists are keen to argue that the possibilities of women's science fiction are endless. Accompanying this is a self-conscious determination to resist narrative closure. As Rachel Blau DuPlessis claims, the key to such resistance lies in 'writing beyond the ending', a point not dissimilar to Zipes's interpretation of the fairy tale. But where, for Zipes, this depends upon a projection outside the text, in the case of science fiction the literary device of time travel enables such futurist projections to be encoded within the text. In this sense an interrogative stance is *required* of the reader, not just an optional extra. The attendant resistance to consolation resides in the recognition that: 'If the future is no longer a resolved place, then in the same way, the past – history itself – no longer has fixity or authority.' And yet a problem remains. However progressive, the generic requirements of any utopian narrative necessitate the adoption of a static narrative framework that will always be primarily dependent upon structural closure for success. This becomes clear when we examine DuPlessis's theory from a more detailed perspective. Her concept of 'writing beyond the ending' is fully articulated in the following terms:

> Most novels begin in the past and end just at or just before the present with a glance at the future. Hence the present and the future are experienced by the reader as unsullied, static, resolved. But when a novel travels through the present into the future . . . social or character development can no longer be felt as complete, nor our 'space' as readers (beyond the ending) perceived as untrammeled.[36]

At first glance this sounds highly plausible. But gradually we unearth a significant flaw. In actuality, DuPlessis conflates narrative time and 'real' time in a misleading manner. Readers do not experience fictional futures as alternative futures, we experience them as alternative visions of the present, because readings only and always take place in the present. This may not conspire against interrogative strategies, but it certainly problematizes DuPlessis's foundational premise.

There is a further difficulty with reading the utopian mode as open-ended. Such forms inevitably channel readings into a singular, complicit narrative stance (even if that complicity functions to critique the dominant order). The reader is expected to agree with the ideological premise instilled within the narrative and very little in the way of narrative pleasure is available as an alternative if we fail. We may resist the framework, but in the process we are far more likely to reject the entire text out of hand than be prepared to radically interact with it. This actually quashes the activity inherent within an interrogative reading. Penny Florence is thus equally misguided in believing that 'The forms of women's writing evidence a growth in consciousness *that means the end of literary genre as "we" know it*', because the only genuine challenge Florence offers to genre derives, not from her reading of form, but from her analysis of fictional content. So, she claims, feminist *sf* pushes closer to the mimetic than conventional *sf* because of what she defines as its 'reality-orientation': 'The free play of signifiers costs too much. Feminist SF writers know that our oppression is inextricably bound up with the "real" . . . in the sense that whoever defines the real holds power.'[37] In part I agree. But this is not challenging 'genre as "we" know it', because 'reality-orientation' in that sense has always been part of the speculative text. It takes more than revolutionary content to revolutionize form, and what Florence overlooks is the sad realization that speculative fictions, however progressive in ideological terms, always remain at least partially compromised by the generic enclosures which give them their voice. Feminist science fiction may well 'cross and recross the boundaries between conventions and form/s',[38] but it does so by retaining an identity in tune with these limits. If we really want complete transformations, perhaps we should begin to concentrate less upon fantasy as a neatly formatted genre and more upon its loose ends, its narrative difficulties and its wilful paradoxes. This is where the fantastic comes into play.

## Tzvetan Todorov Walks the Tightrope

It is unfortunately the case that while most fantasy critics continue to recognize the centrality of Todorov's work to contemporary studies of fantasy and the fantastic, few fully appreciate the crucial role that he has played in our understanding of the application of literary theory to such works. His book *The Fantastic* is, as the subtitle states, 'A Structural Approach to a Literary Genre' and, to that extent, inevitably bears some of the trappings and limitations of structuralism. In essence these underpin a series of divisions and subdivisions through which he defines his terms. Thus, for Todorov, the fantastic inevitably takes up its position in relation to a basic awareness of the centrality of genre issues, even though it refuses to be curtailed by a slavish adherence to their limitations. So, having differentiated the mimetic from the non-mimetic, he identifies two further categories within the latter: the uncanny and the marvellous. We will return to the uncanny in more detail in the following chapter, but for the time being it is enough to note that, as far as Todorov is concerned, the uncanny is primarily associated with supernatural literary devices: 'events . . . which may be readily accounted for by the laws of reason, but which are, in one way or another, incredible, extraordinary, shocking, singular, disturbing or unexpected'.[39] The marvellous, on the other hand, appears a good deal more difficult to define. Separating off four further categories – hyperbolic marvellous, exotic marvellous, instrumental marvellous and scientific marvellous – from what Todorov calls 'the marvelous in the pure state', we recognize here the inevitable complexities and complications that always result when the creativity of the literary text is artificially bound by scientific formulae.[40] Furthermore, when we have jettisoned these problematic sub-categories, the crux of the pure marvellous which is left behind is disappointingly empty, being as unhelpful as it is imprecise. Utilizing Pierre Mabille's definition, Todorov quotes him as follows: 'Beyond entertainment, beyond curiosity, beyond all the emotions such narratives and legends afford, beyond the need to divert, to forget, or to achieve delightful or terrifying sensations, the real goal of the marvelous journey is the total exploration of universal reality.'[41] The problems with this are endemic to structuralism. Todorov, toeing a strict and unequivocal Saussurian line here, has already by this stage asserted that 'a genre is always defined in relation to the genres adjacent to it'.[42] Another way of explaining this is to argue that signs/texts can only ever be understood in terms of what they are *not* (or in this case what they are 'beyond'); not what they are. The resulting assertion that narrative is 'the total exploration of universal reality' is little short of being completely meaningless.

Nevertheless, we remember that at the same time as Todorov adopts a structuralist paradigm, he is simultaneously working beyond its constraints. Recognizing for himself its intrinsic limitations, he repeatedly draws attention to the inadequacies of the very generic distinctions he seems determined to retain. So he refers to his own definition of the uncanny as 'broad and vague . . . [like] the genre it describes', a point that seems particularly telling when we consider the comparative ease with which he describes this in contrast to his intellectual 'wrestling-match' with the marvellous. Ultimately he acknowledges the risk of falling into one of two extremist positions, the first deriving from a schematization which 'reduce[s] literature to pure content' and the second effecting a reductionism that sees literature only as a set of arid structures.[43] The real importance of Todorov's work starts to come to light when he begins to articulate a means of subverting his own classificatory system (although he refrains from putting this in quite these terms). With his focus upon the boundary-marker where the marvellous and the uncanny come into contact, genre delineations start to blur at the edges. This is the site of genuine theoretical renewal, for it is here that we encounter the zone of the fantastic.

That Todorov should need to differentiate between fantasy and the fantastic is not inconsequential, for this is tantamount to thinking beyond the restrictions of genre which, as we have seen, function via 'an intellectually closed system'.[44] What then awaits in the realm of the fantastic? As he approaches this 'tightrope', Todorov's anxiety starts to emerge. How does this structuralist think outside his own limits? As if setting up a safety net, he delineates two new sub-categories on either side of the line: the 'fantastic-uncanny' and the 'fantastic-marvellous'. This is little more than 'pure' prevarication. Suddenly, as if the bonds of the structuralist strait-jacket loosen, Todorov almost gleefully observes: 'The fantastic . . . leads a life full of dangers, and may evaporate at any moment.' Having introduced us to the world of fantastic transgression, even his vocabulary starts to take flight: 'The fantastic is always a break in the acknowledged order, an irruption of the inadmissible within the changeless everyday legality.' Whereas formerly the uncanny exists purely in terms of categories and classifications, here he allows that 'The sentiment of the uncanny originates, then, in certain themes linked to more or less ancient taboos.'[45]

In a number of ways, then, the fantastic functions as a borderline phenomenon. And as part of this, if the structuralist favours the internal workings of the text as sign system, Todorov's reading of the fantastic, looking to address the 'dynamic unity' of a text (a phrase in itself embodying the very tension of his work), opens up the textual borders to intervention from the reader. The fantastic in this sense becomes a site of hesitancy, uncertainty and disquieting ambivalence, and suddenly the reader *is* the main protagonist, not through identification but simply through interaction with the fantastic itself. Todorov, in storytelling mode, sets the scene: 'In a world which is indeed our world, the one we know, a world without devils, sylphides, or vampires, there occurs an event which cannot be explained.'[46] Our primary concern is neither why this happens nor how it can be resolved, but what its effect is on both protagonist and reader. Most significant of all is the manner in which this uncertainty is perpetuated. For the fantastic only occupies the duration of this process and the minute we decide upon a single cause for the event 'we leave the fantastic for a neighbouring genre, the uncanny or the marvellous'.[47] Thus, precisely because the fantastic comes to the fore at the point of interaction between two conflicting worlds/zones/modes, the resulting narrative is always to a greater or lesser extent on the edge between the two, simultaneously acknowledging both, simultaneously cutting across both, or, as Rosemary Jackson later puts it: 'The fantastic exists in the hinterland between "real" and "imaginary", shifting the relations between them through its indeterminacy'.[48] As far as Todorov is concerned, whereas the marvellous and the uncanny might be perceived as spatial enclosures, the realm of the fantastic takes up no space at all. Instead it demarcates frontier territory.

This has further implications for the interaction between text and reader. We have seen that the conventions of genre fantasy push perpetually towards textual closure. This means that although they may present the reader with a fictional world in which certain or even many of the conventions of empirical reality are challenged (perhaps irrevocably), they do so in a manner that prioritizes internal coherence and allows for the consolationist possibilities of narrative closure which keep fantasy on a safely distanced level. As Kathleen Spencer puts it, although 'science-fiction writers . . . construct a text built on a unified non-mimetic world model', they do so, not simply to make it 'probable', but also to render it 'ordinary'. In contrast to this, she reminds us, the reader 'must never be allowed to forget the strangeness of the fantastic'.[49] Perhaps inevitably, this renegade area has its rather reactionary opponents. As Neil Cornwell sees it, 'That PF [the pure fantastic] is represented merely by a line seems at first sight credible, particularly as Todorov suggests so few examples which actually fit such a category. However, it makes little sense to speak of PF as even a sub-genre unless we create a space in the model for it to occupy.'[50] However, in resituating the spatial as a temporal disruption, Todorov offers an illuminating analogy for such resistant voices:

> The classic definition of the present, for example, describes it as a pure limit between the past and the future. The comparison is not gratuitous: the marvellous corresponds to an unknown phenomenon, never seen as yet, still to come – hence to a future; in the uncanny, on the other hand, we refer the inexplicable

> to known facts, to a previous experience, and thereby to the past. As for the fantastic itself, the hesitation which characterizes it cannot be situated, by and large, except in the present.[51]

In essence, then, where genre definitions tend to seal up texts, the fantastic opens them up to an ambivalence that must conspire against the formulaic, despite the fact that Todorov insists on retaining the word 'genre' for what is more usefully seen as an impulse or an interrogative drive. This endlessly open and thus non-containable text must therefore pose a dangerous threat to established notions of fixity and conformity, a characteristic that obviously makes the fantastic a particularly appealing form for the exploration of socio-political marginality and ex-centricity.

As if to underline this, we find that Michel Foucault's definition of transgression follows, almost to the letter, Todorov's reading of the 'pure fantastic':

> Transgression is an action which involves the limit, that narrow zone of a line where it displays the flash of its passage . . . it is likely that transgression has its entire space in the line it crosses . . . [and] incessantly crosses and recrosses a line which closes up behind it in a wave of extremely short duration, and thus it is made to return once more right to the horizon of the uncrossable.[52]

Structurally, then, the two theoretical concepts not only share the same location, but also a similar trajectory. Both exist as tightrope walkers, playing along the limits, frequently threatening to over-balance, but always defying the gravitational pull which tries to force a recapitulation. Intriguingly, this position of nervous hesitancy is endemic even to Todorov's stance. I have already stated that Todorov clings to the very structuralist precepts that his theory of the fantastic threatens to dismiss. Just as transgression seems to have 'its entire space in the line it crosses . . . [and] incessantly crosses and recrosses' and just as the transgressor is *only* a transgressor at the moment that the limit is forced, so the fantastic needs the constraints of genre demarcations in order to function as a disruptive impulse. This is the paradox of its inherent tension. Where Propp finds a typical function-pairing, at the heart of the folktale, between prohibition and violation or, as he refers to it elsewhere, the 'principle of freedom' set against 'little use of this freedom',[53] so Todorov opens this up in true structural style in order to transform generic entrapment into generic disruption. Building upon and yet moving beyond the workings of Propp, no wonder Todorov (himself a transgressor in/of structuralist terms) oscillates throughout between capitulation and transgression.

Nevertheless, in order for us to assert that there is an intrinsic connection between the fantastic and transgression this must also manifest itself on the level of narrative content. Both Foucault and Georges Bataille, perhaps the most clearly acknowledged theorists of transgression, tackle it primarily as a confrontational challenge to and encounter with societal taboos.[54] Those readers familiar with Jackson's work would expect her to agree. Centrally concerned to situate fantasy within a socio-cultural perspective, although it may well be 'naive to equate fantasy with either anarchic or revolutionary politics', Jackson does acknowledge that such fictions 'disturb "rules" of artistic representation and literature's reproduction of the "real"' in a manner we anticipate to be compatible with transgression. But in fact her response is rather disappointing: 'To attempt to defend fantasy as inherently transgressive would be a vast, over-simplifying and mistaken gesture.' Instead, she claims, transgression *per se* has become an obsolete phenomenon: 'the activity is one which is self-consuming, attacking nothing but the human, for without God, transgression is empty, a kind of profanation without an object.'[55] The reasoning behind this observation derives from an assertion made by Foucault himself. In his terms, transgression's relationship with the limit operates as a secularized cultural manifestation of what formerly constituted spiritual sacrilege. But Jackson, in taking issue with Foucault in the most literal of ways, misses out on an important connection. Her criticism of his words here shares (albeit by inference) certain similar characteristics with an earlier charge that she levels at Todorov for 'fail[ing] to consider the social and political implications of literary forms'.[56] Jackson has, as we have seen, categorically argued that it is via strategies of narrative and not simply of content that fantasy fictions can 'disturb' the rules in a way that is analogous to, if not to be equated with, 'anarchic or revolutionary politics'. In the context of Todorov this becomes particularly true. After all, for the structuralist, both text and society can only be fully understood if we situate them as sign systems analogous to language. As Jonathan Culler argues, 'in analysing a language we *are* analysing social facts'.[57] Furthermore, if everything for the structuralist exists only through and within language, then surely one might also argue that language has stepped into God's empty shoes. As Todorov himself observes: 'The supernatural is born of language ... not only do the devil and vampires exist only in words, but language alone enables us to conceive what is always absent: the supernatural. The supernatural thereby becomes a symbol of language.'[58] Bearing in mind his claim that 'there [sometimes] exist necessary and not arbitrary relations between the constitutive parts' of any system of signification,[59] we should not be misled by Todorov's reluctance to invoke the name of God in this case. For the deity and the diabolic gain meaning in terms of each other. Despite his coy evasions, Todorov is cloaked in the discourse of structuralist sacrilege, a point that might explain his own nervous position. In resisting the prohibitive law of the structuralist code, he well and truly offers a framework for 'disturbance' which can equally apply to the social sign system.

Although the importance of Jackson's work cannot be over-estimated, there is one crucial flaw in her reading of Todorov. This not only proves misleading, it is also intrinsic to the rationale behind her negative reading of transgression. This derives from her reluctance fully and thoroughly to differentiate between the terminology of fantasy and that of the fantastic. In a highly uncharacteristic lack of precision, Jackson uses both terms interchangeably, the latter simply forming the adjectival version of the noun. While this may appear a hair-splitting criticism, it is actually crucial to the matter in hand. Jackson is wrong to assert that 'Fantasy is preoccupied with limits, with limiting categories, and with their projected dissolution', for this interrogative role can only be played out by the fantastic. This, as we have seen, is a disruptive and open-ended form which, in Jackson's own terms, 'opens onto the widest spaces'.[60] Fantasy fiction, on the other hand, has a very different structure. When Foucault himself asserts that 'the language in which transgression will find its space . . . lies almost entirely in the future', he carefully avoids asserting that it lies with *fictionalizing* the future.[61] Largely constrained by formulaic constructs, those modes which we might refer to as science fiction, ghost stories, horror fiction and fairy tales offer readers, albeit paradoxically, the consolation of gratified desires. True, we buy ghost stories in order to be disturbed by the narratives they tell, but we anticipate being disturbed by them in a particular manner. If we end up being disturbed because what we took to be a ghost story suddenly seems to be opening up to the hesitant possibility of hallucination or madness, it ceases simultaneously to *be* a ghost story and to fulfil our expectant desires. Ironically, it is precisely this that enables Jackson to argue that: 'Fantasies . . . frequently serve . . . to reconfirm institutional order by supplying a vicarious fulfilment of desire and neutralizing an urge towards transgression.'[62] In contrast to this, the reader of a fantastic narrative is projected into a precarious positionality which, far from 'neutralizing an urge', must inevitably challenge the reader's sense of gratification in reassuring forms and force her to confront the ease with which apparently established limits of all kinds may be transgressed.

The very fact that the concerns of transgression lie with the liminal position and the threshold which is forced, implies in itself that our response to the free play of transgression may often be tentative, equivocal and perhaps even fearful. Nevertheless, the positive side of this is, as W.R. Irwin argues, that the fantasist: 'may really hope that his story will have some lasting effect of modifying the way in which his readers accept the norm that he has playfully violated.'[63] In plotting a journey from the enclosures of structuralism to Todorov's tightrope we have seen the reassuring spaces of genre fantasy come into a confrontation with the discourse of the limit. To return to the terms outlined in the Introduction, this forces the 'child's play' of genre fantasy to lose its consolationist mechanisms and take on the transformative potential of an enticing but frustrating narrative 'foreplay'. But in exchange we pay a price, swapping our comfortable and familiar resolutions for a narrative identification which is '"open", dissatisfied, endlessly desiring'.[64] As we saw in the case of Propp, the dynamics of desire are dependent upon a loss that emerges out of the depths of the unconscious. In Chapter 2 we more fully explore the relevance of these issues to both fantasy and the fantastic, by interrogating psychoanalytic discourses of the uncanny.

## Notes

1 George W. Grace, *The Linguistic Construction of Reality* (London: Croom Helm, 1987), p. 139.
2 Robert J. Branham, 'Fantasy and Ineffability: Fiction at the Limits of Language', *Extrapolation*, Vol. 24 (1983), pp. 66–79 (p. 66).
3 As argued in Donna Haraway, 'The Promises of Monsters: A Regenerative Politics for Inappropriate/d Others', in Lawrence Grossberg, Cary Nelson and Paula Treichler (eds), *Cultural Studies* (New York: Routledge, 1992), pp. 295–337 (p. 304).
4 This is a connection Richard Harland makes with the discourse of structuralism. See Richard Harland, *Superstructuralism: The Philosophy of Structuralism and Post-Structuralism* (London: Methuen, 1987), p. 2.
5 Dieter Petzold, 'Fantasy Fiction and Related Genres', *Modern Fiction Studies*, Vol. 32, (1986), pp. 11–20 (pp. 13 and 11–12 respectively).
6 Vladimir Propp, *Morphology of the Folktale*, trans. Laurence Scott (Austin: University of Texas Press, 1968), p. 9.
7 Jonathan Culler defines *langue* as 'the system of a language . . . a system of forms . . . what the individual assimilates when he learns a language . . . a coherent, analysable object'. Jonathan Culler, *Saussure* (London: Fontana, 1976), p. 29.
8 Propp, *Morphology*, p. 19. Aarne himself defines these as 'Tales of Magic', subdividing them into the following categories:
300–399 – Supernatural Adversaries
400–459 – Supernatural or Enchanted Husband (Wife) or Other Relatives
460–499 – Supernatural Tasks
500–599 – Supernatural Helpers
560–649 – Magic Objects
650–699 – Supernatural Power or Knowledge
700–749 – Other Tales of the Supernatural
Antti Aarne, *The Types of the Folktale: A Classification and Bibliography* (Helsinki: Academia Scientiarum Fennica, 1961), p. 19.
9 Propp, *Morphology*, p. 99.
10 Propp, *Morphology*, p. 100.
11 Louis A. Wagner, 'Preface to the Second Edition', Propp, *Morphology*, pp. ix–x (p. ix).
12 Iona and Peter Opie, 'Certain Laws of Folklore', in Venetia J. Newall (ed.), *Folklore Studies in the Twentieth Century: Proceedings of the Centenary Conference of the Folklore Society* (Woodbridge: D.S. Brewer, 1980), pp. 65–70 (p. 70).
13 Propp, *Morphology*, p. 78.
14 Alan Dundes, 'Introduction to the Second Edition', Propp, *Morphology*, pp. xi–xvii, (pp. xiii–xiv) and Angela Carter (ed.), *The Virago Book of Fairy Tales* (London: Virago, 1991), pp. xx–xxi.
15 Mary Ellen Lewis, 'Some Continuities Between Oral and Written Literature', in Newall (ed.), *Folklore Studies in the Twentieth Century*, pp. 272–6 (p. 272).
16 As argued by Carter, *Virago Book of Fairy Tales*, p. xvii.
17 Carter, *Virago Book of Fairy Tales*, p. ix.
18 Propp, *Morphology*, p. 106. According to Saussure, 'In separating *langue* from *parole* . . .

we are separating what is social from what is individual and what is essential from what is ancillary or accidental.' Ferdinand de Saussure, *Course in General Linguistics*, trans. Wade Baskin (London: Peter Owen, 1960). Cited by Culler, *Saussure*, pp. 30–1. The most significant aspect of this differentiation for our concerns is that the comparatively peripheral stance Saussure ascribes to *parole* is replicated by Propp. This forms the basis of most literary-based criticisms of both.

19 Propp, *Morphology*, pp. 119–27 *passim* (my emphasis) and p. 36 respectively. For a fuller explanation of Freudian readings of sexuality and the family unit see Sigmund Freud, *On Sexuality: Three Essays on the Theory of Sexuality* (Harmondsworth: Penguin, 1977).

20 This wry definition is taken from Madelon Sprengnether, '(M)other Eve: Some Revisions of the Fall in Fiction by Contemporary Women Writers' in Richard Feldstein and Judith Roof (eds), *Feminism and Psychoanalysis* (Ithaca, NY: Cornell University Press, 1989), pp. 298–322 (p. 301).

21 Dundes, 'Introduction', p. xiii.

22 Claude Lévi-Strauss was the most influential theorist to derive a full structural anthropology of kinship relations in the context of myth. My apparent inattention to his work here is due to the differing relationship myth holds to the mimetic, not through any attempt to lessen his significance. Readers interested in pursuing this further should see Claude Lévi-Strauss, *Structural Anthropology*, trans. C. Jacobson and B.G. Schoepf (Allen Lane: London, 1968).

23 Carter, *Virago Book of Fairy Tales*, p. xii.

24 As Selden and Widdowson put it: 'Lacan considers that human subjects enter a pre-existing system of signifiers which take on meaning only within a language system. The entry into language enables us to find a subject position within a relational system (male/female, father/mother/daughter). This process and the stages which precede it are governed by the unconscious.' Raman Selden and Peter Widdowson, *A Reader's Guide to Contemporary Literary Theory* (Hemel Hempstead: Harvester Wheatsheaf, 1993), p. 138.

25 Propp, *Morphology*, p. 36.

26 Tolkien, 'Tree and Leaf', in *The Tolkien Reader* (New York: Ballantine, 1966), pp. 1–84 (pp. 9–10).

27 Tolkien, 'Tree and Leaf', p. 32.

28 Jack Zipes, *Fairy Tales and the Art of Subversion: The Classical Genre for Children and the Process of Civilization* (New York: Routledge, 1991), p. 100. Here Zipes is criticizing Jackson for the lack of attention she pays to this genre in *Fantasy: The Literature of Subversion* (London: Methuen, 1981).

29 Tolkien, 'Tree and Leaf', pp. 13, 14 and 37.

30 Tolkien, 'Tree and Leaf', p. 48.

31 Zipes, *Fairy Tales*, pp. 55 and 174 – original emphasis.

32 Zipes, *Fairy Tales*, pp. 5 and 131.

33 As argued by Jennifer Waelti-Walters, *Fairy Tales and the Female Imagination* (Montreal: Eden Press, 1982), p. 80.

34 Waelti-Walters, *Fairy Tales*, p. 89.

35 Lee Cullen Khana, 'Change and Art in Women's Worlds: Doris Lessing's "Canopus in Argos: Archives"', in Ruby Rorhlich and Elaine Hoffman Baruch (eds), *Women in Search of Utopia: Mavericks and Mythmakers* (New York: Schoken, 1984), pp. 270–6 (p. 273).

36 Rachel Blau DuPlessis, 'The Feminist Apologues of Lessing, Piercy and Russ', *Frontiers*, Vol. 4 (1979), pp. 1–8 (p. 2).

37 Penny Florence, 'The Liberation of Utopia or Is Science Fiction the Ideal Contemporary Women's Form' in Linda Anderson (ed.), *Plotting Change: Contemporary Women's Fiction* (London: Edward Arnold, 1990), pp. 64–83 (pp. 65 – my emphasis – and 69–70).

38 Florence, 'Liberation', p. 70.

39 Tzvetan Todorov, *The Fantastic: A Structural Approach to a Literary Genre*, trans. Richard Howard (Ithaca, NY: Cornell University Press, 1975), p. 46.

40 Todorov offers the following distinction between these sub-categories: The 'hyperbolic

marvelous' deals with 'phenomena [which] are supernatural only by virtue of their dimensions, which are superior to those that are familiar to us'. The 'exotic marvelous' deals with 'supernatural events [which] are reported without being presented as such'. The 'instrumental marvelous' depicts 'gadgets, technological developments unrealized in the period described but, after all, quite possible'. The 'scientific marvelous' brings us very close to what . . . we call science fiction. Here the supernatural is explained in a rational manner, but according to laws which contemporary science does not acknowledge.' Todorov, *Fantastic*, pp. 53–6 *passim*.

41 Todorov, *Fantastic*, p. 57, citing Pierre Mabille, *Le Miroir du Merveilleux* (Paris, 1962).

42 Todorov, *Fantastic*, p. 27.

43 Todorov, *Fantastic*, pp. 46 and 93.

44 As argued by W.R. Irwin, *The Game of the Impossible: A Rhetoric of Fantasy* (Urbana: University Illinois Press, 1976), p. 189.

45 Todorov, *Fantastic*, pp. 41 and 48.

46 Todorov, *Fantastic*, p. 25.

47 Todorov, *Fantastic*, p. 25. Note, then, that in these terms (unlike those we shall see Freud adopting in his essay on 'The "Uncanny"') the uncanny resolves hesitancy, rather than provoking and perpetuating it.

48 Jackson, *Fantasy*, p. 35.

49 Kathleen Spencer, 'Naturalising the Fantastic: Narrative Technique in the Novels of Charles Williams', *Extrapolation*, Vol. 28 (1987), pp. 62–74 (p. 64) citing Andrzej Zgorzelski, 'Is Science Fiction a Genre of Fantastic Literature?', *Science Fiction Studies*, Vol. 19 (1979), pp. 296–303 (p. 299).

50 Neil Cornwell, *The Literary Fantastic: From Gothic to Postmodernism* (Hemel Hempstead: Harvester Wheatsheaf, 1990), p. 136.

51 Todorov, *Fantastic*, p. 42.

52 Michel Foucault, 'A Preface to Transgression', trans. Donald F. Bouchard and Sherry Simon, in Donald F. Bouchard (ed.), *Michel Foucault: Language, Counter-Memory, Practice: Selected Essays and Interviews* (Ithaca, NY: Cornell University Press, 1977), pp. 29–52 (pp. 33–4).

53 Propp, *Morphology*, pp. 64 and 111.

54 See Foucault, 'Preface' and Georges Bataille, *Eroticism* (London: Marion Boyars, 1987).

55 Jackson, *Fantasy*, pp. 14, 175 and 79 respectively.

56 Jackson, *Fantasy*, p. 6.

57 Culler, *Saussure*, p. 51 – my emphasis.

58 Todorov, *Fantastic*, p. 82.

59 Todorov, *Fantastic*, p. 75.

60 Jackson, *Fantasy*, pp. 48 and 22 respectively.

61 Cited by Allon White, 'Pigs and Pierrots: The Politics of Transgression in Modern Fiction', *Raritan*, Vol. 2 (1981), pp. 51–70 (p. 52).

62 Jackson, *Fantasy*, p. 72.

63 Irwin, *Game*, p. 183.

64 An effect that Jackson considers the transgressive text to inspire in the reader. Jackson, *Fantasy*, p. 9.

# 2

# Fantasy, Phantasy and the Realm of the Uncanny

As noted in the Introduction, all fiction has its origins in phantasy and so it comes as no surprise that psychoanalytic theory has had such an impact upon our understanding of literary texts, their writers and their readers. As literary fantasies are particularly preoccupied with encoding the symbolism of the unknown and the unknowable into their narratives, it also stands to reason that psychoanalysis must have a great deal to say of especial use to readers of literary fantasy and the fantastic. To some extent the work of folklorists addressed in Chapter 1 is illustrative of this, for, like these critics, psychoanalytic theorists explore uncharted territory as a means of trying to determine the nature of otherwise indeterminate origins. Remembering Hume's initial analogy between the fantasy quest and literature as quest, we also realize that psychoanalysis is, in itself, a fantastic quest. Thus it sends us on a journey which deconstructs the precepts of linear time and actual space in order to resituate us in only seemingly unfamiliar and alien territory. Confronted by the space of 'elsewhere', we are simultaneously projected into a past that is 'in reality' the present. According to many psychoanalytic theorists, similarly transformative properties reside in the literary text, in particular when associated with fantasy. So Claire Russell, perceiving the existence of a clearly defined parallel between the imagery of dreams and that of folk and fairy-tales, goes so far as to say that the fairy-tale texts which we read or listen to as children may help to introduce us to a cast of dramatis personae or list of possible scenarios which will subsequently (and perhaps repeatedly) find their way into our dreams, even as adults.[1] This is something that Bettelheim also addresses in his own important psychoanalytic study: '[Some] investigators ... emphasize the similarities between the fantastic events in myths and fairy tales and those in adult dreams and daydreams – the fulfilment of wishes, the winning out over all competitors, the destruction of enemies.'[2] This implies, at least at first glance, that it is easy to elide phantasy with fantasy and that the two share a privileged relationship with each other. But clearly this is not always the case. In literary terms we need to add a further layer of differentiation (which psychoanalysis as a whole does not recognize) between phantasy in realism and phantasy in fantasy. This is not made easier by the fact that the German term *phantasie* conflates these in referring simultaneously to 'the imagination . . . the imaginary world and its contents' (fantasy) and 'the imaginings or fantasies into which the poet . . . so willingly withdraws'(phantasy).[3] Beginning with an analysis of the relationship between dreams and fiction, we now explore this problem in greater depth, ultimately considering what happens to phantasy when Todorovian notions of the fantastic enable us to replace the static dream-text with a precariously positioned narrative structure in tension with its own 'pulling mechanisms', those latent encodings which rebel from within.

Freud's preoccupation with dreamwork is an obvious starting-point for this discussion, not least because the dream is so frequently foregrounded as a narrative device in fantasy texts. In an early essay on Jensen's *Gradiva*,[4] Freud uses this as a first step along the road towards an understanding of the nature of the relationship between fictitious dreaming and actual dreaming. Analysing Jensen's dream-text, he sets out by expressing the hope that even if his approach should do little to enlighten us about the workings of dreams, it should nevertheless expand our understanding of literary narratives. Furthermore, making a point of stressing the generic 'fantasy' status of *Gradiva* suggests he will go on to explore the status of such dreams, not as phantasy but as (literary) fantasy. Dreams, in fiction as in phantasy, function primarily as borderline phenomena. In psychoanalytic terms they form the boundary-marker between conscious and unconscious realms, while in their literary guise (at least as far as fantasy texts are concerned), they enable characters (and thus readers) to manoeuvre between the realms of mimesis and those of fantasy. While analogous, these two borderline functions are not interchangeable. The fictional dream has never been dreamt and, in that sense, is no closer to psychoanalytic dreams and the unconscious than any other fictional device. It can of course simulate dreamwork (as Freud shows *Gradiva* to do) but it is not and never will be dreamwork itself. Indeed, despite Freud's initial promise, what emerges from his essay is that Freud is far more interested in what his observations can tell us about the workings of the unconscious of *Gradiva's* elusive author than he is about the nature of the dream as a text.[5]

From our perspective, then, Freud's work on the relationship between dreams and fiction is more interesting in terms of what it implies about the generic structure of fantasy fictions than it is about the nature of dreams as their content. Freud's subsequent work makes it possible to differentiate between (day-)dreams that *frame* a narrative and night-dreams that occur within one. It is in 'Creative Writers and Day-dreaming' that he claims that the role of the creative writer can be compared with both the role of the day-dreamer and that of the child at play.[6] Like the child/day-dreamer, this writer willingly suspends disbelief, immersing herself into an imagined fictional world *as if* it were real. It is this 'as if' that is important here, because as Freud goes to great pains to acknowledge, neither child nor dreamer/writer ever genuinely mistakes that fantasy for the world of real life, the parameters bordering the limits always being clearly marked (a distinction not so clear in the case of the night-dream). Once again though, it is important to remember that Freud is not differentiating between fantasy and mimesis here; his ideas hold true for all literary texts. As I have noted, nevertheless, his work does open up avenues for the discussion of genre as narrative formula. Precisely because Freud's parameters of play are so firmly set, it is as if (as in the case of his reading of Jensen's narrative) only the content of the dream-text has scope for change. The structure itself and the relationship the reader holds to the text is in his view very firmly fixed.

The argument he sets out in this essay feeds into our understanding of the workings of narrative closure as we have seen them to impinge upon the fantasy formula. As we saw in the previous chapter, irrespective of the number or manner of ways in which the conventions of empirical reality are challenged within the text, the prioritization of internal narrative coherence always enables the reader to leave that realm at will, returning to a real world which is just as it was before the reader 'left' it. That Propp situates lack at the centre of his chosen generic mode has also been explained. But a psychoanalytic reading of the dynamics of the generic structure helps to enlighten this preoccupation still further. Freud, making the apparently sweeping generalization that 'a happy person never phantasies, only an unsatisfied one', relies upon our awareness that it is those same dynamics of lack and desire that take us to fiction (both as writers and readers) in the first place. Leaving aside Freud's belief that the writer is able to utilize written texts as a socially acceptable medium for sharing her fantasies in a therapeutic manner,[7] the beauty of formulaic fantasy for readers is that we know it offers us certain reliable and fulfilling consolatory criteria. The fictional dynamics of any reading strategy follow a complex interaction between a revealing and a reveiling of information that keeps us in a perpetual state of pleasurable arousal, torn between a desire for immediate total gratification and a competing one for delicious delay. Situated, according to psychoanalytic theory, within a presiding state of lack, our narrative day-dreaming, unlike Todorov's non-formulaic fantastic counterpart, gives us precisely this experience while never letting us down in the end. The ability to take the climax for granted makes the delay no more than a fenced-in Freudian playground where the toys come to life and return to inanimation always and only at our own beck and call.

Of course psychoanalysis is an approach frequently viewed with suspicion by literary critics, and for a number of reasons. The complexity of some of its terminology does not help, but perhaps more significant has been its historical tendency to offer unilateral readings of symbolism in particular and narrative modality more generally. In some ways this has tended to earn it a reductionist reputation not dissimilar to the one I have ascribed to structuralist readings of genre fantasy. Certainly, however interesting Freud's work is in terms of the parallels one may perceive between narratology and the dreaming process, he does remain remarkably flawed in his reading of aesthetics. Elizabeth Freund has argued that the problem with Freud's reading of texts is that he remains incapable of maintaining a sustained differentiation between 'readers and writers, subject and object, analyst and analysand'.[8] Far more problematic in my view is the fact that Freud seems incapable of recognizing that there is anything of interest in literature beyond that of the implied author's perspective. Indeed, if the reader exists in any way at all for Freud, it is only as a passive sap to authorial control. As he says in his later essay on 'The "Uncanny"': 'The imaginative writer has this licence among many others, that he can select his world of representation so that it either coincides with the realities we are familiar with or departs from them in what particulars he pleases. *We accept his ruling in every case.*'[9] Fortunately, of course, we do nothing of the kind. Nor is he always correct in his assessment of the 'literary' qualities of a narrative. For him, the language of textuality, rather than contributing to (indeed forming) the magic mirror of the fantasy text, seems to function as a transparent pane of glass, a vista upon the author's day-dreams rather than a canvas upon and into which they are woven by both author *and* reader.

## Sinister Mirrors and Uncanny Reflections

It is perhaps Freud's omnipotent view of the author that explains his own blinkered reading of fantasy forms such as the fairy tale. For as we have seen, the fairy tale is partially cut loose from and thus conspires against authorial appropriation by its presence as shared cultural artform and collocation of competing narrative voices. Freud, in consequence, dismissively consigns it to the realms of the facile and the fabulous, a narrative so divorced from the complexities of the psyche that we can never expect to be seriously affected by it: 'Apparent death and the re-animation of the dead have been represented as most uncanny themes. But ... [w]ho would be so bold as to call it uncanny, for instance, when Snow-White opens her eyes once more?'[10] Once again we find Freud failing to account for the differing impact a variety of readers can have upon a particular text. Just as, elsewhere in this same essay, he vastly over-generalizes in asserting that 'children have no fear of their dolls coming to life, they may even desire it', so here his inattention to the impact of the fairy story upon very young or anxious child readers is completely overlooked.[11] One can only presume that he is ascribing the unilateral status 'reader' here to an adult reader well-versed in the formulaic structure of the fairy tale and probably equally well-versed in and thus well-prepared for the particularities of this specific narrative. This reader we recognize as Freud himself.

It is perhaps shortcomings such as these which have enabled Bettelheim's psychoanalytic reading of fairy-tale narratives to be received in such a favourable light. Unlike Freud's, Bettelheim's analysis opens with the clear understanding that: 'The delight we experience . . . comes not from the psychological meaning of a tale (although this contributes to it) but from its literary qualities.'[12] As his use of the word 'we' implies, his emphasis falls throughout upon the role of the reader, a point that loosens the shackles of what I have been arguing to be the narrative constraints of the fantasy genre as frame. Bettelheim's study is important for what it tells us about the unconscious workings of fairy-tale narratives and the impact (good and bad) that they have upon readers. It has also undoubtedly paved the way for any number of further deconstructive readings of the form, some of which have already been mentioned in the previous chapter. But there are aspects of his reading, too, that remain unconvincing, even (perhaps particularly) as they relate to the dynamics of reading. For throughout his study, Bettelheim is determined to differentiate between the child and adult reader's relationship with the fairy tale as a mode. Of course in some ways he is right to do so, for in returning to the charge levelled against Freud's evasion of the 'literary' aspects of a narrative, it seems probable that a child and an adult may well have a differing response (conscious or unconscious) to the presence of various literary tropes in a tale. But this is not the basis of Bettelheim's differentiation. Instead, he relies on a rather assertively fixed and yet somehow contradictory conceptualization of the child's unconscious that seems out of keeping with any of the major psychoanalytic perspectives on the subject: 'Children's dreams are very simple: wishes are fulfilled and anxieties are given tangible form . . . [But a] child's dreams contain unconscious content that remains practically unshaped by his ego . . . for this reason, children cannot and should not analyze their dreams.'[13]

As a close textual analysis of this statement shows, the second part undermines its opening gambit. If children *cannot* analyse their dreams, then their manifest content (as narrated to a third person) will obviously *appear* to be facile, even if in 'truth' the original version is far more complex. Ironically, Bettelheim is falling into precisely the same trap here as not only Freud, but also those fantasy critics like Jackson who seem determined to dismiss the fairy tale for its facile consolations, having failed to theorise it in any but the most superficial of ways.[14] In addition, we should remember that there is a profound difference between the rather glib connection Bettelheim draws here between children being *unable* to analyse dreams and children being *forbidden* to analyse them. In fact the two conspire against each other. As our exploration of transgression in the previous chapter made plain, prohibition usually functions as an open invitation to transgress. Who, exactly, will take it upon themselves to do the forbidding here and how, exactly, will this strange embargo be enforced? There is a sense, of course, in which Bettelheim's observations on the relationship between children, dreaming and the unconscious really function as an admonitory warning to adults – 'do not attempt to analyse the child's unconscious fantasies, for harm can only result' – a point, in fact, he later makes explicit. It is indeed telling that Bettelheim concerns himself with the fairy tale, for his reading of the relationship between child readers and fairy stories is obsessed, throughout, with the type of false optimism that the traditional fairy tale has been criticized for adopting as a narrative technique. It is this protective, cotton-wool cladding that leads Bettelheim to read the fairy tale as a way of 'the child [becoming] less and less engulfed by unmanageable chaos' and which perhaps finds its sentimentalist pinnacle in his Mills-and-Boon-style maxim that: 'fairy tales . . . prepare the child's mind for the transformation demanded by, and brought about by, being in love'.[15]

Generically, we have seen that the conventional fairy story follows the formula of romantic fiction. In both modes the protagonist is motivated by a quest, undergoes struggles in the process of attaining the desired object and ultimately succeeds to the almost audible cheers of the reader. Narrative consolation is the clear and (we are led to believe) desirable end result. But it is only in the context of this type of textual comparison that Bettelheim's sentimentality can be argued to be valid. For in fact it is not love (that intangible, inconceptualizable and usually unsatisfactory phenomenon) that is the key to the success of the fairy tale, but the far more motivational structures of desire: a desire to succeed, to attain fulfilment, to grow to adult/giant size. And for the child, just as much as for the adult, this will inevitably produce, not Bettelheimesque consolation, but what we have seen to be a Proppian lack. After all, the child is unmistakably aware that, whatever her day- or night-dreams may offer, real-life attainment of any of these things is endlessly deferred by the realities of her social position as 'inferior'.

And here we find the political subtext to Bettelheim's approach. Far from being unaware of the importance of desire to these narrative fictions, he uses them to reinforce the power imbalance that exists between child and adult readers. For of course the truth behind this over-protective dynamic is that withholding information is one of the most effective and duplicitous ways of maintaining superiority (as fairy tales themselves so often remind us). Consider Bettelheim's observations about the adult as 'analyst': 'Startling and incomprehensible as an adult's dreams may be, all their details make sense when analyzed and permit the dreamer to understand what preoccupies his unconscious mind ... [Indeed] new insights into oneself from dreams permit a person to arrange his life much more successfully.'[16] Bettelheim's false optimism is not, it would seem, restricted to the child alone, for observations such as this appear surprising, not only to any adult reader of fantasy, or to any adult reader of psychoanalysis, but simply to any adult reader. Each one of us, recounting our dreams, knows full well that there is an intangible and elusive background to their surface narrative which remains beyond our cognitive reach and which can neither be located nor articulated once we have passed into waking mode. Only if we 'dishonestly' manipulate, reorder and re-create the remaining dream fragments can we string them out into a 'sensible' structure, but this inevitably conspires against their originary form. As we have seen, this is the basis of 'secondary elaboration' or 'secondary revision' and forms the crux of the relationship between night-dreaming (as opposed to day-dreaming) and the literary construction of fictional forms. In that sense the irrevocable distinction that I have implied should be drawn between fictionalized dreams and real dreams is not an entirely true one. After all, in the sense that 'real dreams' are always partially (perhaps largely) beyond conscious cognition, then all dreams are, in the sense in which we use the term, fantasy fictions.

What our analysis of Bettelheim does enable us to observe is the proximity of the fairy tale to fantasy forms such as the gothic. For, as was the case with Propp, it is not so much what Bettelheim says, but what he *implies* here that really strikes a chord, and a sinister one it is at that. Thus Bettelheim's adult, this surrogate analyst, is cast in the role of a duplicitous voyeur, not only prising open the secrets of the child's mind but also jealously keeping the nature of those secrets to herself. Once again, he tries to convince us, such evident duplicity is in the child's own interests: 'If the parent indicates that he knows [the child's inner thoughts] already, the child is prevented from making the most precious gift to his parent of sharing with him what until then was secret and private.'[17] Profound misgivings surround this approach, and they are the type of misgivings that James R. Kincaid deals with in his study of the child as eroticized object. Bettelheim seems to be coercing his child reader, either into the role of an exploited and objectified other, or into what Kincaid refers to as the disturbing allure of the false/naughty child, who knowingly plays games with our adult assumptions in order to flatter our pride while retaining her distance.[18] Whatever the choice, Bettelheim's adult 'analyst' seems to me to be a sinister wolf indeed, luring the child into a truly *unheimlich* sense of false security and misplaced trust. And yet in a strange sense this functions as the most interesting aspect of Bettelheim's work. In the apparent guise of protecting the child reader, Bettelheim reveals (albeit unwittingly) one of the least rigorously explored aspects of fairy-tale narratives: just how frequently the fairy tale's apparent consolations are really 'false friends'. Behind them lurk a series of uncanny confrontations with what can only be referred to as a gothic *dis-ease*.[19]

At first glance, that I should be arguing for a central interrelationship between the fairy tale and the gothic may appear anomalous. But although there is apparent distinction between the sinister ambivalence of the gothic narrative on the one hand and the seemingly playful fantasies of the fairy-tale formula on the other, in fact the two are far more similar than it may at first appear. So the child-devouring witches and ogres that lurk in the forest are an early introduction to the dangerous possibilities of the (only-apparently) familiar, and one has simply to consider the imaginative impact of the house of sweets in 'Hansel and Gretel' or Granny's bedroom in 'Little Red Riding Hood' to recognize the abiding presence of gothic motifs such as the sinister mansion or Bluebeard's bloody chamber. It is also perhaps shared characteristics such as these that explain the presence within Grimm's *Household Tales* of other related tale-types such as 'ghost stories, legends about evil spirits, witches and the malevolent dead'.[20] Here, too, we find fascinated readers identifying with vulnerable interlopers. Here, too, we find the alluring facade of hearth and home so easily shifting into an imprisoning structure, *unheimlich* secrets and the textual encoding of latent desires. In addition, as several feminist re-readings of fairy tales have shown, any number of latent messages in the fairy-tale form render them deeply uncanny narratives for all-too-aware women readers.

In these terms, Gilbert and Gubar refer to the image of the so-called wicked stepmother in '*Snow White*' as a simple gothic metamorphosis of the 'good' queen prior to childbirth. This is an important interpretative manoeuvre, as it helps to situate motherhood as an initiation into the realm of gothic entrapment (a theme we will return to in the context of *The Yellow Wallpaper*). But of course it is the presence of the 'magic' mirror that is so powerfully destructive in the context of this narrative, setting up rivalries between 'mother and daughter, woman and woman, self and self'. Moreover, this central symbol 'frames' this 'wicked woman', forcing her 'to be driven inward, obsessively studying self-images as if seeking a viable self'.[21] It is in motifs such as this that the work of Jacques Lacan is seen to have application to fantasy texts. For in his well-known ideas about the mirror stage of infantile development he wrestles (albeit unconsciously!) with a central image of the literary fantastic. As Carroll's *Alice Through The Looking-Glass*, George MacDonald's *Lilith* (1895) and any number of fantastic narratives show, the mirror is repeatedly found as a double-sided symbol which, as well as having its conventional, mimetic properties, likewise functions as a metaphorical gateway facilitating entry into another world, realm or stage of character development. As Lacan informs us, the necessary psychological rite of passage that takes us from the undifferentiated place of desire that constitutes the imaginary realm into the socially organized and recognizable everyday world of the symbolic order necessitates two things. The first of these is that we must enter what he calls *le stade du miroir* (the mirror phase), whereby we begin to shape our own sense of self through a paradoxical recognition of otherness. As Richard Boothby argues, 'We are to think here of the infant whose wide-eyed gaze, fixed on the face of its mother, seems to deliver it momentarily, as if by magic, from the chaos of movements that characterize most of its waking life.'[22] So, in perceiving mother as other and, as part of this process, reflected self as simultaneously self and not-self, we begin to 'make sense' of the world in terms of boundary enforcement, separation (and therefore loss). Importantly, as in fantasy fictions, Lacan takes pains to assert that the literal presence of a mirror is not required. The mirror exists simply as the ubiquitous metaphor along the road to the symbolic.

The second requirement of the mirror phase, however, returns us in part to our concerns in the previous chapter, for this is the role played by language in the initiation process. In Lacanian terms, the journey into the symbolic is a journey into and through language. Indeed, the mirror itself becomes a site of first articulation (although usually mental rather than oral). In his terms this revolves around a perceived distinction between the lexical choices 'I' and 'not-I' or, as he puts it, the subject of the enunciating and the subject of the enunciation,[23] the former comprising the infant who does the recognizing and the latter the 'reflected' image of the infant which is simultaneously self and other. But for our purposes, the important issue surrounding this is the relationship that the mirror holds to language as power. Returning to Snow White's 'wicked stepmother', we recognize that her sense of loss is well and truly initiated by her recognition that the mirror exists *primarily* as a site of language: 'Mirror, mirror, on the wall, who is the fairest one of all?' How strange, though, that she should ask about the 'fairest *one*' and not the fairest woman (which is surely the real question behind her enquiry). And yet of course the answer she receives fractures her own sense of self-containment and she learns in the process that she is not 'one' at all, but a split-subject, caught in the trap of the mirror that divides, in this case, the subject of the enunciating (the Queen) from the subject of the enunciation (mirrored self but not self): the step-daughter, Snow White. Finally, another point made by Gilbert and Gubar is crucial to this scene. For they position the King at the site of that splitting: 'His, surely, is the voice of the looking glass, the patriarchal voice of judgment that rules the Queen's – and every woman's – self-evaluation.'[24] As French-school feminists have convincingly argued, the woman's relationship to the symbolic realm is one of double loss. Severed from an awareness of what Hélène Cixous refers to as the voice of the mother – 'that omnipotent figure that dominates the fantasies of the pre-Oedipal baby'[25] – the law of the father here replaces this cruel site of reflection with another mirrored distortion, this time set up between woman and woman.

Lacan's work on the mirror stage is, of course, heavily indebted to Freud's work on narcissism. When we attend to what Cixous also has to say about the latter's reading of 'The "Uncanny"', we see that a similarly narcissistic compulsion underlies the Freudian gothic. As many readers of his text have acknowledged, Freud's essay tends to mystify as much as it illuminates. And this is not because it is particularly 'difficult', it is simply that it follows a typical gothic narrative strategy, in revealing itself only in order to reveil. Thus multiple conflicting definitions and illustrations masquerade as exposition, placing the reader in the position of detective and, in that sense, *embodying* the uncanny as much as explaining it. As Cixous observes: 'What does the disconcerted reader do? He "selects" the most salient themes in order to seek out what he hopes to find. And what about the rest? One pulls a thread. The tapestry remains.'[26] This 'tapestry', however, as we shall come on to see, bears more than a passing resemblance to the seductively alluring veil. For the essay draws us into its confidence as unsuspecting interlopers, playfully offering us a pleasurable but frustrating form of (anti-)logic which, at the same time as it mimics the structures of a rhetorical argument, continually and even flirtatiously subverts and eludes this structure by means of a number of compulsive reminiscences of a playful (even at times a personal) nature. Paradoxically, this compulsive repetition/reminiscence is strung together as an elaborate form of wilful denial. As Cixous observes, in the essay as a whole, repetition is 'regulated by the allusion "should not have repeated itself"'.[27] What we are dealing with, then, is not simply an essay *about* the manner in which the uncanny insists upon its own absent and unspecified presence in gothic texts, but one which encrypts this within itself. A clearly evident though unspoken subliminal message erupts between the lines of the page and in the realm of half-hints, disturbing and disrupting with its uncannily 'absent' presence. The name attached to this '[thing] which ought to have remained hidden but has come to light'[28] is Freud's own obsessive day-dream of being a creative writer. No wonder he begins this, like so many of his 'literary' essays, by apologizing for his lack of narrative expertise. After all, without such perceptible 'lack' where might the issue of desire spring from? Nevertheless, its usefulness to us remains in its ability to facilitate a deconstruction of genre by furthering our understanding of Todorov's fantastic (particularly as it impinges upon gothic narratives).

The substance of Freud's argument can be summarized as follows. The essence of the uncanny (*unheimlich*) is that which fearfully but deliberately situates itself upon a central paradox. In part the nature of the paradox derives from the uncanny's etymological antithesis 'homely' (*heimlich*), insofar as two of the latter's possible meanings seemingly contradict each other:

I ... belonging to the house, not strange, familiar, tame, intimate, friendly ...
II Concealed, kept from sight, so that others do not get to know of or about it, withheld from others ...[29]

Yet once we note the shared connection (set up in the German original) with the world of domesticity, these convolutions and, along with them, those surrounding the mystical nature of this distinction between the *heimlich* and *unheimlich*, start to unravel. For the intimacy which we desire to create in the sharing of personal space initiates, in its turn, a sense of privacy and general exclusion which does, indeed, result in certain possessions, patterns of behaviour or activities being 'concealed' or 'kept from sight' within the four walls of the home. There is nothing contradictory or even uncanny about this. It is precisely what endows our cultural fantasies of 'hearth and home' with their pleasurable/wish-fulfilment dimensions. The issue becomes still clearer when the definition of the *unheimlich* is fully spelt out: '"*un-*": eerie, wierd, arousing gruesome fear ... *"Unheimlich" is the name for everything that ought to have remained ... secret and hidden but has come to light*' (Schelling).[30] In other words, we are not simply dealing with the concealed here, but with something sinister or disturbing that is actually in the process of being revealed. We can summarize this distinction a great deal more succinctly than Freud does by suggesting that whereas the *heimlich*/homely deals with the issue of privacy, the *unheimlich*/uncanny deals with the discovery of something formerly clandestine or secret.

Freud is therefore correct in differentiating between the uncanny and 'what excites fear in general', the uncanny being a particularly poignant version of fear.[31] In order for us to feel something to be uncanny, it must derive from a situation, object or incident that ought to feel (and usually has felt) familiar and reassuring, but which has undergone some form of slight shift that results in what I have referred to as a form of *dis-ease*. This is one of the reasons for the powerful uncanny potential inherent in the presiding imagery of the gothic mansion. Rather than giving us anticipated home comforts, the mansion unnerves us by offering the 'strange' instead. Here, far from conveying security, a locked door functions to 'shut up' secrets and keep the interloper or others ensnared by their fears. It is important that this fear hinges upon an awareness of reassurance denied, for it is at this point that the psychoanalytic element begins to emerge. If we think about this connection more closely, for example, it becomes clear that many of the motifs of the gothic bear a striking resemblance to the everyday objects of the analytic procedure. So we find ubiquitous references to the dwarfing presence of furnishings (couches), interior settings, and the presence of a presiding, powerful mediator who is both gothic/romantic hero and interloper into the realms of the analysand's interior locked chest/mind and its guilty secrets. When we also bear in mind that psychoanalysis is basically a 'family' narrative located in the realms of private space, such uncanny connections are made all the more obvious. In summary, then, the uncanny is a confrontation with 'concealed' repressions; not perhaps 'everything that ought to have remained . . . secret and hidden but has come to light' as Schelling puts it, but certainly something that we might *wish* had 'remained . . . secret and hidden but has come to light'.

Freud continues his argument by offering a number of examples of typical uncanny devices, a categorizing approach that seems worryingly close to those reductive, genre-based readings of fantasy forms that were disparaged in the previous chapter. These categories comprise four major groupings. The first of these refers to the existence of an apparently precarious dividing line between animate and inanimate objects, as is frequently conveyed by the presence of puppets, waxwork figures and clockwork toys. The second relates to the presence of doubles in the form of identical twins, mirrored reflections or shadows. The third refers to certain types of 'involuntary repetition', as in the case when: 'caught in a mist, perhaps, one has lost one's way in a mountain forest, every attempt to find the marked or familiar path may bring one back again and again, to one and the same spot, which one can identify by some particular landmark.'[32] The final major category of uncanny stimulus derives from what Freud refers to as 'omnipotence of thoughts', or apparently bringing into being or into our presence something/someone that we have dreamt up or spoken about without having any apparent reason for doing so. In summary, he argues that 'an uncanny effect is often and easily produced when the distinction between imagination and reality is effaced, as when something that we have hitherto regarded as imaginary appears before us in reality.'[33]

Here our fears of generic reductionism begin to abate. For it is this aspect of the uncanny, above all, that takes us away from fantasy as genre fiction and much closer to Todorovian readings of the literary fantastic which share this ability to distort apparently defined boundaries between the real and the unreal. Like Freud's reading of the uncanny, we have seen that Todorov's reading of the fantastic derives from the perpetuation of uncertainty as to whether an event is caused by psychological or supernatural devices. And if it were not for the fact that Freud is almost pathologically opposed to the recognition of the supernatural as a possible phenomenon, both perspectives may have shared even more common ground. Both Todorov and Freud have their limitations in this respect. Jackson, for example, is quite condemnatory about what she perceives to be Todorov's evasions of the psychoanalytic dimensions of uncanny structures. Thus, although he recognizes their presence as 'fear, or horror, or simply curiosity', he refuses to discuss them as anything other than part of that safe territory surrounding the disruptive borderground of the literary fantastic.[34] But it remains the case that, while the two share many characteristics, the fantastic is more versatile than the uncanny, including all of the latter and some more besides (a point that many critics have failed to acknowledge). Rather more important is Freud's lack of attention to the type of readerly strategies that Todorov's theory facilitates. Indeed, Freud's continued refusal to differentiate between the reading strategies adopted when reading realism as opposed to the fantastic makes his work inevitably flawed in its application to the latter. For example, in the context of William Shakespeare's *Macbeth* (1623) (a play that we might loosely subsume under the auspices of the gothic), Freud suggests the following analysis: 'the supernatural apparitions . . . may be gloomy and terrible enough, but they are no more really uncanny than Homer's jovial world of gods. We adapt our judgement to the imaginary reality imposed on us by the writer, and regard souls, spirits and ghosts as though their existence had the same validity as our own has in material reality.'[35] But do we? Certainly we 'willingly suspend disbelief' when confronted with fantastic forms in literature – *Macbeth* included – but this is not to reduce its gothic aspects to the realm of the mimetic. Instead, as Todorov recognizes, we hesitate over the perpetuation of an uncertainty that revolves around the distinction to be drawn between the supernatural and psychological hallucination. Undoubtedly one of the intriguing dilemmas of this play for any twentieth-century reader/spectator derives from this very prevarication. On the one hand we do, following the terms of the theatrical setting, read these characters as witches. But alongside this we also acknowledge a psychological interpretation that renders them nothing more than hallucinatory manifestations: the grotesque embodiment of a compulsive obsession. The key lies, not in deciding between the two, but in juggling with both.

Irrespective of what we have seen to be Freud's authorial aspirations, the fact is that in 'The "Uncanny"' we do not allow him to adopt an author/itarian role. Indeed, far from 'accept[ing] his ruling in every case', his argument about the interrelationship between the presence of the uncanny in reality and its manifestation in literature often seems both arbitrary and unconvincing. In one of his characteristically sweeping generalizations, Freud confidently asserts: 'The uncanny as it is depicted in literature . . . is a much more fertile province than the uncanny in real life, for it contains the whole of the latter and something more besides.'[36] While agreeing that literature offers us plentiful examples of the uncanny, I regard the second part of Freud's statement as quite simply untrue. First, his belief is founded on the spurious assumption that every incident which we would find uncanny in reality would also strike us as uncanny if we were to encounter it in literature. This can only be the case if we believe (and unfortunately Freud does seem to believe this) that all readers read texts in exactly the same way and that literary style and structure account for nothing. An example drawn from his own essay conveys this. Seeking to illustrate the uncanny qualities of the 'compulsion to repeat', Freud offers the following anecdote by way of an example:

> we naturally attach no importance to the event when we hand in an overcoat and get a cloakroom ticket with the number, let us say, 62; or when we find that our cabin on a ship bears that number. But the impression is altered if two such events, each in itself indifferent, happen close together – if we come across the number 62 several times in a single day, or if we begin to notice that everything which has a number – addresses, hotel rooms, compartments in railway trains – invariably has the same one, or at all events one which contains the same figures. We do feel this to be uncanny.[37]

Though accepting the validity of this as an uncanny 'real-life' event, it is rather unconvincing that such a series of events in a literary narrative would *necessarily* strike a reader as uncanny. At best they might appear intriguing. At worst they would soon become predictable or contrived and the uncanny be ironically submerged by the all-too-familiar. But one aspect of this example is undoubtedly uncanny. Wishing politely to play along with our 'author' here, the reader humours Freud and, in the process, simultaneously pretends acceptance while partly rebelling against (among other things) the specific choice of the number 62. This passage well and truly fractures the reader into a split readerly/writerly subject. The readerly subject simply complies: any number must be selected at random for the purposes of illustration and, as we have seen, Freud seems to believe that the reader of a text is always compliant. Not surprisingly, then, no rationale is offered for the selection of this number. But the writerly subject is by no means appeased. In any work of psychoanalysis nothing can be seen as genuinely incidental. Why choose the number 62? Surely it must in some way hold a concealed, repressed, 'uncanny' significance that Freud is refusing to bring to light. Again, it is Cixous who unearths the secret and, just as Schelling argues, its effect upon us is indeed uncanny. Typically, the answer to the riddle lies with Freud's authorial narcissism. Born in 1856, Freud is 63 (almost but not quite 62) in 1919, the year of first publication of the essay. But what is the meaning of this 'almost but not quite'? How can this have any place within the uncanny? Cixous patiently elucidates further:

> if you are writing . . . a text which the instinct (*trieb*) of death haunts, then you will be the reprieved author, who escapes this anouncement of his end, masked by a you where the I becomes identifiable with the reader. Freud is palming off his own death on us . . . and isn't the one who has lived a year beyond the age foreseen for his own disappearance in some way a ghost?[38]

The full irony of this is not even seen by Cixous herself. This author-centred text, which prides itself on its uncanny reveilings has, encrypted within it, its very own paradox. Buried within and speaking out of its own playful masquerade is the very 'death of the author' that Freud, the 'capricious stage-setter',[39] narcissistically strives to repress. Few uncanny doubles could be as uncanny as this!

## The Gothic Text and/as 'Space Between'

In summary, Freud and Bettelheim, theorising the relationship between creative writing and day-dreaming, site a rather fixed conceptualization of play at the centre of both the resulting (textual) secondary elaboration and the unconscious wish-fulfilment phantasy out of which the former emerges. Play, in this respect, forms a parallel with what child psychologists refer to as 'pretend play' (or the exploration of unreal scenarios through a controlled 'daylight' use of phantasy). This notion of play is likewise adhered to by later theorists such as Winnicott, who goes so far as to argue that 'play and playing . . . form the basis of cultural experience in general . . . '. The subject of play is, as I have said, crucial to all literary forms. As Holland puts it: 'Both play and literature can be understood . . . as first, letting a disturbing influence happen to us, then, second, mastering that disturbance . . . When literature "pleases", it, too, lets us experience a disturbance, then master it, but the disturbance and mastery distinguishes our pleasure in play and literature from simple sensuous pleasures.'[40] Perhaps this is never more true than when applied to fantasy fictions. Object-relations theorists' preoccupations with space and its relationship to play as boundary demarcations, render frontier territory central. So, as well as the child utilizing play in the manner that the adult utilizes fantasy (and vice versa), play also becomes a means of adapting to 'the boundaries between self and not-self'. The same could be said of adult relationships with the pleasures of fantasy texts. Once object-relations boundaries have been established, literature permits us to loosen and thus subject them to interrogation. Fantasy fiction enables not only the self/not-self boundary, but also the boundaries between 'inner and outer' and 'past, present, and future' to be placed under scrutiny in this manner.[41] Ultimately this offers more productive strategies for facilitating our readings of fantastic forms.

The gothic is a good example of such textual interrogations, for we need to remember that a gothic text only *becomes* a gothic text when the apparently fixed demarcations between the interior nightmare realm and the outside world of so-called daylight order are called into question. The means by which this occurs is through the presence of an interloper who stirs up the fixity of the frame and forces the night-dream out into a daylight interaction with this 'rational' world. On one level, as we will see in the context of *The Strange Case of Dr Jekyll and Mr Hyde*, this role is performed by a fictional character within the text. But on another level, it is also fulfilled by the reader. We have already seen that Todorov's own fantastic chink of light helps to cut through the rigidity of Freud's closed day-dream text. What of the material that the reader brings to the narrative? As Istvan Csicsery-Ronay Jr. asserts, we can locate 'two linked forms of hesitation, a pair of gaps' at the centre of all fantasy texts[42] and it is these two 'gaps' that are the important issue here. From the perspective of psychoanalysis, they could be seen to refer to the 'willing suspension of disbelief' on the one hand and the unconscious repressions that we carry around with us on the other. In this way the reader, in the guise of the interloper, stirs up the fixity of the frame to produce a disruptive text of fantastic destabilization. In contrast to Zipes, then, who believes that: 'it is practically impossible to determine what direct effect a [text] will have upon an individual reader in terms of validating his or her own existence',[43] Holland theorises this relationship precisely, a point that makes his work particularly interesting. Like Todorov, he works through and with the tension between the schematic and a more fluid, dynamic, reader-response approach. As part of this, he also agrees that the reading process necessarily involves a degree of compartmentalization: 'The skilled reader organizes the details of the text into recurring images and themes. Essentially, he abstracts repeated or contrasted words, images, events or characters into categories.'[44]

In a sense, then, Holland is offering a way of explaining the drive towards ordering and satisfying that all readers impose upon literary texts, arguing that this mirrors the psychological ordering and phasing that the child undergoes on her journey of development.[45] For our concerns, it is his work on the oral and anal phases that is of most immediate relevance. The oral phase is the one which impacts most significantly upon our reading/devouring of all texts (the term 'Reader's Digest' coming to mind at this point). So literary narratives create a hunger to know more (through suspense and other means) which stimulates the attendant desire for gratification that keeps us turning the pages. But while the text functions as 'food' to be ingested as we 'take in' the narrative, we reciprocate in becoming the object which is 'taken in' by its plot. The oral phase, in this sense in conjunction with the anal phase, is therefore intrinsically called upon to help us form distinct reader/text boundaries between 'out there' and 'in here'. We not only relate to the content of narratives in the manner described above, we also interact unconsciously with their structural devices, a dynamic far more complex than anything Freudian readings can offer: 'We generate expectations from our general balance of defense and [ph]antasy and test the new novel against them: "pleasing terror", "bland language", suspense'.[46]

It is quite clear that Freud's belief in the text as a static site of play is very much challenged under these theoretical terms. But as well as being intrinsic to the reading process in general, this distinction is also specifically central in the context of fantasy modes such as the gothic or science fiction, where 'in here' and 'out there' form crucial narrative pivots. Thus the gothic mansion becomes '"potential space" . . . a space between',[47] while in the case of science fiction we find a similar depiction of boundaries as limits to interrogate. This paradigm can be used to deconstruct genre, but more significantly it imposes itself upon the reader of texts: 'Often, when literary works ask us to enter an environment explicitly labeled as fantastic, we are being asked to merge orally into that new world . . . We must "trust" [it] . . . as we would a nurturing mother.'[48] Rather than being a utopian desire, such an envelopment might strike us as profoundly threatening. It is one thing to be asked to 'merge' and to 'trust', but the realm we are dealing with here is that alien, strange foreignness that we will see Kristeva perceiving as intrinsic to the *loss* of the nurturing mother. And in a sense this is always the play of the fantastic text, a form necessitating readerly risk. We have already addressed the intrinsic connection that fairy tales have with gothic narratives (even horror narratives if we take this oral projection to include threats of being devoured by giants, cooked in stoves by witches, or poisoned by apples). If even these supposedly reassuring forms are so precariously placed, then what of the realm of a Stephen King chiller? This issue of the paradox of fearful pleasures is often perceived to derive from the work's ability to order the disturbing in a satisfying (and thus aesthetically consoling) manner. Usually this is taken to be an issue for readers rather than writers but, as Hume reminds us, it is actually one for both, authors 'project[ing] their own anxieties into their stories as a means of handling their own subconscious tensions, and readers enjoy[ing] literature in part because it plays with these sensitive issues in a way that keeps them from seeming too threatening.'[49] In itself, of course, this mirrors psychoanalysis, which aims to provide order through narrative articulation, working through the repetition of imagery and symbolism and the power of association to render up meanings. But this argument, though persuasive, fails to account for the fact that not all readers *will* find Stephen King's narratives 'pleasurably' fearful and ultimately reassuring. Some will simply find them disgusting and terrifying. This is why Holland's view is far more persuasive.

Holland looks to analyse the individuality of reader response in terms of psychoanalytic repression. Consequently, although he argues that 'most men and women can tolerate a wide variety of infantile fantasies – a tribute to the polymorphous perversity of our early years', on occasions a particular individual will react in what is commonly seen to be a generically 'inappropriate' manner by screaming, fainting, vomiting or calling out.[50] This he ascribes to an inability to recognize the aforementioned distinctions between 'in here' and 'out there' and interestingly, in these cases, the results return to their bodily origins. But all reader response is more or less conditioned by such strategies as they are encoded within the trappings of the text. Some of the examples that Holland gives of this demonstrate the varying degrees of condensation and displacement that may be at work in any particular transformation and the extent to which such eruptions might control or shape the surface narrative. In the context of the 'anal' text, for example, he claims that: 'Images of dirt are the essential clue . . . [as are] fears of being enveloped by what is foul, dirty, or sordid.' In this case, the relationship between phantasy and secondary elaboration can be seen to be fairly metonymic/mimetic. When he develops this theme further, however, a gradual shift towards the metaphorical structures of condensation becomes apparent: 'As for imagery, one [also] finds . . . a preoccupation with dirt, with smells . . . and then with their transformations: fog, mist, sweet smells, pure air, light, even, ultimately, *logos*, the word of God.'[51] The distinction between these two spheres is important. As one journeys progressively through this continuum, the distance between what we might refer to as the tenor and the vehicle begins to widen. What possible connection, one may ask, genuinely exists between the anal phase and the word of God? Admittedly one might reply that the child is gradually encouraged verbally to articulate the desire/need to defecate and urinate, in response to which the God-like parent imposes spoken commands, rewards and perhaps even punishments. But Holland is wary of the ease of such classificatory approaches. Just as 'children do not behave so neatly as adults with schemes might wish', so 'symbols are flexible and dynamic: they vary with the context',[52] including, of course, their literary context.

Such metaphorical structures are the essence of the relationship between phantasy and fantasy. They reflect the fact that all literary structures are entirely dependent upon the centrality of metamorphic transformations, being secondary elaborations of an originary phantasy which has no fixed and final form. If, for example, a fictional event, description or character functions as a secondary elaboration of an originary anal phantasy, although it will be associated with a clearly locatable developmental phase, it cannot be connected with a specific real-life scenario. As Meredith Skura points out, the eruption of any particular 'kind' of phantasy can only *interact* with the surface narrative, perhaps going so far as to '[pull] the surface into new patterns', but never accounting for a text's full significance. Overall, in fact, 'A single primal [ph]antasy preempts first one and then another aspect of the text, repeating its own pattern beneath what otherwise appears to be a changing surface.'[53] The modifications that the formal aesthetic devices of the text inflict upon the elaboration of the phantasy will also work as psychoanalytic defence mechanisms. In the case of enjambement or ellipsis, for example (both clear instances of Skura's 'pulling' mechanism in the sense of respectively overspilling and reducing the line demarcations), we are given a perfect example of the inherent tension between the anarchic kaleidoscope erupting beneath the surface and the formal constraints which articulate and explore while concealing and containing. And yet, as if to underline the difficulty of fully divorcing phantasy from fantasy, this comparison between the analytic scenario and the un-masking of charged textual material compulsively returns us to the world of the gothic: 'Repression, in effect, buries alive an impulse or fear or feeling or fantasy, buries "alive", because the drive does not lose its force . . . the repressed can return . . . rise up from the tomb to trouble the living.'[54] In textual terms, our individual 'matrix' of personal repressions interacts with those encoded into the text. It seems feasible to presume then that those readers who are especially drawn towards or away from a particular fantasy genre or text are thus drawn because of the complex combination within it between the phantasy material and the method, style and structure of elaboration chosen. At the same time, as fantasy genres such as horror or the gothic illustrate, the function of some forms is to push us as close to those limits as they can, while ultimately maintaining our 'safe place' within them.

Just as Freud, in 'Creative Writers and Day-Dreaming', recognizes that part of the writer's role is to overcome the inevitable embarrassment or even repulsion that we would expect to experience on being told the content of another person's fantasies, so Holland observes that, under normal circumstances, 'These fantasies, our own and the work's, would not be acceptable to our egos . . . a 'censor' would reject them in their raw form'.[55] Only via literary mediation is such censorship side-stepped. So we are duped by means of defences (aesthetic structuring) and introjected satisfied desires into accepting what aims to be the perfect textual combination of 'drive-satisfying and anxiety-arousing aspects'. This strikes me as a far more credible and useful theory of the reader's fascination with fantastic fears than the static and compromised enclosures of aesthetic bracketing or, as Donald Palumbo puts it, the 'paradoxical ability to exorcise fear of the unknown by revealing [it and] . . . safely containing it – in familiar, known formats'.[56] Thus when Holland argues that, 'In a way, we seek literary forms because we wish we could manage life itself as adroitly as a sonnet does', he is recognizing that, far from containing, there is always an overspill between gratification and denial that leaves us in a state of ongoing desire.[57] As the horror critic Dennis Giles has acknowledged, a text is 'not a finished product but a process of production', a perspective that replaces the static dream-screen with a 'structure of conflict' resistant to assimilation but interactive with those parts of the psyche in which lurk unspecified fears and buried desires.[58]

## Frontier Territory, Or Playing in Space

Returning again to the type of 'free play' that we have seen to be in operation in Freud's reading of the uncanny, we recognize that once generic boundaries start to become deconstructed the process of secondary elaboration moves at least one step beyond the control of the dreamer/writer. In the process it turns both her and the reader into nothing more than playthings of the text. As Roger Abrahams asserts: 'playing subverts as it amplifies . . . In this way we can, in any situation we call play, sense the presence of absent things doubly – in the fiction that gives place, substance, and meaning to the things.'[59] Ultimately, perhaps, it is this playful disruption which signals the distinction between gothic fictions and traditional fairy tales. Whereas we have seen the latter sheltering within a clearly delineated dream-text, gothic narratives are always struggling to come to terms with a problematic paradox between licence and control that consistently undermines straightforward textual categorization. The very relationship that exists between readers of gothic texts and the texts themselves helps to unveil this playful, if problematic dialectic. Considering, once again, Schelling's belief that 'everything is *unheimlich* that ought to have remained secret and hidden but has come to light', does this not effect a double negative that actually prevents a gothic narrative from being uncanny? After all, a fictional text is designed to be read and, in the process, its 'secret and hidden' contents *intended* to come to light. Nevertheless, the complex combination of revealing and reveiling that comprises the gothic enables what, in the hands of the fairy tale, would be a cryptic encoding of repressed fears and desires, to be transformed in a gothic context into a rather more problematic *en*-crypting of the same. Morris Dickstein's observation that 'Filmmakers realized early on that the darkened theater and the flickering images created a kind of dream space'[60] is worth considering in this light, for what we might at first take to be a fenced-in Freudian playground of lack and desire becomes, in the terms of the 'flickering images' through which it is perceived, an interactive site of fantastic destabilization far more in tune with Skura's psychoanalytic reading of phantasy:

> [Ph]antasy's role cannot be predicted; it crops up wherever it can, taking over or slipping out like a taboo subject in polite conversation, and it affects not only the story or plot but the character configurations, the landscape, the props, the imagery, and the language. The presence of [ph]antasy is anything but a mere substitution of a hidden story for an open one. [Ph]antasy is present in the proliferation of scenes arising from different elements of the text, sometimes more, sometimes less directly and obviously; it is sometimes literally part of the text and sometimes only a distant echo.[61]

Finally, this takes us on to the work of Julia Kristeva, whose ability to inform theories of the fantastic has been largely undervalued. Transforming Lacan's static playground of the imaginary realm into a far more disruptive site of disruption, Kristeva perceives the location of the split subject to be one in which our position within the symbolic is continually displaced and destabilized by the fantastic possibilities of the semiotic. This, just like the uncanny itself, continues to threaten and disrupt, haunting the order of the symbolic with its unrepressible phantoms. But this is also, of course, the zone of the fantastic: 'the inside or underside of realism, opposing the novel's closed, monological forms with open, dialogical structures, as if the novel had given rise to its own opposite, its unrecognizable reflection.'[62] We should not be distracted by the Lacanian inflection in the use of the phrase 'unrecognizable reflection' here, for a continual interrogation of the symbolic is implied overall. It is this which leads Jackson to refer to the fantastic in a manner that is entirely Kristevan in its terms: 'The fantastic, then, pushes towards an area of non-signification. It does this either by attempting to articulate "the unnameable" ... attempting to visualize the unseen, or by establishing a disjunction of word and meaning through a play upon "thingless names".'[63] That the semiotic has a connection with the fantastic in general and the uncanny in particular is made clear by Kristeva's work in *Strangers to Ourselves*. Situating her argument within an exploration of psychoanalytic readings of foreignness, she concludes her study with a reading of Freud's uncanny: 'Henceforth the foreigner is neither a race nor a nation ... foreignness is within us: we are our own foreigners'.[64] Quite aside from the fact that it is perhaps this, above all, that fantasy fiction explores in general, it also reminds us that Freud's ultimate source of the uncanny derives from precisely the same 'place' as the Kristevan semiotic: our repressed awareness of the pleasures of the mother's body.

Concealed and repressed (indeed literally kept out of sight), that once all-too-familiar territory is now a prohibitive site of taboo. We have seen that the uncanny is different from 'what excites fear in general', but surely we cannot be blind to Freud's playful use of oxymoron here.[65] This space of the stranger/mother/other is not simply fearful; it is also a profound source of repressed pleasurable excitement/arousal. Indeed, it is a space to which we are complusively and repeatedly drawn, even as we assert our own separateness from it. This, more than anything else, is what draws the attention of Kristeva, who explains this phenomenon in the following terms: 'A first step was taken that removed the uncanny strangeness from the outside, where fright had anchored it, to locate it inside ... the familiar potentially tainted with strangeness and referred ... to an improper past.'[66] Her use of the term 'improper' is obviously loaded. Kristeva, like all French-school theorists, negatively endows the term 'proper' with ap-propriation and the usurpation of the law of the father. Like the 'un-' of the 'un-' canny then, this 'im-' prefix (playfully mirroring the splitting of the affirmatory statement of identity 'I(')m'), conspires against straightforward disencoding, asserting legitimacy in the guise of the illegitimate/improper. In Kristeva's terms, rather than functioning as a powerful image of horror, the body of the mother is that lost site of play from which we are exiled. Permanently expelled from this 'land of our birth' we remain forever refugees, wishing to return to the lost utopia, haunted by a wish-fulfilment phantom pregnancy which *is* the fantasized body of the mother: an image undoubtedly at the heart of so many uncanny inter(n)ments.

In addition to this, Kristeva's own perceptions of the interrelationship between space and textuality render her voice an interesting addition to those of the postmodernists we will encounter in the next chapter. In 'Women's Time', for example, she explicitly argues that one of the functions of literature is to operate as 'a game, a *space* of fantasy and pleasure'. This is not dissimilar to the approach taken by Massey, who argues that 'Words themselves create a space between themselves and experience: a time-space, because they take time to speak or read, and a life-space, because they postpone action.'[67] In some ways, however, Kristeva's perspective proves more encompassing. For she brings together the various competing readings of textual play already addressed and the centrality of space as an issue for both speculative fictions and postmodern theory. Henri Lefebvre nevertheless offers a salient warning: 'any search for space in literary texts will find it everywhere and in every guise: enclosed, described, projected, dreamt of, speculated about. What texts can be considered special enough to provide the basis for [such] a "textual" analysis?'[68] Perhaps this is the crux of the project which the fantastic shares with both the postmodern and the psychoanalytic. Whatever Lefebvre's reservations, it is true that in the case of popular fiction, the typical prioritization of pleasure, desire and consolationist wish-fulfilment and the situation of these within a clearly defined spatial/formulaic enclosure renders projected space especially central. As I have noted elsewhere, it is also the case that no single popular mode offers a more sustained treatment of the relationship between fantasy, pleasure and concepts of the spatial than that of science fiction.[69] Of course psychoanalysis also shares with the fantastic its preoccupation with the mysterious territory which forms the site of the transactions between private and public realms, a point which, in Kristevan terms, renders psychoanalysis itself a (perhaps fantastic) 'journey into the strangeness of the other and of oneself'.[70] Indeed, one begins to wonder, taking the recurrent fascination with space and time into account, whether in fact it is not space which is the ultimate 'stranger to ourselves' and psychoanalysis merely the means by which its journey is mapped out. But if Freudian notions of space are reconfigured as 'innerspace ... internally coherent clusters of belief and desire', then Kristeva's *sujet-en-proces* can be read as an intrepid voyager through space as well as being, in David Crownfield's terms, a subject at play.[71] After all, it is through Kristeva's early work on the importance of the free-playing counter-structures of textual pleasure and desire that she embarks, *sf*-like, upon a metaphorical journey into the psyche, prioritizing as she goes, 'All functions which suppose a *frontier* ... and the transgression of that frontier'.[72] Endowing such territory with corporeal definition, the following chapter moves on to consider the narrative and ideological implications of this alien encounter with fantastic metamorphosis. Siting this interaction, not simply on the frontiers of outer space, but at many and various cultural locations, we re-encounter

Kristeva's stranger at the end of this road, engaged in an ongoing struggle to the death with her postmodern antagonist, Haraway's cyborg.

## Notes

1 Claire Russell, 'A Study of the Folk Symbolism of Kinship; The Tooth Image', in Venetia J. Newall (ed.), *Folklore Studies in the Twentieth Century: Proceedings of the Centenary Conference of the Folklore Society* (Woodbridge: D.S. Brewer, 1980), pp. 366–70 (p. 366).

2 Bruno Bettelheim, *The Uses of Enchantment: The Meaning and Importance of Fairy Tales* (Harmondsworth: Penguin, 1991), pp. 35–6.

3 As defined by Jean Laplanche and Jean-Bertrand Pontalis, 'Fantasy and the Origins of Sexuality', in Victor Burgin et al. (eds), *Formations of Fantasy* (London: Routledge, 1989), pp. 5–34 (pp. 5–6).

4 Sigmund Freud, 'Delusions and Dreams in Jensen's "*Gradiva*"', trans. James Strachey, in Albert Dickson (ed.), *The Penguin Freud Library, Vol. 14, Art and Literature* (Harmondsworth: Penguin, 1990), pp. 27–118.

5 Throughout his essay Freud displays an obvious and recurrent curiosity in using it as a means of psychoanalysing the author's unconscious. Indeed, as Freud's own postscript to the second edition testifies, he subsequently approached Jensen, requesting 'to know the material of impressions and memories from which the author . . . built the work' (p. 117). Jensen, declining co-operation with this, died prior to the publication of this postscript, thereby removing any subsequent possibility of such revelations. Ironically, of course, this simply functioned to further stimulate the curiosity of Freud the 'archeological' analyst.

6 Sigmund Freud, 'Creative Writers and Day-Dreaming', trans. I.F. Grant, in Dickson (ed.), *The Penguin Freud Library, Vol. 14, Art and Literature*, pp. 129–41.

7 Freud, 'Creative Writers', p. 134.

8 Elizabeth Freund, *The Return of the Reader: Reader-Response Criticism* (London: Methuen, 1987), p. 117.

9 Sigmund Freud, 'The "Uncanny"', trans. Alix Strachey, in Dickson (ed.), *The Penguin Freud Library, Vol. 14, Art and Literature* , 335–76 (pp. 373 – my emphasis).

10 Freud, 'Uncanny', p. 369.

11 Freud, 'Uncanny', p. 355.

12 Bettelheim, *Enchantment*, p. 12.

13 Bettelheim, *Enchantment*, p. 54.

14 See Rosemary Jackson, *Fantasy: The Literature of Subversion* (London: Methuen, 1981), pp. 153–6 *passim*.

15 Bettelheim, *Enchantment*, pp. 155, 66 and 278 respectively.

16 Bettelheim, *Enchantment*, p. 54.

17 Bettelheim, *Enchantment*, p. 18.

18 For a fuller discussion of this see Chapter 7, 'The Naughty Child', in James R. Kincaid, *Child-Loving: The Erotic Child and Victorian Culture* (New York: Routledge, 1992).

19 This use of the term *dis-ease* is one I adopt throughout this book. Usefully combining the obvious connotations of 'unease' with that pervasive sense of sickness intrinsic to the gothic, it is also a coinage particularly applicable to the type of disturbance gothic narratives inflict upon their readers.

20 This offers an answer to Linda Dégh's puzzlement about their inclusion. See Linda Dégh, 'Grimm's *Household Tales* and Its Place in the Household: The Social Relevance of a Controversial Classic', *Western Folklore*, Vol. 38 (1979), pp. 83–103 (p. 91).

21 Sandra Gilbert and Susan Gubar, *The Madwoman in the Attic: The Woman Writer and the Nineteenth Century Literary Imagination* (New Haven: Yale University Press, 1984), pp. 36–44 passim.

22 Richard Boothby, *Death and Desire: Psychoanalytic Theory in Lacan's Return to Freud* (New York: Routledge, 1991), p. 31.
23 Selden and Widdowson illustrate this in the following manner: 'When I say "Tomorrow I graduate", the "I" in the statement is known as the "subject of the enunciation", and the ego which makes the statement is the "subject of the enunciating". [Lacanian] thought enters the gap between these two subjects'. Raman Selden and Peter Widdowson, *A Reader's Guide to Contemporary Literary Theory* (Hemel Hempstead: Harvester Wheatsheaf, 1993), p. 138.
24 Gilbert and Gubar, *Madwoman*, p. 38.
25 This is Toril Moi's definition. See Toril Moi, *Sexual/Textual Politics* (London: Methuen, 1985), p. 114.
26 Hélène Cixous, 'Fiction and Its Phantoms: A Reading of Freud's *Das Unheimliche* (The 'Uncanny')', *New Literary History*, Vol. 7 (1976), pp. 525–48 (p. 538).
27 Cixous, 'Phantoms' p. 540.
28 This phrase being central to Freud's essay. See Freud, 'Uncanny', pp. 345 and 364.
29 Freud, 'Uncanny', pp. 342–4 *passim*.
30 Freud, 'Uncanny', p. 345 – original emphasis.
31 Freud, 'Uncanny', p. 339.
32 Freud, 'Uncanny', p. 359.
33 Freud, 'Uncanny', p. 367.
34 Tzvetan Todorov, *The Fantastic: A Structural Approach to a Literary Genre*, trans. Richard Howard (Ithaca, NY: Cornell University Press, 1975), p. 92.
35 Freud, 'Uncanny', pp. 373–4.
36 Freud, 'Uncanny', p. 372.
37 Freud, 'Uncanny', p. 360.
38 Cixous, 'Phantoms', p. 541.
39 This being Cixous's phrase. 'Phantoms', p. 525.
40 Clare Winnicott, Ray Shepherd and Madeleine Davis (eds), *D.W. Winnicott: Psycho-Analytic Explorations* (London: Karnac Books, 1989), p. 205. Norman Holland, *The Dynamics of Literary Response* (New York: Oxford University Press, 1968), p. 202.
41 Holland, *Dynamics*, pp. 100–1.
42 Istvan Csicsery-Ronay, Jr., 'The SF of Theory', *Science Fiction Studies*, Vol. 18 (1991), pp. 387–404 (p. 387).
43 Jack Zipes, *Fairy Tales and the Art of Subversion: The Classical Genre for Children and the Process of Civilization* (New York: Routledge, 1991), p. 55.
44 Holland, *Dynamics*, p. 6.
45 One could summarize Holland's seven phases of infantile psychic repression in the following manner:

| | |
|---|---|
| Oral | narratives obsessed, not only with eating and being eaten, but with engulfment, being overwhelmed, being enclosed and being buried |
| Anal | narratives depicting prim, precise, repressed characters, or dealing with tales of greed, money, and possessions (hoard, filth and corruption) |
| Urethral | images of flood and drowning and fire |
| Phallic | risk, adventure and aggression, testing the limitations of the body, fears of bodily mutilation |
| Oedipal | familial conflicts, the loss or discovery of parents |
| Latency | (often in children's narratives) problems with understanding and progression – little narrative displacement |
| Genital | again, little displacement (erotica and pornography). |

See also Kathryn Hume's analysis of Holland's seven-point schema in *Fantasy and Mimesis: Responses to Reality in Western Literature* (New York: Methuen, 1984), pp. 173–6.
46 As argued by Norman N. Holland and Leona F. Sherman, 'Gothic Possibilities', in Elizabeth A. Flynn and Patrocinio P. Schweickart (eds), *Gender and Reading: Essays on*

*Readers, Texts and Contexts* (Baltimore: John Hopkins University Press, 1988), pp. 215–33 (p. 229).
47 Holland and Sharman, 'Gothic Possibilities', p. 223.
48 Holland, *Dynamics*, p. 35.
49 Hume, *Fantasy and Mimesis*, p. 173.
50 Holland, *Dynamics*, p. 223.
51 Holland, *Dynamics*, p. 40.
52 Holland, *Dynamics*, p. 57.
53 Meredith Anne Skura, *The Literary Use of the Psychoanalytic Process* (New Haven: Yale University Press, 1981), pp. 87 and 91.
54 Holland, *Dynamics*, p. 53.
55 Freud, 'Creative Writers', p. 140. Holland, *Dynamics*, pp. 91–2.
56 Donald Palumbo, 'Sexuality and the Allure of the Fantastic in Literature', in *Erotic Universe: Sexuality and Fantastic Literature* (Westport, Conn.: Greenwood, 1986), pp. 1–17 (p. 3).
57 Holland, *Dynamics*, p. 161.
58 Dennis Giles, 'Conditions of Pleasure in Horror Cinema', in Barry Keith Grant (ed.), *Planks of Reason: Essays on the Horror Film* (Metuchen, NJ: Scarecrow, 1984), pp. 38–52 (p. 38).
59 Roger Abrahams, 'Play', in J. Newall (ed.), *Folklore Studies in the Twentieth Century*, pp. 120–5 (p. 122).
60 Morris Dickstein, 'The Aesthetics of Fright', in Barry Keith Grant (ed.), *Planks of Reason*, pp. 65–78 (p. 67).
61 Skura, *Literary Use*, p. 96.
62 See Jackson, *Fantasy*, p. 25.
63 Jackson, *Fantasy*, p. 41.
64 Julia Kristeva, *Strangers To Ourselves*, trans. Leon S. Roudiez (Hemel Hempstead: Harvester, 1991), p. 181.
65 Freud, 'Uncanny', p. 339.
66 Kristeva, *Strangers*, p. 183.
67 Julia Kristeva, 'Women's Time', trans. Alice Jardine and Harry Blake, in Toril Moi (ed.), *The Kristeva Reader* (Oxford: Basil Blackwell, 1986), pp. 187–213 (p. 207 – my emphasis). Irving Massey, *The Gaping Pig: Literature and Metamorphosis* (London: University of California Press, 1976), p. 148.
68 Henri Lefebvre, *The Production of Space* (Oxford: Basil Blackwell, 1991), p. 15.
69 Some of the ideas contained in this closing paragraph are more fully elaborated upon in Lucie Armitt, 'Space, Time and Female Genealogies: A Kristevan Reading of Feminist Science Fiction', in Sarah Sceats and Gail Cunningham (eds), *Image and Power: Women in Fiction in the Twentieth Century* (London: Longman, 1996), pp. 51–61.
70 Kristeva, *Strangers*, p. 182.
71 See Jane Flax, *Thinking Fragments: Psychoanalysis, Feminism, and Postmodernism in the Contemporary West* (Berkeley: University of California Press, 1990), p. 217 and David Crownfield, 'Inter-Text 7', in David Crownfield (ed.), *Body/Text in Julia Kristeva: Religion, Women and Psychoanalysis* (New York: New York State University Press, 1992), pp. 139–40 (p. 139).
72 Julia Kristeva, 'The System and the Speaking Subject', trans. Seán Hand, in Toril Moi (ed.), *The Kristeva Reader* (Oxford: Basil Blackwell, 1986), pp. 24–33 (p. 29 – original emphasis).

# 3

# Re-Theorising the Body, Re-Thinking its Spaces

Perhaps, above all, it is our obsession with the body that comes to the fore in reading fantasy. Whether the fantasy aspect manifests itself in terms of the colonization and exploration of other planets, the erotic pleasures of the pornographic, or the anthropomorphic creations of George Orwell's *Animal Farm* (1945) or Richard Adams's *Watership Down* (1972), it is the relationship between the body politic and body politics that often forms the narrative pivot. Even postmodernism, for all its rhetoric of endings and entropy, situates this 'sacred icon of the essential self' at the centre of some of its more interesting ideas.[1] Thus, speaking out against the assumptions of an Enlightenment legacy which subordinates the body to the 'higher echelons' of the cognitive self, recent theories of the cyborg frustrate this denial of the body while equally resisting the goal-orientated 'truth-searching' that motivates the psychoanalytic. Of course one need not be a critical theorist to recognize the centrality of the body to fantasy. As Hume observes: 'Fantasy is not bodiless; like a living creature, it is affected by the limitations of the particular body it inhabits.'[2] Such metaphors may even be central to all forms of writing. As Iain Chambers puts it, 'contemplating writing is the difficulty of thinking the metaphor, of thinking the metamorphosis',[3] and the literary narrative, as previous discussions of secondary elaboration have demonstrated, is nothing if not a linguistic metamorphosis.

Massey's work on the relationship between literary language and fantastic metamorphosis is particularly significant in this regard. What makes Massey interesting is that, like structuralists, he situates language at the *forefront* of all transformations but, unlike structuralists, he looks to move beyond those paradigms which reduce *all* signifying systems to language. Instead, as only a critic of the fantastic could, he forges a path in the opposite direction in a quest to find that fabulous location where

'Meanings are immediately collapsed into things'. This is the world of fictional metamorphosis, a world which 'seems to express the assumption that all things we know turn immediately into the Other even before we grasp them consciously'.[4] In his terms metamorphosis reflects the connotative excesses central to all literary transformations. Thus the body *in* the text becomes uncontainable in the terms of the body *of* the text. Massey's whole project continually wrestles with the impact of language upon literary theories of the body and, in so doing, furthers our understanding of that common dynamic Susan Gubar finds at the heart of all readerly pleasures:

> A 'passage' of a text is a way of knowing a 'corpus' or 'body' of material that should lead us on, tease us – but not too obviously. 'Knowing' a book is not unlike sexual knowing . . . Not only do we experience gratification orally as we 'devour' books voraciously, we also respond subliminally to the 'rhythms' of the plot, looking forward to a 'climax'.[5]

Massey rethinks this in fantastic terms. Ditching the mimetic need for the arbitrary but necessary relation between signifier and signified, he argues that the fantastic explores a series of endlessly shifting signs cast adrift from their system of signification. So whereas Gubar anchors her argument in metaphor, Massey irreversibly severs tenor from vehicle, and while Chambers draws a connection between metaphor and metamorphosis, Massey roots both in a struggle to the death, the metamorphic 'tak[ing] refuge in the physical, not because that is where it chooses to go, but because that is the only place where language cannot follow it'. As he asserts at the opening of his book: 'Although [metamorphosis] is a critique of language . . . It is set up on the other side of language – after one has gone mad through preoccupation with language, taking it so seriously that it has become a physical thing again.'[6] If we wish to formulate a definition of the fantastic in contradistinction to the reductive classificatory arguments criticized in Chapter 1, we may find an alternative in metamorphosis: at least as understood in its widest application. For alongside those narratives which cite the metamorphic body as the central source of pleasure, empowerment, terror or horror, the fantastic in general takes us into a realm where the static and the finite shift, be it ever so slightly, to metamorphose the formerly familiar into a defamiliarized state. This is the basis of science fiction, the gothic and Tolkien's reading of fantasy. The presiding question perhaps revolves around why.

## The Body Politic and Anatomical Excess

If we adopt the theoretical premise of defamiliarization as the basis of all fantasy forms, the connections between the body and the body politic start to become fully apparent. That ability to look anew and afresh at something familiar reminds us of the ways in which change can be brought into being. What it also reminds us of is that even the most apparently frivolous of fantasies can and does have a social dimension. On the face of it, nothing could be more personal than the body of the individual: be it short, gross, anorexic or leprous. Our bodies, we may feel, are strictly our own business. But when we consider that social prejudices often evolve on the basis of our anatomies – our sex, our skin colour, our physical deformities and disabilities – we realize that this, too, is a source of power. Take, for a moment, the stock fantasy figure of the giant. As fictional construct, this larger-than-life figure is generally feared, hated and cheerfully destroyed. Its antagonist is smaller, usually younger, often poorer than (usually) him. Archetypally, this antagonist is Jack the young boy, the imaginative and adventurous protagonist with whom we, numerous children and numerous parents, identify.

The story, we think, is 'just for children', a bedtime adventure, of no political consequence. Yet even the most fleeting of glances at its literary genealogy convincingly shows this not to be the case. Evolving from the source text 'Jack and the Giants', this is a narrative that acquires its popularity because of its ability to function on a socio-political level. The fitting hero of a tale originally read by poor 'common' folk with a poor to moderate level of literacy, Jack is the fictional embodiment of the peasant farmer who has to sell his produce for the equivalent of a handful of beans, hoping against hope that his 'seed' will produce plenty of food in return. The giant, of course, is the wealthy landowner whose physical size is simply a metaphor for his financial and social superiority. Jack's only hope, having usurped his place on the hierarchy by climbing up the social ladder and gaining entry to the castle and its wealth by unsanctioned means, is to outwit this ogre, for cunning and desperation are his only weapons. No wonder we take pleasure in the giant's overthrowing, even if Jack has to return to his original place in order to escape a fate that will have consequences for the whole body (politic). Lining both his coffers and his stomach with the blood, sweat and tears of his tenants, these people form the bones which the giant grinds to make his bread. In addition, as it is not only this Jack but all Jacks everywhere who will suffer if attempted revolution is detected, it is vitally important that 'magic' is on the side of the ordinary people in order to aid them to evade their oppressors. All this is well and good, but 'Jack and the Beanstalk' is a child's tale of terror, not a story about liberation. Read in its childhood form it becomes a gothic narrative about danger and desire, detailing the wish to transgress the restrictions we face, be they physical (the beanstalk), financial, or social. Gigantism in children's stories is a common phenomenon because the child *is* surrounded by giants: parents, nannies, teachers, shoppers; all of whom are freer, stronger, older and wiser. As Leslie Fiedler argues, the male giant here is simply a textual version of the immense and at times oppressive father. Even for adults this remains the case, since the memories of such fears as can only haunt children never really go away: 'in our deepest consciousness we remain forever little Jacks'.[7]

What happens, then, when the oversized body *becomes* the common-folk? This is the project of Bakhtin. Bakhtin's work on carnival and the grotesque has been central to our understanding of the literature of the body as a political aesthetic. In differentiating, as carnival does, between stereotypical notions of low and high cultural forms, it soon becomes clear that the 'low' realm of the non-mimetic is far more in tune with carnival structures than the 'high' literary ranking of traditional realism. Like the fantastic, Bakhtin perenially deals in gross exaggeration and hyperbole. As Jackson puts it, 'He points towards fantasy's hostility to static, discrete units, to its juxtaposition of incompatible elements and its resistance to fixity. Spatial, temporal, and philosophical ordering systems all dissolve; unified notions of character are broken; language and syntax become incoherent.'[8] In taking the motif of the individual body in excess he 'expands' upon this to explore its social, collective significance as politically interrogative. Again, like so much fantasy fiction, these disruptions of the fixed have a serious agenda: '[such work] is finally about freedom, the courage needed to establish it, the cunning required to maintain it, and – above all – the horrific ease with which it can be lost.'[9] And yet how can these issues be quite so connected? The answer in part derives from the etymological origins of the word 'carnival', although even here there are two commonly differing interpretations. The Latin derivation is *carne levare* which, in Michael Bristol's reading, is literally translated as 'the taking away of meat/flesh' (after the festivals immediately preceding Ash Wednesday and the fasting season of Lent).[10] In this sense holiday excess precedes and pushes against a rigidly enforced prohibitive limit which returns the populace to restrictive conformity. In the process, carnival situates itself in contradistinction to the sacred, a point that reminds us that carnival is basically a sacrilegious activity at which the devil himself presides as the ultimate lord of misrule. Allon White, however, though by no means dismissing such doctrinal applications, pays far more attention to the secular politics of carnival. He adopts a rather more metaphorical application of the term in associating its etymological origins, not so much with the religious taking *away* of meat/flesh but with the profane aspects of the taking of the flesh (as oral gluttony and erotic pleasure).[11] Other critics have also associated sexual ecstasy with the breaking apart of the body and an attendant political power imbalance. Leo Bersani, for example, sharing this fascination with the body, argues that 'Because sexual excitement momentarily shatters the will and disintegrates the constructed self' it facilitates a perfect situation for 'one person gaining mastery over another person'.[12] Thus, under the spirit of the carnivalesque, the body is not only the central reference point, but also the limits of its concerns – a preoccupation that provides it with its primary socio-political significance as a crucial site of power and manipulation.

It is particularly common for myths and legends concerning gigantism to utilize fantasy motifs as a commentary upon topography. Mountains, rocks and islands are said to exist as the (usually dismembered) bodies or organs of giants, as sea and earth take on bodily proportions. Never perhaps in the whole of recorded history has it been more true than now that the earth itself is a grotesque body, only precariously held in place as damage to the ozone layer, climatic abnormalities and poor air quality start to take effect upon its own surface layer. Bakhtin has always connected 'cosmic catastrophe' with upheaval 'in the material bodily lower stratum', resulting in degradation and the transformation of its populous into grotesque monsters.[13] Post-apocalyptic fictions show how clearly connected these two really are. In line with this, the grotesque is the 'flip-side' of festival laughter, the point at which 'something ominous and sinister' emerges out of 'something playfully gay and carelessly fantastic'.[14] For Wolfgang Kayser, whose study of the grotesque is generally considered the most informative, the typical characteristics of this form articulate a clear pathway between the world of realism and that of the fantastic. Differentiating between 'true caricature' (or the representation of actual distortions), 'exaggerated caricature' (the enhancement of found monstrosity) and 'purely fantastic caricatures . . . where the [creator] . . . gives rein to an unchecked fancy', the grotesque is seen to function in a manner that opens up an entry-point between the two worlds. In this respect, as in all fantastic fictions, the grotesque takes us into a fictive space that 'is – and is not – our own world'; a world of anxiety, insecurity and 'the terror inspired by [individual and collective] disintegration'.[15] It is in contexts such as these that some of the gothic tropes we have encountered in the previous chapter come to take on a collective political application. According to Fiedler, in the context of the nineteenth century, the 'spectre' emerges from between the pages of the ghost story to make an appearance in the form of a haunting threat to the politics of the gothic mansion as aristocratic inheritance. In this sense it functions as a 'ghost not out of the past but a future already embodied in the expropriated proletariat dreaming of expropriating its expropriators'.[16]

Kayser, retaining the connection between the grotesque and the fabulous, also insists upon a retention of the carnivalesque notion that the individual body is merely a synecdochic representative of the collective: 'The distortion of all ingredients, the fusion of different realms, the coexistence of beautiful, bizarre, ghastly, and repulsive elements, the merger of the parts into a turbulent whole.'[17] If strictly precise, we might argue that it is often via the disruptive and disturbing presence of the individual grotesque anatomy that the sinister collective excesses of carnival are conveyed. Consequently, although it is Massey's eponymous 'gaping pig' that tends to encapsulate most fully the ambiguities of this form (with its 'dead-alive look' and the unsettling jaw posture which simultaneously suggests the shriek of laughter and the 'squeal or scream' of the abbattoir death[18]), the typical grotesque body is a monstrous hybrid of human and inhuman parts. The carnivalesque, on the other hand, tends to function by mingling the 'upper' and the 'lower' parts of the human body, so making excrement its own *raison d'être*. The social significance is clear even here, the king being the 'head' of the nation while the tramp remains a 'bum' of the streets. So the body revolts and becomes, in the process, 'mass-ively' revolting. Individual gluttony is politically restrictive, being 'torn away from the process of labour and struggle'. Only the orgy, the banquet, the street-brawl show us the 'fat belly' of the public at large. But an irony emerges in this use of body parts. While protruding eyes may be a source of comic humour for Bakhtin and the nose a mockery of the phallus, it is the mouth itself that is the dominant image, for it forms the literal connection point with those same 'gross' parts. Bakhtin's mouth is not for fine words. It is a 'trap', a 'cakehole' a 'gob' which sucks, spits, gorges and vomits, while 'the entire mechanism of the word is transferred from the apparatus of speech to the abdomen'. Just as it is rarely shut, so Bakhtin's primary orifice is rarely shut up. Only its choice of vocabulary shifts, clamouring to articulate those parts of the body with which it is most vulgarly connected: 'men's speech is flooded with genitals, bellies, defecations, urine, disease, noses, mouths, and dismembered parts . . . The common human fund of familiar and abusive gesticulations is also based on these sharply defined images.'[19] As part of this drive for freedom then, the grotesque body is always in the process of breaking open: orifices gaping, fluids overrunning. As a form which is continually resistant to closure, the openings of the body also mimic the openings of the text: gaps to be explored, crevices to be fingered, folds and creases which invite a smoothing out. So the reader becomes the coy seducer, gradually allowing herself access to the inner mysteries of the fantasized other, imprinting herself upon the blank page like a malleable tattoo. As Marcel Tetel puts it 'The space, the interface, between the ingestion of food and drink and the cathartic experience is that occupied by the book . . . All ingestion . . . leads to the valorization of the transformational, the creative process . . . the book [is] the ultimate and inevitable catharsis.'[20]

Another of the reasons for the relevance of Bakhtin's work on the body to the literature of the fantastic is the particular manner in which it deals with excess in the form of the overreaching of presently fixed limits: be they social, spatio-temporal or anatomical. As Peter Stallybrass and Allon White argue, the world of carnival is 'a world of topsy-turvy, of heteroglot exuberance, of ceaseless overrunning and excess where all is mixed, hybrid, ritually degraded and defiled'.[21] Even temporality enters the realm of fantastic disruption, the 'past [being] fasting and the present, to combat fasting, [being] feasting which in turn prepares the way for an open-ended future'.[22] Such utopian readings still have their dark side. Critics such as Allon White insist upon the need to maintain a differentiation between the grotesque as a world of dark introspection and the positively transgressive (carnivalesque) world of collective politics. And in many ways it is through fantasy fictions that the literary manifestations of this become most apparent. According to White, the dangers of introspection revolve around the world of the modern-day gothic which tends to effect a metamorphosis upon the 'public carnival of the day', turning it instead into a 'private "carnival of the night"'. The very imagery of the gothic narrative seems to contribute to this, with its 'chamber games of bed and torture', its 'airless linguistic spaces' and what White refers to as 'the interior darkness of the individual unconscious'. In this suffocating and claustrophobic space, imprisoned by its *unheimlich* secrets, 'the carnivalesque will increasingly turn inward upon itself, transgressing its own transgressions' and, in the process, contaminating the spirit of carnival with 'the emblems of alienated desire, paranoid fantasy, and the individual will-to-power'.[23] Ultimately, then, rather than depending upon the fractured images of the grotesque body alone, it is the context of the imagery that supplies the important political insight. Even beyond these introspective parameters, Bakhtin's terminology can be opened up to the typical ambiguities of any grotesque image. Referring to the characteristic activities of an oversized form which 'swallows, devours, rends the world apart, is enriched and grows at the world's expense'[24] we see that this cancerous presence is, once again, as comparable with the imagery of a post-apocalyptic novel as it is of the liberating body in excess.

One particular strand of the dark side of the carnivalesque has recently flourished under the scrutiny of feminist theory. Intrisically concerned with the centrality of the body to subjectivity, sexuality and the politics of power, feminist literary critics have frequently argued a case for woman's existence as monster under patriarchal law. Woman may be the body *in* society, but she is excluded or marginalized by the body *of* society, even as she employs such carnivalesque processes for her own revolutionary ends. The female body politic is, we hear, a 'shrieking sisterhood' or a ridiculed mass of rabid 'bra-burners' even (perhaps especially) to the public body at large. Nevertheless, such 'grotesque' associations can have genuine transformative impact. Transgression itself necessitates risk. Simultaneously driven by pleasure and anguish, like Massey's 'unhappy' state of metamorphosis it drives itself towards that point at which 'the limits of the self become unstable, "slipping"'.[25] But the 'self' in this sense is not the just the individual consciousness, it is also the realm of the body politic. And as feminists such as Mary Russo and others have acknowledged, there is a necessity, albeit uncomfortable, for the collective body of feminism (along with all cultural sub-groupings) to continually interrogate (perhaps even destabilize) the comfortable fixity of its own limits in order to move on.[26]

Thus, if patriarchy remains determined (as it seems to be) to read women as monstrous whatever they do, then there is every reason for feminism to confront it with female monstrosity on its own terms. As Russo argues, it is a mistake for feminism to try to appeal, when the collective grotesque body has far more impact as a force which appals: 'Feminism in the 1990s has stood increasingly for and with the normal . . . [which] has led to a cultural and political disarticulation of feminism from the strange, the risky, the minoritarian, the excessive, the outlawed, and the alien.'[27] What strikes us is not simply that this final list of adjectives relates to the carnivalesque, but that it also encapuslates the qualities of fantasy. Taking as her focus a specific reading of the grotesque *as* (to some extent fantastic) female form, Russo looks to redress this misplaced diversion. One of the most interesting aspects of this approach is the centrality she gives to the notion of 'stunting'. Focusing in a number of contexts on the figure of the 'flying' woman (as pilot, trapeze artist or feminist activist) Russo delights in the play of the term: 'The double meaning of the word "stunt" bifurcates the notion of the extraordinary into 1) a model of female exceptionalism (stunting) . . . and 2) the doubled, dwarfed, distorted (stunted) creatures of the sideshow.'[28] As we see, the aim is not to shun the grotesque, but to 'fly in the face' of patriarchal reductionism, reclaiming the carnivalesque in feminist forms. So, as often seems to be the case with comparative theoretical approaches, it is partly through a consideration of gender that a bridge is built between the apparently oppositional discourses of psychoanalysis (dealing with the individual, the hidden and the clandestine) and the carnivalesque (fixated by the public, the pleasures of display and the gratuity of excess). As Russo explains, 'The Freudian canon, with its "creature features" as case studies, is filled with horrific dismemberments, distortions, hybridities, apparitions, prostheses . . . The figure of the female hysteric . . . is as foundational to psychoanalysis as the image of the "senile, pregnant hags" is to the Bakhtinian model of grotesque realism.'[29]

It is easy to forget, when reading so much liberal theory on carnival as freedom, that carnival humour is often horrific. Because it pleasures in disgust and licence that is genuinely excessive, in its most extreme guise it is dangerous and violent, pushing us towards (perhaps over) the limit. One of the central theoretical foundations upon which it is based is the precarious relationship between prohibition and transgression and the linked concepts of the taboo, the abject and the grotesque. But as we have seen, the relationship between prohibition and transgression is not only precarious, it is also paradoxical, because the prohibitive limit cannot exist without the temptation to transgress it. In other words, although the relationship between prohibition and transgression is one of apparent mutual denial, in actuality each necessitates the existence of the other. This is one of the anchorpoints of theories of transgression, as Bataille's book on *Eroticism* shows. Like Bakhtin, Bataille commonly elides the sacred and the profane, his view of transgression going so far as to argue that: '*transgression does not deny the taboo but transcends it and completes it*'.[30] Massey, on the other hand, reads this as the site of the unhappy realm of the metamorphic, with its dark secrets and unsettling inconsistencies which, 'with all its pain, is about a reconciliation of silence with speech, and of the damned with the divine'.[31]

In dealing with the fantastic, then, we are looking at fiction that is obsessively interested in the precariousness of apparently fixed structures, their transgression, and the problem of the small-scale individual who finds herself amid large-scale circumstances beyond her control. These are all important qualities of fantasy fiction which, like carnivalesque cultural forms, 'situate themselves exactly at the frontier between elite and popular culture . . . and it is precisely in these mongrel or heteroglot texts that the repressed or excluded meanings of popular culture become most intelligible.'[32] According to postmodern critics, such cultural locations require spatial recognition, for 'the production of texts cannot be conceived outside of the production of diverse and exacting spaces'.[33] From the perspective of speculative fictions, one might also add that, alongside 'exacting' spaces, neither can this take place outside the textual (re)production/conception of *existing* spaces: 'That possibility is called the Earth, here, now, this elsewhere, where real, outer, inner, and virtual space implode.'[34] Science fiction, of course, has always preoccupied itself with issues of space. Now, as well as fictionalizing a new vision of spatial relations, it also has a key function to perform in terms of a postmodern reconceptualization of generic and inter-generic/canonical and extra-canonical spatial relations.

## Postmodern Forms and the Challenge to Origins

One of the major contributors to dialogues surrounding these areas is Jean Baudrillard, whose theories of the simulacrum and its impact upon contemporary culture are both deeply seductive and deeply dangerous. For Baudrillard, space, far from defining itself in terms of 'the final frontier', has simply become the space of representation. Cut adrift from any sense of an original upon which 'the map, the double, the mirror or the concept' imprint themselves, we have come to inhabit the realm of the 'hyperreal'. Not insignificantly, just as the term 'hyperreal' itself appears to allude to the world of the fantastic, so Baudrillard's chosen analogy of maps, mirrors and doubles has immediate impact upon theories of the fantastic. This is not simply because they are associated with what Baudrillard refers to as the 'era of the counterfeit',[35] but also because they operate as the central motifs which pull together the sense of spatiality and subjectivity we are exploring throughout this book. Charlie Blake, for example, cautioning us to remember that 'there will be many who enter this world of wall-to-wall simulation and prefer to remain there',[36] is merely updating the terminology typically used for that 'dangerous' relationship that has always been perceived to exist between science fiction and escapism. But postmodernism refuses to answer such charges. Unlike the carnivalesque, the latter stands accused of transforming the non-canonical, not into a radical critique of hierarchies, but into a mere 'self-annihilati[on]'.[37] Thus Baudrillard, situating his reading of American culture in the context of Disneyland, uses this popular cultural phenomenon, not as a distorted mirror-image to be held up to society at large, but as a mask that conceals the fact that Disneyland is really all that there is. The western world has, in his terms, become a theme park of representation whereby 'all hold-ups, hijacks and the like are now as it were simulation hold-ups, in the sense that they are inscribed in advance in the decoding and orchestration rituals of the media'.[38]

Clearly this feeds into the aforementioned discussion regarding transgression and the taboo. For Baudrillard, the order of the simulacra is far more disturbing than what one might perceive as rather more 'orthodox' readings of transgression (if such a term can be adopted), the very concepts of law and order becoming reduced to mere self-referential systems of representation. Here White's warning rings in our ears. Such introspective undercuttings must ultimately result in a denouncing of their own discourse and thus, paradoxically, a strengthening and reinforcing of Enlightenment hierarchical distinctions. It becomes, in both senses of the term, then, the discourse of 'self-annihiliation': simultaneously self-defeating and a denial of subjectivity. But what of its application to theories of the fantastic? Despite Baudrillard's assertion that 'This isn't a science fiction dream' the clear possibilities of his argument for speculative fictions seem self-evident. What else do such fictions give us other than visions of the 'hyperreal' or, as Baudrillard himself calls it at times, a '*hallucinatory resemblance of the real within itself*'? Surely this is simply a postmodern reconceptualization of what has already been referred to as defamiliarization, even if 'The cool universe of digitality has absorbed the world of metaphor and metonymy.' The problem presumably revolves around this notion of 'vision' or representation. Just as Disneyland is not a space of play but the game itself, so fiction is not a site of speculation upon the real, but simply a misplaced tautology: 'There is no more fiction that life itself could possibly confront . . . it is reality itself that disappears utterly in the game of reality.'[39] But even if we choose to ignore or critique Baudrillard's riddling insistence upon the futility of representation, his ideas remain central to current readings of speculative fictions and the power of the fantastic.

The primary means via which postmodernism tackles this issue tend to revolve around two related areas: the concept of the simulacrum ('the cool and cybernetic phase following the hot stage of fantasy'[40]) and the retheorising of the body and/in its relationship to space. It is ironic from this point of view that Baudrillard seems to have a transparent preoccupation with mirrors, even if only to insist upon their insignificance/irrelevance to the contemporary subject. This, of course, functions to veil his suspicion of Lacanian psychoanalysis, postmodern readings of bodies and/in space refusing to engage with any search for a unified subject, for, as Chambers puts it: 'Inside the simulating machine, on the other side of the screen, there are no fixed images, no finished sounds, no final text.'[41] Instead of Lacan's realm of the imaginary, then, 'the distorting and fragmenting reflections of [this] enormous glass surface' merely suck us into the nebulous wastes of cyberspace.[42] The glass surface, which simultaneously encapsulates the immense glass structures of contemporary city architecture, the presiding *leitmotif* of the computer screen, the objectifying lens of visual cinematic images and the shattered fragements of celluloid collage is, in itself, a predominant synecdoche for the postmodern aesthetic. According to Scott Bukatman it is this which renders the cinematic so open to postmodern readings, as it 'enacts an always present-time *experience* of physical, bodily spatial reality . . . [where] vision and spatial participation combine'.[43] As we shall see in Chapter 6, Carter's *The Passion of New Eve*, with its preoccupation with the artifice of celluloid representation, the 'sacred iconography' of the cinema, and her complex treatment of the self as simulacrum, is admirably well suited to readings such as these.

Indeed, fiction in general lends itself to these Baudrillardian precepts. Long before the advent of virtual reality, reading enabled us to 'enjoy virtual relationships, virtual sex or virtual reunions without leaving our homes'.[44] All novels, plays, poems and stories are simulations of the 'real' and, to some extent, theories of language have concentrated upon its existence as self-referential system with no connection with/belief in pre-existing 'truth'. None the less, it is undoubtedly with the rise, not only of postmodernism in general, but cyberspace in particular, that science/speculative fiction has begun to take on far more than a 'paraliterary' role. As Istvan Csicsery-Ronay, Jr. observes, 'I suggest, then, that we think of cyberpunk not as a movement . . . but as a more encompassing aesthetic . . . with profound philosophical and aesthetic premises.'[45] One can see how easily such discourses lend themselves to various forms of literary fantasy – especially those of science fiction. It is also the case that such notions, deriving from science fiction, have now become crucial to contemporary thinking in a variety of disciplines: 'This mode cannot speak a static present; thinking in the 'as if' throws us forward, not into the securities of a definite future but into the practicalities of getting from here to there.'[46] So, after a period in which science-fiction criticism has lagged behind more explicitly theoretical fields, it is now enjoying a central status as the impetus behind and stimulus for one of the most influential of all critical discourses. Thus even 'high' postmodernist texts (the apparent contradiction here only being an apparent one) draw heavily upon the language and tropes of popular science fiction. This is reflected in the reading of science fiction offered by Csicsery-Ronay, Jr. For him, the label *sf* has recently come adrift from its fictional referent. Instead it becomes a 'monogram' or 'insignia' which links together a grouping of aesthetic and philosophical perspectives which oscillate around cybernetic concerns. In line with the workings of this realization, *sf* 'clings to its traces' in the very act of setting itself free from its originary roots, a point that partly assuages Roger Luckhurst's reservations about the attendant tendency for this to reinscribe the cultural marginalization of science fiction as little more than a feeder for the postmodern theoretician.[47]

In this context the work of Donna Haraway is complex, wilfully grandiose in its claims and both alluring and disquieting as a contemporary polemic. For Haraway, political theory itself has a science-fictional trajectory: 'to produce a patterned vision of how to move and what to fear in the topography of an impossible but all-too-real present'. As part of this, her whole vision of society takes as its focus a challenge to the belief in the 'natural' as being oppositional to culture. So, she argues, our 'natural' environment is culturally produced, even down to the existence of the organism itself, because 'knowledge' is not a recording but a construction of existence: 'Biology is a discourse, not the living world itself.' And yet this is not to remove theory from the world of the body. Haraway's theory is intrinsically corporeal and the body a site of full articulation. Her aim, which situates itself within a feminist worldview, is to break down those restrictive dualistic hierarchies of thought that always inscribe the woman as 'natural' (read 'primitive') and the man as 'cultured' (read 'superior'). Taking on the ultimate 'proof' of woman as body and thus biological function, she deconstructs the 'naturalness' of this phenomenon, biological mothering being replaced by reproductive technology and all technology becoming inherently reproductive. One only has to look to such radically different examples of 'canonical' science fiction as *Brave New World* (1932) and *Woman on the Edge of Time* (1976) to see how central these ideas have been to fantasy. But Haraway expands upon this to relate it to the interpersonal 'network'/'interface' on a number of levels: 'Science fiction is generically concerned with the interpenetration of boundaries between problematic selves and unexpected others . . . The emerging social subjects called 'inappropriate/d others' inhabit such worlds.'[48] Taking this terminology of reproduction and/as technology she effects a playful connection between the birthing process, the borderline territory between worlds where self and other meet and, in all senses, the reconciliation between belonging and non-belonging instilled within the body politic by the presence of the alien outsider/within. All this can be encapsulated within cyborgian politics; it can also be encapsulated within the framework of *sf*.

This is also significant to the work of Baudrillard and Frederic Jameson. Like Haraway, both of these theorists, latching on to a political re-reading of postmodern cybernetics, read human proliferation in terms of technological advancement. But for Jameson a historical distinction exists between what he considers to be the 'relatively mimetic idolatry of the older machinery of the futurist movement' (for him encapsulated by objects/icons such as the motor car and the machine gun) and 'the computer, whose outer shell has no emblematic or visual power'.[49] It is through such distinctions in the relationship between ideology and representation that the mimetic gives way to fantastic projection and, in accordance with this, technology situates itself in terms of reproduction (including, presumably, the reproduction of images associated with mass culture as opposed to the production of original and unique *objets d'art*). This is important to our understanding of the fantastic as a whole but, as Haraway's work demonstrates, it has particular consequences for a feminist polemic.

According to Haraway, the discourses as well as the structures of Enlightenment thinking revolve around the ideological hierarchies of phallocentric legitimation. In contrast to this the cyborg, who is 'not utopian nor imaginary; s/he is virtual', is situated as a model of alterity with no sense of dualistic difference and therefore no subordinated other.[50] A complex hybrid of 'machine and organism', Haraway's cyborg bears more than a passing resemblance to its grotesque ancestor. As Kayser observes, 'The fusion of organic and mechanical elements offers as easy a target as disproportion did in the past. In modern [texts], airplanes appear in the form of giant dragonflies . . . and tanks move as if they were monstrous animals.'[51] The differences perhaps lie in their political motivations. Whereas, in Kayser's terms, these manifestations of the '"technical" grotesque . . . are demonically destructive and overpower their makers', the cyborg has no clearly defined 'maker' upon whom to turn. Instead, its political impact lies within its own self-definition, the cyborg becoming a metaphorical means of moving beyond the dualisms of gender politics by using technological hybridity as a form of self-reproduction. For Haraway, the biological mother is always the phallic mother, a figure entrenched in patriarchal codes and forged by repressive mythologies, a disempowered and disempowering masquerade embodying 'unity, fullness, bliss and terror'.[52] Called upon necessarily to reject this omnipotent image (even when/as mothers ourselves), we situate ourselves and are situated within a mythology of loss that is equally a misconception of a lost sense of paradise. Certainly this is borne out by Madelon Sprengnether's textual analysis of a number of feminist reappraisals of the Eve motif.[53] According to Sprengnether, while male writers are preoccupied with the Genesis story as a narrative about lost innocence and woman as temptress, for women Eden becomes a site of banishment from the nurturant mother. Not surprisingly, to reiterate a point made in the Introduction, whereas for Sprengnether this becomes a positive springboard for the feminist utopia, Haraway's re-reading renders it a site of temptation to be rigorously resisted: 'Cyborg writing must not be about the Fall, the imagination of a once-upon-a-time wholeness ... Cyborg writing is about the power to survive ... on the basis of seizing the tools ... that marked [women] as other.'[54] Marilyn Edelstein's re-reading of postmodern 'nihilistic' tendencies and outlooks, to some extent articulates Haraway's position: 'In contrast to this nostalgic language of *loss*, we can see postmodernity as *gain*, enabling a proliferation of new meanings, media, narratives, and identities.'[55] In these terms Haraway's means towards this semantic proliferation is, in itself, a utopian dream in which, looking to the image of the cyborg as a means of forging a world without/post- gender, women are freed from their bodily harness and its reproductive trappings. Without the phallic mother there can be no originary fantasies of woman as loss, lost, tempter or traitor.

Although apparently uneasy with the label 'postmodern', Haraway is undoubtedly one of postmodernism's most powerful weapons in the current fascination with science fiction and cyberpunk. Utilizing these related discourses, like Russo she propounds a theory of shape-shifting monstrosity as the basis for a new feminist re-reading of the body: 'The goal of this journey is to show ... metamorphoses and boundary shifts that give grounds for a scholarship and politics of hope in truly monstrous times.'[56] But hers is a monstrosity of a rather different kind. Taking as its title an apparent amalgam of the utopian and the dystopian, 'The Promises of Monsters' situates, among other things, the play of textuality within a sense of space and place understood by Haraway as 'the womb of a pregnant monster'. Her concerns can be summarized as a postmodern critique of the patriarchal obsession with origins as power and woman as 'space'. Typically for her, the originary symbol of the tree of knowledge is synchronically retheorised as a reproducing technology in itself. In amalgamating its Judeo-Christian mythological symbolism with the type of hag-ographical symbolism that radical feminists such as Mary Daly have re-read as intrinisic to female creativity and spirituality,[57] she simultaneously secularizes and technologizes both, creating a metamorphosed image that is itself transformative: 'a Web, a vast system of computer connections' (what we know, perhaps, as the *World Wide Web*).

The central concept around which explorations of the cyborg revolve, derives primarily from the perceived function of origins as linear structures. Again, this is one seemingly irreconcilable distinction between the postmodern and the psychoanalytic. But contradictions emerge even here. Frederic Jameson, talking about the concept of the simulacrum (upon which so much postmodern theory depends), ascribes the term a Platonic genealogy, a point which equates such 'radical' retheorising with one of the originary thinkers of the classical period. Notwithstanding this, he still goes on to argue that bourgeois genealogies are now replaced by a collage of fragments or, as he puts it, 'a multitudinous photographic simulacrum'. In addition, there are other ways in which postmodern dislocations of the time/space dynamic fail to fully challenge the presiding framework of other (meta-)discourses. In perceiving 'personal identity' as 'a certain temporal unification of past and future with the present before me',[58] Jameson simply articulates the dynamics of the analysand's search for self and the 'unification' of the split subject. Nevertheless, what Jameson's comment does help us to come to terms with are the literary disjunctions of the time/space dynamic so common in any number of fantasy texts. On one level this manifests itself in that common science-fiction trope of space and time travel, but in other texts such as Carter's *The Passion of New Eve* it works its way through in a feminist demythologizing of creation myths.

Origins need not be patrilinear. In negating the power of original creation Haraway actually negates the power of the maternal, reproduction becoming replication (even in the sense that Jameson uses it). As is the case with patriarchal readings of the female grotesque we may even say that postmodernism's apparent deconstruction of Enlightenment beliefs and patrilinear discourses ultimately effects a shunning (even a hatred) of the body of the mother. For although the apparently paradoxical amalgamation of the feminine and/as the technological appears to render the cyborg a revolutionary phenomenon, we could argue that woman has always been culturally positioned in that impossible embodiment of two irreconcilable but inseparable factions. Caught between aesthetic/fantastic idealism and basic mechanical reproduction we find the Virgin Mary and Mother respectively. Cut adrift from her mental capacities, woman is valorized in purely bodily terms, whereas the cyborg (again in carnivalesque mode) integrates both in a manner that refuses to recognize a hierarchical duality between head and body. Admittedly, a collective application can be derived from Haraway's model: '"woman" [being] no longer singular, but rather, a commodified, technological object whose unique human status is challenged by radical technological transformations'.[59] What remains ambiguous, however, is the extent to which such strategies are genuinely revolutionary. Although 'social interactions' are the key to our understanding of this, once cut adrift from the singularity of the subject (even when radically split), surely, as both Lacan and Kristeva have notoriously claimed, 'woman does not exist' in that place.[60]

## The Stranger, the Cyborg and the World of the New Canon

More than one critic has claimed Kristeva to be in line with the postmodern. In essence this depends upon a corporeal localizing of the political, which in Edelstein's opinion 'run[s] far less risk than the master narratives [of Marxism and feminism] did of effacing difference, and of doing violence to the other'.[61] Advocates of Kristeva as postmodernist may argue that because her work revolves around the related issues of the body, its social constraints, its pleasures and its discourses, she is an obvious companion for Haraway herself. But in fact it is through a comparative reading of Kristeva's concept of the stranger and Haraway's concept of the cyborg that Kristevan psychoanalysis waves farewell to this postmodern counterfeit. As defined in *Strangers to Ourselves*, strangeness and foreignness are 'the hidden face of our identity', being a projection on to others of our self-concealment. Permanent exiles from the mother's body, we are uncomfortably reminded by the presence of the stranger of home: 'that invisible and promised territory, that country that does not exist but that [we bear] in [our] dreams, and that must indeed be called a beyond'.[62] Herein lies the key to the discrepancy between the two.

We have seen that, as well as being a creature without origins, Haraway's cyborg is a creature with no sense of loss. This removes it from any relationship with the maternal at all, despite sharing the stranger's illegitimate status. Though both appear to be bastardized aliens, Haraway's figure is simply without parentage. Only Kristeva's stranger is an orphaned outsider. In that sense the stranger is conceived of through an absence paradoxically dependent upon a past sense of presentness. This also indicates a further distinction. Situated as a melancholy figure, the albeit travelling stranger is nevertheless rigidly rooted in a personal time/space continuum and history. The cyborg, on the other hand, is as close to being time-less as any cultural construct could be. Inevitably, this affects their respective readings of time, space and feminist ontology. Haraway's belief that 'the boundary between science fiction and social reality is an optical illusion' presumably means that her ideal futurist narrative searches, like her political theory, for a world without gender, an approach in large part challenged by Kristeva's sceptical enquiry 'is a society without foreigners possible?'.[63] More particularly, one wonders if such a society would be *desirable*, not least for the foreigner herself. Implied in Haraway's argument is a challenge to the validity of a science fiction which actively pleasures in the depiction of the alien's role as *ongoing stranger* in a world searching, not only for the space but also the *time* for cultural and sexual difference.[64]

Just as Kristeva's own theories can inform the postmodern, so are there connections between the grotesque hybrid and the cyborg. Likewise there are structural similarities between carnival's relationship to high and low culture and the cultural location of cyberpunk. Quite aside from the fact that Bakhtin draws upon the topography of outer-space fiction in referring to the grotesque body as a 'cosmic and universal' phenomenon, he also asserts that 'grotesque imagery constructs what we might call a double body . . . it retains the parts in which one link joins the other, in which the life of one body is born from the death of the preceding, older one.'[65] This also looks similar to the image of the cyborg, both bringing together opposing facets to be integrated into a 'double' body which is 'simultaneously object and subject'.[66] This is particularly clear as it manifests itself in science-fiction cinema narratives such as *Robocop* (1987), the hero being born out of a physiological death of the human form with which its cybernetic parts are amalgamated. But the crucial and central distinction between the two once again revolves around body politics. If, in Bakhtinian terms, conceptualizing the body as individual entity actively conspires against and cuts across its potential to operate as body politic, the political implications of body imagery under postmodern readings of it by Baudrillard and Haraway become more problematic again. According to Bakhtin, what the grotesque body ignores is 'the impenetrable surface that closes and limits the body as a separate and completed phenomenon' and what it displays are 'not only the outward but also the inner features of the body: blood, bowels, heart and other organs'.[67] When we read this, we realize that in essence we are dealing with the opposite of the cyborg physique. In truth, Haraway's cyborg comes much closer to Bakhtin's classical body (or what he also refers to as 'the body of the new canon'): the closed, perfect form whose outlines refuse any sense of interaction. Despite her assertion that 'Bestiality has a new status in this cycle of marriage exchange',[68] both the libertarian and the interpersonal aspects of this image are false. At best, as Blake argues, we have no more than 'a delirium of cybernetic surfaces in contact and friction', whereas at worst, as Veronica Hollinger claims, we may go so far as to equate the cyborg with a precarious tendency towards self-destructiveness: 'the self/body [being] in danger of being absorbed into its own technology'.[69] In these terms breaking down hierarchical dualities is achieved only at the expense of producing a type of fantastic carcinogen or an ecstasy-induced paralysis. Thus liberation from anxiety occurs only at the expense of 'a liberation from every other kind of feeling as well, since there is no longer a self present to do the feeling'.[70] Again, this is similar to Russo's perspective on grotesque reproductions: 'Through the dark models of pathological anatomy, counter-nature, and death, the illumined modern body emerges . . . [as] "a syntactical reorganization of disease" . . .'.[71] Skin may well be a problem for the cyber-technician, but is the alternative a preferable one?

Bearing in mind White's reservations about the 'carnival of the night' as political regression, it is interesting that Blake's own reservations about the cyborg return us once more to gothic *dis-ease*. Referring to the work of cyberpunk writers, Blake locates the cyborg as the most haunting of spectres: 'human neuro-systems can be downloaded long after their corporeal vessels have ceased to function – only to be retrieved, like unwilling ghosts . . . cyberspace is haunted not only by the voodoo gods and virtual zombies of a pre-millenial age . . . but by vampires, shapeshifters and chimerae of every conceivable kind.'[72] Intriguingly, these reservations about cyberspace can be in many ways mirrored by White's reservations about the grotesque body in its depoliticized form. Where White expresses concern about self-perpetuating and self-fulfilling transgression, Blake expresses concern over 'the demise of the political and its re-emergence as an executive or cybernetic function of libidinal flows and forces'.[73] Consequently, rather than focusing upon the interface between the individual and the state, the politics of the cyborg relate to the impact of technology upon the individual and her interface with the 'other' who is the self. Rather than Lacanian readings of the split subject, we end up with 'a technically controlled self-identity so complete that it leaves . . . no shadows'.[74] And when the shadows of history include the spectres of international and domestic atrocities, one cannot help but share Blake's unease about an ideology which 'prepare[s] us intellectually, morally and culturally for a cyber-modernism in which we no longer interact with technology, but become it'. Just as White returns us to the collectivity of carnival as political subversion, so Blake looks hopefully towards the development of those aspects of popular youth culture which have opened up around 'cyber-tech' resistance to authority and which, in being collective, ever-mobile and located around common land, seem to have far more in common with carnival festivity than they do with the classical new canon of the cyborg.[75]

Again we see the relevance of this to fantastic literature. Bakhtin's 'new canon' is also a reference to the body of literature that closes off argument, engages in 'classical' aesthetic practice and sets itself up as a 'high' rather than a 'low' fictional form. But science fiction, ghost stories, fairy tales and fantasies are generally considered to be popular, mass-market forms situated, like Bakhtin's reading of the mouth, at 'the open gate leading downward into the [textual] underworld'. Furthermore, their intertextual, somewhat formulaic structures also locate them in an openly interrogative space 'on the boundary dividing one body from the other . . . at their points of intersection'.[76] Where Bakhtinians theorise fantastic body images in terms of performance and display, postmodernists rethink them in terms of inner and outer spatial and cultural inter/faces: 'The blasted scenes, sumptuous textures, evocative colors, and ET monsters of the immune landscape are simply there, inside us . . . the hillocks of chromosomes lie flattened on a blue-hued moonscape of some other planet . . . the auto-immune disease-ravaged head of a femur glows against a sunset on a dead world'.[77] And yet comparisons remain. Haraway, also picking up on the generic lack of fixity of the umbrella abbreviation *sf*, comments that in simultaneously referring to 'science fiction, speculative futures, science fantasy, speculative fiction', such terminology encapsulates the presiding note of tension which articulates, in itself, the situation of difference within the apparent reproduction of technology; a paradoxical stratagem with a clear spatio-textual positioning.[78]

What we have seen in this chapter is a very different reading of the spaces of fantasy than is available in either structuralist or Freudian terms. Here, the text, rather than being an enclosed space or playground of fantasy as desire, sets up a series of competing discourses or free-playing counter-structures that threaten to disrupt the very narrative they comprise. There are inevitably positive and negative implications of this. On the one hand we have found 'play' and 'playing' to be synonymous with a number of carnivalesque activities, as their derivations 'playing up' and 'playing about' imply. We have also noted that the terms themselves come from the same etymological root as the word 'pleasure', a connection that also includes ecstasy (and thus, from the perspective of carnival, the dubious pleasures of drug culture and acid-house forms). Barthes, taking this theory of pleasure a stage further, centrally aligns the dynamics of the text with the sensory and the erotic. Where that returns us to competing discourses is in the awareness that, as a result, the narrative is transformed from being an objectified other into a far more assertively reciprocal presence: 'The text you write must [also] prove to me *that it desires me.*'[79] This interactive quality (like its bodily manifestation the cyborg) produces a positively flirtatious arena of pleasurable 'combat'. In its most celebratory of guises it endows fantasy fictions with a fleshly dimension whereby, as Bersani argues, 'The literary imagination reinstates the world of desiring fantasies as a world of reinvented, richly fragmented and diversified body-memories.'[80] But uncompromising celebration is inevitably utopian and this would return us to the dangers of genre. For the conventional utopia inevitably silences through closing off/shutting up all possible counter-articulations. As Irwin reminds us, behind, beneath and within fantastic masquerades lie 'tactical manoeuvres instrumenting some serious strategy'[81] and, in the context of interrogative fictions, this sometimes includes a serious resistance to straightforward wish-fulfilment. It is at this point that our dilemma comes most sharply into focus. For the one positive aspect of the traditional utopia is its undoubted ideological stance. Precisely because it is a monological vision of change its polemical message is always fully apparent. Once we set up an endlessly free-playing alternative, we risk projecting ourselves into what Jane Flax perceives as a futile, even perilous, postmodern stance of self-referentiality: 'Those engaged in other games (e.g. state/power/law/economy) may tolerate postmodernist . . . practices precisely because of their irrelevance to and in the others. Hence postmodernists may be playing with texts while a fundamentally oppressive and destructive social system continues unfazed and unaltered.'[82] When applied to the world of fantasy fictions this casts them adrift from their characteristic association with ideological and narrative subversions. Instead Flax's words return us to an old-fashioned, largely obsolete reading of fantasy which perceives it to have nothing to say beyond its own fabulous parameters. In these terms, far from transforming the word into flesh, in the most nihilistic of ways the word imitates God, language (however playful) being all that there is. But while interrogative, free-playing strategies may seemingly to conspire to deny the utopic, its transformative impulses need not be lost. As we move on, in the second section of this book, to a fuller appraisal of the ideas raised within the first three chapters by contextualizing them in specific fictional terms, one of the key issues raised will be the ideological effect of these competing theoretical and critical voices upon the still (but not static) transformative potential inherent within all fantastic fictional forms.

## Notes

1 This is a phrase adopted by Veronica Hollinger. See 'Cybernetic Deconstructions: Cyberpunk and Postmodernism', in Larry McCaffery (ed.), *Storming the Reality Studio* (Durham, NC: Duke University Press, 1991), pp. 203–18 (p. 207).
2 Kathryn Hume, *Fantasy and Mimesis: Responses to Reality in Western Literature* (London: Methuen, 1984), p. 150.
3 Iain Chambers, *Border Dialogues: Journeys into Postmodernism* (London: Routledge, 1990), pp. 115–16.
4 Irving Massey, *The Gaping Pig: Literature and Metamorphosis* (Berkeley: University of California Press, 1976), pp. 20 and 19 respectively.
5 Susan Gubar, '"The Blank Page" and the Issues of Female Creativity' in Elaine Showalter (ed.), *The New Feminist Criticism* (London: Virago, 1986), pp. 292–313, (p. 294).
6 Massey, *Gaping Pig*, pp. 187 and 1 respectively.
7 Leslie Fiedler, *Freaks: Myths and Images of the Secret Self* (New York: Simon and Schuster, 1978), p. 91.
8 Rosemary Jackson, *Fantasy: The Literature of Subversion* (London: Methuen, 1981), p. 15, referring to Mikhail Bakhtin, *Rabelais and His World*, trans. Hélène Iswolsky (Bloomington: Indiana University Press, 1984).
9 Bakhtin, *Rabelais*, p. xxi.
10 Michael D. Bristol, *Carnival and Theatre: Plebeian Culture and the Structure of Authority in Renaissance England* (New York: Routledge, 1989), p. 41.
11 Allon White, 'Pigs and Pierrots: The Politics of Transgression in Modern Fiction', *Raritan*, Vol. 2 (1981), pp. 51–70, (p. 56).
12 Leo Bersani, *A Future for Astyanax: Character and Desire in Literature* (London: Marion Boyars, 1978), p. 302.
13 Bakhtin, *Rabelais*, p. 356.
14 As argued by Wolfgang Kayser, *The Grotesque in Art and Literature* (New York: Columbia University Press, 1981), p. 21.
15 Kayser, *Grotesque*, pp. 30, 37 and 52.
16 Fiedler, *Freaks*, p. 207.
17 Kayser, *Grotesque*, p. 79.
18 Massey, *Gaping Pig*, p. 11.
19 Bakhtin, *Rabelais*, pp. 302, 309 and 319.
20 Marcel Tetel, 'Carnival and Beyond', *L'Esprit Créature*, Vol. 21 (1981), pp. 88–104 (p. 103).
21 Peter Stallybrass and Allon White, *The Politics and Poetics of Transgression* (London: Methuen, 1986), p. 8.
22 Tetel, 'Carnival', p. 102.
23 White, 'Pierrots', pp. 54–5.
24 Bakhtin, *Rabelais*, p. 281.
25 As argued by Susan Rubin Suleiman, 'Pornography, Transgression and the Avant-Garde: Bataille's *Story of the Eye*', in Nancy K. Miller (ed.), *The Poetics of Gender* (New York: Columbia University Press, 1986), pp. 117–36 (p. 120).
26 Mary Russo, *The Female Grotesque: Risk, Excess and Modernity* (New York: Routledge, 1994), pp. vii-viii.

27 Russo, *Female Grotesque*, p. vii.
28 Russo, *Female Grotesque*, p. 22.
29 Russo, *Female Grotesque*, p. 9, citing Bakhtin, *Rabelais*, p. 25.
30 Georges Bataille, *Eroticism*, trans. Mary Dalwood (London: Marion Boyars, 1987), p. 63 – original emphasis.
31 Massey, *Gaping Pig*, p. 195.
32 Bristol, *Carnival and Theatre*, p. 39.
33 As argued by Jody Berland, 'Angels Dancing: Cultural Technologies and the Production of Space', in Lawrence Grossberg et al. (eds), *Cultural Studies* (New York: Routledge, 1992), pp. 38–55 (p. 39).
34 See Donna Haraway, 'The Promises of Monsters: A Regenerative Politics for Inappropriate/d Others', in Grossberg et al. (eds), *Cultural Studies*, pp. 295–337 (p. 328).
35 Jean Baudrillard, *Simulations* (New York: Semiotext(e), 1983), p. 98.
36 Charlie Blake, 'In the Shadow of Cybernetic Minorities: Life, Death and Delirium in the Capitalist Imaginary', *Angelaki*, Vol. 1 (1993), pp. 128–37 (p. 135).
37 As argued by Istvan Csicsery-Ronay, Jr., 'Cyberpunk and Neuromanticism', in McCaffery (ed.), *Storming the Reality Studio*, pp. 182–93 (p. 183).
38 Baudrillard, *Simulations*, p. 41.
39 Baudrillard, *Simulations*, pp. 48, 142 (original emphasis), 152 and 148 respectively.
40 Baudrillard, *Simulations*, p. 148.
41 Chambers, *Border*, p. 7.
42 As argued by Frederic Jameson, 'Postmodernism, or the Cultural Logic of Late Capitalism', in McCaffery (ed.), *Storming the Reality Studio*, pp. 219–28 (p. 226).
43 Scott Bukatman, 'The Cybernetic (City) State: Terminal Space Becomes Phenomenal', *Journal of the Fantastic in the Arts*, Vol. 2 (1989), pp. 43–63 (p. 57).
44 This is a playful re-reading of Blake, 'Shadow', p. 135.
45 Istvan Csicsery-Ronay, Jr., 'Cyberpunk', p. 185.
46 As argued by Elspeth Probyn, 'Technologizing the Self: A Future Anterior for Cultural Studies', in Grossberg et al. (eds), *Cultural Studies*, pp. 501–11 (p. 511).
47 Istvan Csicsery-Ronay, Jr., 'The SF of Theory: Baudrillard and Haraway', *Science Fiction Studies*, Vol. 18 (1991), pp. 387–404 (pp. 390–1). See also Roger Luckhurst, 'Border Policing: Postmodernism and Science Fiction', *Science Fiction Studies*, Vol. 18 (1991), pp. 358–66 (p. 364).
48 Haraway, 'Promises', p. 300.
49 Jameson, 'Postmodernism', p. 225.
50 Haraway, 'Promises', p. 329.
51 Kayser, *Grotesque*, p. 183.
52 Donna J. Haraway, 'A Cyborg Manifesto: Science, Technology, and Socialist-Feminism in the Late Twentieth Century', in *Simians, Cyborgs and Women: The Reinvention of Nature* (London: Free Association Books, 1991), pp. 149–81 (p. 151).
53 Madelon Sprengnether, '(M)other Eve: Some Revisions of the Fall in Fiction by Contemporary Women Writers', in Richard Feldstein and Judith Roof (eds), *Feminism and Psychoanalysis* (Ithaca, NY: Cornell University Press, 1989), pp. 298–322 (p. 318).
54 Haraway, 'Cyborg', p. 175.
55 Marilyn Edelstein, 'Toward a Feminist Postmodern Poléthique: Kristeva on Ethics and Politics,' in Kelly Oliver (ed.), *Ethics, Politics, and Difference in Julia Kristeva's Writing* (New York: Routledge, 1993), pp. 196–214 (p. 197).
56 Haraway, 'Promises', p. 306. Cyberpunk is usefully defined by Veronica Hollinger as 'an analysis of the postmodern identification of human and machine' in a manner that 'is about the breakdown of these oppositions'. Hollinger, 'Cybernetic', pp. 204–5. The current fascination with these ideas, which is simultaneously 'celebratory and anxious', is the determining feature of much postmodern debate. What is particularly interesting for our concerns is that theoretical argument and speculative fictions continue to be engaged

in an interactive debate over this which makes it impossible to attribute originary status to either.

57 As Mary Daly argues, 'For women who are on the journey of radical be-ing, the lives of the witches, of the Great Hags of our hidden history are deeply intertwined with our own process. As we write/live our own story, we are uncovering their history, creating Hag-ography and Hag-ology.' In that sense the term 'hag' is positively reclaimed as a symbol of woman-centred creativity and thinking. Mary Daly, *Gyn/Ecology: The Metaethics of Radical Feminism* (London: Women's Press, 1979), p. 15.
58 Jameson, 'Postmodernism', pp. 221–2.
59 As argued by Anne Balsamo, 'Reading Cyborgs Writing Feminism', *Communication*, Vol. 10 (1988), pp. 331–44 (p. 337).
60 Or, to put it in Kristeva's own words, '[woman] does not exist with a capital 'W', possessor of some mythical unity – a supreme power, on which is based the terror of power and terrorism as the desire for power'. Julia Kristeva, 'Women's Time', trans. Alice Jardine and Harry Blake, in Toril Moi (ed.), *The Kristeva Reader* (Oxford: Basil Blackwell, 1986), pp. 187–213 (p. 205).
61 Edelstein, 'Toward', p. 199.
62 Julia Kristeva, *Strangers to Ourselves*, trans. Leon S. Roudiez (Hemel Hempstead: Harvester, 1991), pp. 1 and 5.
63 The ideas contained in this paragraph are more fully developed in Lucie Armitt, 'Space, Time and Female Genealogies: A Kristevan Reading of Feminist Science Fiction', in Sarah Sceats and Gail Cunningham (eds), *Image and Power: Women in Fiction in the Twentieth Century* (London: Longman, 1996), pp. 51–61.
64 See Haraway, 'Cyborg', pp. 149–50 and Kristeva, *Strangers*, p. 127.
65 Bakhtin, *Rabelais*, p. 318.
66 As argued by Csicsery-Ronay, Jr., 'SF', p. 396.
67 Bakhtin, *Rabelais*, p. 318.
68 Haraway, 'Cyborg', p. 152.
69 Blake, 'Shadow', p. 129 and Hollinger, 'Cybernetic', p. 206.
70 As argued by Jameson, 'Postmodernism', p. 220.
71 Russo, *Female Grotesque*, p. 116.
72 Blake, 'Shadow', p. 133.
73 Blake, 'Shadow', p. 129.
74 As argued by Csicsery-Ronay, Jr., 'SF', p. 392.
75 One example Blake gives of this is the movement 'Spiral Tribe' which, 'in spite of perpetual harassment, fines, confiscations and imprisonment by the state – continues to organize vast and technically illegal "raves" on the common land across Britain, uniting travellers and settlers, and confounding the authorities with the spontaneity, popularity and mobility of these events'. Blake, 'Shadow', pp. 129–30.
76 Bakhtin, *Rabelais*, pp. 325 and 322 respectively.
77 See Haraway, 'Promises', p. 320.
78 Haraway, 'Promises', p. 300.
79 Roland Barthes, *The Pleasure of the Text*, trans. Richard Miller (Oxford: Basil Blackwell, 1990), p. 6 – original emphasis.
80 Bersani, *Future*, pp. 314–15.
81 W.R. Irwin, *The Game of the Impossible: A Rhetoric of Fantasy* (Urbana: University of Illinois Press, 1976), pp. 90 and 190.
82 Jane Flax, *Thinking Fragments: Psychoanalysis, Feminism, and Postmodernism in the Contemporary West* (Berkeley: University of California Press, 1990), pp. 39–40.

# Part Two

# READING TEXTS

# 4

# Drifting In and Out of the Unconscious: Lessing's *Briefing* and Banks's *The Bridge*

*Briefing For A Descent Into Hell* is a particularly interesting fantasy text to consider in relation to the reductionist attitudes of genre theory or 'border policing'.[1] Lessing scholars tend to struggle to accommodate its challenging parameters, not because they necessarily dislike it, but because it quite obviously functions as a 'misfit' narrative at the chronological centre of Lessing's writing career. While undoubtedly complex and diverse, her *oeuvre* nevertheless prides itself on its painstaking working and reworking of several central motifs which help to anchor it to a form of reassuring coherence. Thus, although Patrick Parrinder recognizes within *Briefing* the presence of three motifs central to much of Lessing's work, namely the sea, the earthly paradise and the ideal city,[2] it is nevertheless the novel's problematic relationship to fantasy and the fantastic that disorientated so many 'typical' Lessing readers at the time of its first publication. Taking this into account, one might expect that science-fiction criticism would offer more useful insights into the narrative. But even this is confronted with an apparently irreconcilable paradox. Central to this narrative is a deconstruction of the very generic precepts through which such critics inevitably read it. Lessing explores the concerns of inner (mental) space by situating them in the context of a possible outer-space scenario. In this sense it is a text that plays with and consistently frustrates readers' expectations of a fictional text, be that text realism- or fantasy-orientated. And while it comes too early and (if Lessing herself is to be believed) is too generically distinct to be considered in the same context as her later 'Canopus in Argos' outer-space series, *Briefing* nevertheless explores similar concerns while retaining a more resistant relationship with the science-fiction form.

Katherine Fishburn takes one of the most significant perspectives on this novel for our purposes and for that reason I have chosen to engage with it in detail. Analysing its competing claims as science fiction on the one hand and what she refers to as 'psycho-drama' on the other, she concludes by ascribing to the text a generic connection with the former category. Overall, her argument is one with which I have some sympathy, not least because it challenges a presiding counter-argument which is based far more in canonical prejudice than in close textual reading. But this is not to say that I unequivocally accept it, for it inevitably complies with that reductive utilization of genre that we have already critically addressed. In summary, Fishburn goes so far as to deem it 'essential' for the text to be read in this way, despite her recognition of its own explicit and inherent resistance to unproblematic issues of identity (including generic identity). The basis of her argument derives from the effect that the narrative has upon its readers, rather than a detailed analysis of its imagery. For, as she rightly says, both science fiction and 'psycho-drama' can and do have the ability to offer us 'various alien worlds of experience that are all equally valid and real, even though they are accessible to only one person'. In that sense imagery alone is largely insufficient as a means of demarcating genre.[3]

Immediately this is an improvement upon some of the reductionist generic readings critiqued in Chapter 1. At least Fishburn engages with what Holland would refer to as the dynamics of literary response. Unfortunately, the precise claims she makes cannot always be supported. In her terms, science fiction is much better placed than 'psycho-drama' as a means of producing interrogative fictions which will, she asserts, 'achieve nothing less than a *total transformation* of the way we perceive reality'. But as my added emphasis here implies, how can any text result in a 'total transformation' of the way in which we see the world? Undoubtedly it can and (in the best of cases) will challenge our assumptions, perhaps even 'broadening our horizons' on the way. But it cannot in and of itself turn the world (or even our perceptions of it) into something/somewhere else. This is just one of the difficulties with criticism such as this. Another important weakness lies in the way in which Fishburn dismisses 'psycho-drama' as mere escapism in a manner that carries a very clear echo of the usual slur aimed (often equally imprecisely and inaccurately) at science fiction by 'mainstream' critics: 'In psycho-drama, we always seem to have an internal escape valve as we read: we can remind ourselves that what we find disturbingly strange in the work is only the product of the diseased imagination of one (or more) of the characters.'[4] If we were to replace the term 'psycho-drama' with 'science fiction' and substitute 'the author' for the final phrase 'one (or more) of the characters', the typical mainstream 'put-down' of science fiction would be complete. Fishburn also makes a further distinction based upon readership: 'The conventions of SF work to make believers of us, while the conventions of psycho-drama work to make sympathisers of us'.[5] Hence she reinforces a claim already implicit in the argument she offers, which is that where the supposed profound escapism of 'psycho-drama' requires/constructs *lisible* (readerly) readers, the interrogative potential of science fiction requires/constructs *scriptible* (writerly) readers.[6] But escapism quite simply is not the point. Irrespective of whether we read the protagonist, Charles Watkins, as a space/time traveller or a man suffering from mental delusions, his perennial status as outsider means that he already holds an ex-centric relationship to the society in which he is 'realistically' situated. If any form of escape is to be found in this text, it is more likely to be that which I have elsewhere referred to as 'the need to escape into . . . an alternative reality within which centrality is possible'. This is a very different issue to fictional escapism.[7]

One device Fishburn does correctly analyse is that of textual disturbance. *Briefing* is, by design, a profoundly unsettling 'read' which sets out to disorientate the reader by severing her moorings from those of literary realism. Nevertheless, what seems very strange is Fishburn's belief that this is one reason why the text is *precluded* from functioning as 'psycho-drama'. On the contrary, trapped as we are within the limits of Charles's psyche (the first-person narrative rendering the limits of his mind also the limits of the text), the extent of readerly disturbance becomes all the more significant. Far from providing an 'internal escape valve' this actually denies us any way out beyond the limits of insanity. And this is where Fishburn's argument becomes surprisingly restrictive: 'Once we accept that Lessing's entire novel is an attempt to make real that which we ordinarily find not-real, we will recognize that she intends us not to see Charles as a madman . . . but as the guide-leader.'[8] Rather like the mysterious leopard-like creatures who guide Charles's ascent up the seemingly insurmountable obstacle of the glassy slope, Charles is, according to Fishburn, our mysterious (but ultimately benevolent) narrator/helper. This is an extraordinarily wilful reading of his position. The only benevolence that any narrator can bestow upon us is to be utterly trustworthy and therefore reliable, and the most scant reading of this text shows that Charles is neither of these two things. This is where Fishburn takes the extraordinary step of refusing to read him as an unreliable narrator. Doing so, for her, would necessitate agreeing with Doctors X and Y and, in the process, dismissing most of the novel as the ramblings and fragmentary utterances of a lunatic. At best, rather than offering us strategies for rethinking our relationship with the 'real', this can only offer us a new understanding of 'how we think about the mentally ill'. Rightly concluding that this is not the effect that this text aims for, she is left with the only option of reading the text as science fiction. In accordance with this, 'the worlds we see as "inside" Charles are also "outside" – accessible to us if only we will learn to see them'. Charles, in these terms, is telling the 'truth'.[9]

But the 'truth' is a difficult issue, a point undoubtedly central to Lessing's depiction of her protagonist and his world-view. It is not that we need to decide whether Charles is sane or insane (for quite evidently the doctors' obsession with this is shown to be misplaced). Rather, by centring the narrative largely around the presence of a first-person narrator, Lessing projects us into the realms of a defamiliarized uncertainty that deliberately invites and sustains a textual prevarication.[10] Fishburn is right in arguing that at no stage do we 'dismiss' Charles's perspective of events. Neither do we ever fully trust him. Instead we are forced grimly to cling to him, just as he clings to his raft, going 'round and round and round' (BDH, 27) until we too find it 'hard to tell whether [we are] looking at the white of the sails or at foam on a distant swell' (BDH, 26). And the reason behind our narrative tenacity is that we recognize this narrative to be, paradoxically, *both* science fiction and psycho-drama while actually being *neither*. Ascribing *Briefing* to a generic reductionism denies a crucial aspect of its power as a narrative. In her determination to tie up any and all loose ends, Fishburn denies the novel its fully transgressive impact. Effectively (although not explicitly) aligning herself with what we saw, in Chapter 3, to be a misplaced reading of *sf* as 'writing beyond the ending', she likewise falls into the trap of believing that content can overcome what we have seen to be the rigid constraints of the formula mode. Lessing's novel can only be subsumed under the generic label 'science fiction' if we see it in Bruce Sterling's terms as one of those hybridized 'slipstream' texts, 'bizarre works from both the mainstream and SF [which] meet in the "non-space" between the two'.[11] But even this possibility is challenged by those critics who argue that the dichotomy conventionally set up between science/speculative fiction and the mainstream demonstrates the latter also to be a product of the genre itself: a necessary 'outside' against which to define itself.

Lessing's attitude towards genre is also worthy of consideration, as she is well known (even notorious) for setting tasks and riddles for the readers of her work. Although superficially keen to compartmentalize her writing into discrete phases or sections (such as the 'Children of Violence' and 'Canopus in Argos' series)[12] and differentiate between 'inner' and 'outer' space fictions respectively, in fact she does so in a manner that (rather like Todorov's) somehow manages to hold in tension the rigidity of compartmentalization with an attendant perpetual undercutting of its limits. *Briefing* is a perfect example of this. Rather than seeing it as a continuation of the preoccupation with madness that runs through her earlier work, perhaps the best way of 'placing' this difficult novel is to see it as a bridge in Lessing's work which straddles the divide between the futurist dystopia of the Appendix to *The Four-Gated City* (1969) and the later 'Canopus in Argos' novels. But the nature of this bridging point is not simply fictional futurism. Perhaps more significantly it is their shared preoccupation with the shifting dynamics of the spatial dimension. *The Four-Gated City* is a piece of domestic fiction which shows how easily personal space is translated into public/political space, whereas the 'Canopus in Argos' novels take the vast panorama of an entire fictional galaxy in order to defamiliarize 'smaller' earthly preoccupations. Precisely like these, *Briefing* forces the inner and the outer into a complex (perhaps even incompatible) confrontation with/interrogation of each other. As if to place this within her own terms, Lessing stamps a defining epitaph on the frontispiece of the text:

*Category:*

Inner-space Fiction
For there is never anywhere to go but in.

At first sight this authorial definition seems wholly contradictory to the line adopted so far in this book. Closer scrutiny, however, reveals it to be far more in keeping with a dialectical reading of the inner and the outer than might at first be apparent. For although Lessing insists that all fictional exploration delves into the recesses of the psyche (something that inevitably classifies *Briefing* as 'inner-space' fiction), she does so in a manner that challenges not only psychoanalysis but also structuralism. What an attuned reading of Lessing's words reveals is that the presence of inner-space fiction need not exclude the simultaneous presence of outer-space fiction as well. Indeed, in these terms outer-space fiction is simply a sub-set of inner-space fiction. Consequently then, in the guise of being an exclusory comment, Lessing's 'categorization' is shown to be entirely inclusive and entirely in keeping with Todorovian perspectives. And, as Todorov reminds us, while the fantastic overreaches generic constraints, it does so through recognizing its relationship with them. So before going on to address this text as an example of the literary fantastic in practice, we will see how it also relates to genre science fiction.

## Science Fiction or System of Signification?

Somewhat inevitably, Fishburn's definition of *Briefing* depends less upon a positive alignment of it with science fiction and more upon a negative differentiation of it from 'psycho-drama'. This is anathema to the very spirit of Lessing's text, which is precisely why Charles spends so much of the narrative struggling against such binary choices. Like the blatantly reductive diagnosis of Frederick's condition as 'male menopause and manic depression', Fishburn's reading is 'interesting in an academic way, but unhelpful' (BDH, 163). Admittedly, traditional linguistics reads language usage as a similar set of binary choices (between the synchronic and the diachronic; between the noun or the verb; between the transitive or the intransitive). And obsessed (like structuralist readings) with definitions and counter-definitions, although both doctors disagree in almost every other way, they are adamant about the need to append a firm and unchallengable 'name' to Charles's condition. After all, only by being named can he return to or take up an established place within the sign system. Nevertheless, names contribute to the difficulties with identity which we have seen to be central to this text. And just as generic identity is a problem to be overcome rather than an aid to understanding here, so attempting to fix particular signifiers to particular signifieds is seen to be a false resolution. Most basically this manifests itself on the level of character.

As Claire Sprague has shown, the figure of the double is the motif which, above all, functions as the focus for Lessing's career, and this frequently manifests itself within the word-play of character naming.[13] In the case of *Briefing*, characters function as what DuPlessis refers to as 'cluster protagonists', whereby multiple signifers endlessly attach themselves to a group of protagonists who may 'actually' (if such a word can be used in this context) be quite small in number.[14] In other words there is an overspill beyond the framework connecting layer with layer. Variously referred to as Jason, Ali Baba, Sinbad and others, Charles is on one level the archetypal questor who searches out truths, albeit that the minute they are found, such truths are endlessly displaced. For if Charles is as much Jason as he is Charles, it is equally true to say that he is not Charles (as he consistently denies such an identification), just as he is not Jason. A similar argument could be applied to Charles's other cluster doubles, such as Conchita/Konstantina/Constance. It is not simply that identity is consistently tied up with the notion of belonging and classification, but that existence itself (in structuralist terms) is, we remember, seen to be valid only insofar as it has an 'arbitrary but necessary' relationship with its signifier. Early on in the narrative, Doctor Y asks Charles for the name of his wife and the surnames of George and Charlie, characters that Charles has 'named' while unconscious. Implied within this questioning is the belief that (by negative definition) only if Charles is capable of naming others, is the existence he has fabricated for himself legitimate; the recognition of the function of other signifiers implying that he too has validity as part of the same system. Quite clearly the exercise has less to do with the ability to match signifiers with the 'correct' signifieds and a great deal more to do with Charles's own willingness to enter into the system of signification. What critics such as Fishburn overlook, is that their readings conspire against this central narrative stance.

Quite clearly a coherent and sustained science-fiction 'thread' does run throughout the scope of the narrative. After all, in the early stages where we find Charles 'all at sea', it is the emergence of the shining crystal disc that gives the narrative its first anchor-point:

> The disc came closer, though so unnoticeably, being part of the general restless movement of the blue and white, that it was resting on the air just above the waves ... What we felt was a sensation first, all through our bodies ... The disc that had been in our eyes' vision a few yards away ... seemed to come in and invade our eyes ... Yet when it was on us, it seemed no longer a disc, with a shape, but it was more a fast beating of the air ... then I looked to see if George ... was still alive. But he was gone, and when I turned in terror to see where he was, and where the others were, they weren't there. No one. Nothing. The disc ... was lifting into the sky. It had swept away or eaten up or absorbed my comrades ... (BDH, 22–3)

Any reader of fiction, presented with this passage out of context, would be likely to classify it as that science-fiction 'mainstay' scene whereby a UFO sweeps down into the Earth's atmosphere and 'beams aboard' human beings for exploratory observation. It is, in fact, only the aforementioned uncertainty created by the lack of objective consensus surrounding Charles's perceptions that leads to any form of narrative doubt in this case. Such science-fiction devices recur throughout. Under the terms of this reading an interpretation is gradually built up by means of which Charles is shown, far from being a human who has become isolated due to being the sole survivor of an alien 'snatching' of fellow crewmembers, to be an alien planted on Earth to observe and, indeed, inform alien cultures about human life and subjectivity. In that sense his occupation of classics professor is a perfect cover. For in the guise of *professing* truths he is able to mask them, just as pretending an obsession with the origins of western culture enables him to deter any investigation of his own 'alien' roots. But it is of course with the eponymous 'Briefing' section that the science-fiction reading becomes most dominant. Why, for example, does the following *caesura* occur where it does:

> As a result, the Permanent Staff on
> Earth are reinforced and
>
> *The Conference*
> was convened on Venus ...
> (BDH, 116)

if it is not to signal the centrality of this conference to our reading of the text? And why does this scene offer the only available definition of the title if it is not to be read as a narrative pivot? For it is here that we learn that Earth is the 'Hell' into which this descent takes place.

Of course, if we decide along with Fishburn that this is the answer to all textual doubts, then we still have to resolve the issue of Charles's apparent amnesia. One possible explanation for this is that Charles, having indeed lost his memory (and thus his relationship to past time), severs himself less from his connections with Felicity and the Terran family unit (for such connections are no more than a masquerade to begin with), and more significantly from his role as intergalactic space/time traveller: 'there was something I had to remember. Have to remember. I know that' (BDH, 237). A reading of this kind (in line with all generic classifications) would enable full and final closure to be well and truly asserted. Thus, just as he is on the verge of grasping this recognition, the shock therapy which he agrees to undergo against the advice and will of fellow aliens such as Rosemary Baines seems to put his alien status beyond his recall. In the process, it not only kills off his alien double and the text (as science fiction), it simultaneously kills off Charles's function as first-person speaking subject/narrator. But fortunately the loose ends are not tied up in this way. Instead they are deliberately left fraying at the edge of the tapestry by Charles's final words to Violet, uttered as he takes leave of her before having ECT. In telling her that, 'There are people in the world all the time who know . . . But they keep quiet . . .' (BDH, 249), he implies a full and clear awareness of his own alien status. He is, in that sense, far from being Fishburn's reliable 'guide', actually the ultimate unreliable deceiver, whose claim to be 'himself again' (BDH, 245) prior to his decision to undergo shock treatment could define his identity in any number of ways. After all, as the continuation of this passage implies, there is a clandestine message encoded within it: 'the ones who have got out . . . become the ones to live quietly in the world, just as human beings might if there were only a few human beings on a planet that had monkeys on it for inhabitants, but the monkeys had the possibility of learning to think like human beings' (BDH, 249). The analogy here between 'the ones who have got out' and Charles's possible role as alien interloper on a human planet is only the first part of the equation. In a rather complicated act of mirroring and word association (two of the central narrative techniques of the whole text), what Charles implies here is that he will, in simian fashion, 'ape' conformity while in fact going on to live an undercover existence (just as he claims to have done as part of the resistance movement in Yugoslavia). This makes it entirely appropriate that Charles himself should utter the words which most saliently criticize the workings of genre theory: 'If you have shaped in your mind an eight-legged monster with saucer eyes . . . you will not see anything less, or more – that is what you are set to see. Armies of angels could appear out of the waves, but if you are waiting for a one-eyed giant, you could sail right through them and not feel more than a freshening of the air' (BDH, 21). In summary, then, a hesitant, anti-generic reading poised between the psychological and science fiction enables us to come to terms with what otherwise seems an extremely uninspiring ending to a fascinating journey through contradiction and paradox. In this case the 'ending' becomes merely a hiatus, an uncomfortable and irresolvable riddle with which Charles leaves Violet and therefore the reader.

So Lessing's novel functions as a 'fantastic' text, structured in terms of Todorovian hesitancy, awkwardly oscillating (like Todorov himself) between structuralist (generic) conformity and the transgression of its own limits. But we should also remember that transgression lies at the root of the fantastic, not only as structure but also as content. This is the dual nature of the role of Lessing's protagonist. On the one hand Charles's very resistance to binary demarcations and his liminal situation in a number of scenes renders him a Todorovian tightrope-walker of fantastic proportions. On the other he is also morally transgressive in the mould of Bataille. Undoubtedly the most powerful example of the transgressor 'at play' concerns the scene of orgiastic abandon which he witnesses and joins in with in the forest at night. Perfectly in keeping with my reading of Shakespeare's witches in Chapter 2, these visions of gluttonous and potentially cannibalistic excess quite clearly hover on that ambiguous territory between the realms of the supernatural and those of hallucination, as Charles's experience of the aftermath so clearly illustrates:

> The bloody hide of the dead cow lay in its rough folds . . . where the women and the boys had thrown it. I ran to it, and was about to wrap myself in it, all wet and raw as it was, when I chanced to look up, and saw that the sun stood over the trees and the treacherous moon had gone. And so had the fire, the pile of bloody meat, the dead baby – everything. There was no evidence at all of that night's murderous dance. (BDH, 64–5)

As Todorov reminds us, via the fantastic we are enabled to journey beyond limits we would otherwise not dare to cross. Just as reference to the supernatural can absolve us from taking responsibility for such diabolical fantasies, so in this case the element of disavowal offers an attractive prohibitive limit: attractive because it marks the point at which excess is denied by casting doubt on its 'actual' existence in textual terms. Likewise, just as transgression requires the affirmation of the limit in the very act of crossing it, so this apparent prohibition re-stimulates the transgression. In casting doubt upon its existence it permits us to linger over this limit in our minds a little longer. Throughout the text, where Charles's liminal stance is not taken up by confrontations with the abject and the taboo, it is clearly circumscribed in two further ways: either in terms of the interloper role, or in terms of the usage of language. For, as Todorov asserts, literature (especially of the fantastic variety) 'is a kind of murderous weapon by which language commits suicide'.[15]

As far as the interloper is concerned, we see a hesitant figure whose very presence pushes against established limits. Just as a number of geometric shapes are adopted as structuring principles aiming to give meaning to spaces, so Charles hovers upon their limits, aiming to imprint his own resisting patterns along the edges of such lines. Cautiously penetrating to the heart of the ruined city, he 'took up a waiting position at the outer edge of the circle, looking in towards the centre' (BDH, 87), aware of his role as interloper forcing this space into a new sequence of signification. And, when he later informs the doctor that 'All these words you say, they fall into a gulf, they're not me or you' (BDH, 141), we see that this resisting impetus is equally reflective of his attitude towards language and its effect upon subjectivity. We have seen that Foucault likewise locates transgression within the space of the limit and the limitations of language. As he reminds us, the transgressor's relationship with subjectivity is always and inevitably problematically tied up with the very limits that she oversteps. But he also goes on to argue that part of this positioning involves a clear identification with the self as site of loss and its linguistic trajectory as that which has moved beyond control: 'the language . . . that has now separated itself from him . . .'.[16] Hence, unlike the anti-transgressive Doctors X and Y, who firmly believe in the existence of an unproblematic and singular 'I', Charles himself argues that 'saying I, I, I, I, is their madness this is where they have been struck lunatic, made moonmad, round the bend, crazy . . . never can they say I, I, without making the celestial watchers roll with laughter or weep with pity' (BDH, 103). Right from the start, Charles's relationship to language is that of Foucault's transgressor. For it, too, 'continually breaks down at the center of its space, exposing in his nakedness, in the inertia of ecstasy, a visible and insistent subject . . . who now finds himself thrown by [language], exhausted, upon the sands of that which he can no longer say.'[17] Intrinsically paradoxical, transgression's relationship with the limit means that it must always articulate itself 'from precisely the place where words escape it'. Even Foucault's topography is that of *Briefing*: 'Essentially the product of fissures, abrupt descents, and broken contours, this misshapen and craglike language describes a circle; it refers to itself and is folded back on a questioning of its limits.'[18] This also has a spatio-temporal dimension. Like Todorov's schizophrenic,[19] Charles adopts a 'private language' which, in its denial of a collective consensus over the nature of the relationship between linear progress and grammatical tense, infers that he lives in 'an eternal present' despite being a classics professor (a point that self-evidently connects him with the language of the past and, as we shall see, the function of dreamwork).

In terms of dreamwork being a structuring principle, the same tension exists between levels of consciousness. At times the language and events via which the dream sequences are related show an obvious connection with the 'surface' level of the mimetic. Thus the raft of the early shipwreck scenes bears a one-to-one correspondence to his hospital bed, the white-winged bird to the nurse who tends him, and the soothing noises she makes ('Hushhhhhhh. Shhhhhhhhhhhhhhhhhhhhhhh' (BDH, 36)) to the sounds of the sea as the waves break around the shore. And in the midst of all this, the recurrent dream imagery which alternates between drowning and being saved is very much in keeping with his position regarding medication and consciousness. Thus, as he tries to rouse himself:

> I can feel myself struggling and fighting as if I were sunk a mile deep in thick dragging water but far above my head in the surface shallows I can see sun-laced waves where the glittering fishes dance and swim, oh, let me rise, let me come up to the surface like a cork or a leaping porpoise into the light. Let me fly like a flying fish, a fish of light. (BDH, 130)

Instead, however, he is 'pushed back to sleep . . . as they drown a kitten' (BDH, 127) as the drugs once again start to take effect; forcing him to mimic the very tidal motions that seem to be determining the direction of his journey. Furthermore, as if to project both ways between levels of consciousness, this ambivalent relationship with the hospital staff is to some extent mirrored by the equally ambivalent relationship he holds with the 'dream-beasts' he encounters at various stages of his fantasy quest.

Yet in case we move to the opposite extreme to Fishburn and align ourselves with Joan Didion's rather dismissive observation that 'The reality Charles Watkins describes is familiar to anyone who has ever had a high fever',[20] we must remember that this psychological element of the text is not only interrupted but also destabilized by certain elements that prevent us from clearly accounting for all aspects of the text as simple strata neatly superimposed upon each other. One such element is the competing (because retrospective rather than present) 'mimetic' layer of the narrative concerning Charles's involvement in Yugoslavia. Intriguingly, a number of critics dismiss this as pure fabrication.[21] The rationale behind this derives from Charles's relationship to Miles Bovey, a protagonist whom the former believes to have died in action. As we later see, Miles is still very much alive and, furthermore, in answering Doctor Y's enquiry, asserts: 'No, I am very sure that Charles Watkins was not at any time in Yugoslavia' (BDH, 224). This statement either suggests that Charles is lying, or that he is genuinely confused. Yet one further possibility exists. Why, in this novel created from a panoply of conflicting and unreliable voices, should we trust the testimony of Miles Bovey any more than we do that of Charles Watkins? Could it not be that Miles (either as well as or instead of Charles) is deceiving us about the truth? A closer look at the wording of Miles's assertion shows that another reading of him is also available. Describing his own entry into Yugoslavia as 'two descents' (BDH, 224), he immediately reminds us of the other *Briefing* scene of the novel and the words spoken by Merk Ury. Taking on board the character-doubling we have already considered, we should note that the name Miles Bovey is similar enough in syllable count and phonetics to Merk Ury to suggest a connection here. If we accept the two to be one cluster protagonist named differently on two levels of the text, we understand absolutely why Miles Bovey/Merk Ury needs to divorce himself from any connection with Charles in order for the clandestine nature of the mission to be maintained. This is just another of the ways in which this text refuses completely and utterly to account for its competing fictional worlds.

## The Archeology of the Unconscious

According to Samuel H. Vasbinder, the 'lost civilization' motif as it functions in fantasy fictions offers a means of 'provid[ing] special access to periods of the past through the activities of contemporary characters'.[22] That this is effectively a psychoanalytic strategy is borne out by Freud's own essay on Jensen's *Gradiva*, in which the central protagonist (a young repressed archeologist called Norbert Hanold) sets off on a quest to find a young woman of peculiarly 'graceful gait', but ends up finding 'himself' by finding her. The topography of Jensen's tale follows that of the 'lost civilization' motif, for during the course of his journey Hanold travels to Pompeii, a fitting site for his own 'excavation'. As Freud himself remarks, 'There is, in fact, no better analogy for repression . . . than burial of the sort to which Pompeii fell a victim and from which it could emerge once more through the work of spades.'[23] Ironically, then, this archeologist discovers that it is in the land of the living that his quest will be fulfilled. Far from dredging up the historical past, he comes face to face with his own personal past in the form of an old childhood sweetheart. Although it is to her that the 'graceful gait' in actuality belongs, it is made clear that he has repressed all memory of her in favour of an apparent interest 'only in women of marble and bronze'.[24] As I have already implied, Charles's role as classics professor projects him into a paradoxical position in terms of temporality and origins. In precisely the same way as Jensen's protagonist, it enables him to cover over his own roots while concentrating on unveiling those of a collective culture. Small wonder, then, that while he can withstand the (at times) impudent interrogations of Doctor Y/why, he is determined to repress any knowledge of the 'presence' of Doctor X/ex-, for what is 'ex-'/past to him is securely buried in the realms of the 'unconscious' (in both the psychoanalytic and the physiological senses of the term). Ultimately (and fittingly) it is his own dreams that find him out.

In entering the 'lost' city, Charles is reluctantly forced into a face-to-face confrontation with the very thing from which he is hiding, albeit that his approach to this site locates its position as an abandoned space of utopian proportions:

> This forest . . . was full of birds and the chattering of troops of monkeys. There was a heavy scent. It came from a tree . . . [with] large mauvish-pink flowers, like magnolias, and the light breeze had spread this scent so that it seemed to come from every tree and bush. There was no feeling of hostility towards the intruder in this place. On the contrary, I felt welcome there, it was as if this was a country where hostility or dislike had not yet been born. (BDH, 40)

Even during his first few days in the city, the fellow inhabitants he senses but cannot see endow him with a feeling of security and 'homely' benevolence. Slowly but surely, however, the presence of the *unheimlich* starts to emerge: 'the ruined houses . . . had set themselves from me, they had turned away, and when I came up to a jut of wall, or the corner of a building, or a threat of shadow, my hands clenched themselves, and my eyes darted of their own accord to every place that might shelter an enemy (BDH, 59). What Charles does come face to face with is the figure of the rat-dog, Lessing's grotesque inversion of the beautiful Gradiva which, far from 'step[ping] trippingly' in the manner of Norbert Hanold's ideal,[25] appears to have only just evolved to the stage of walking on hindlegs: 'staggering, or jerking . . . at each step' (BDH, 74). But both have a parallel role to play, for it is immediately apparent that the rat-dog is simply a defamiliarized version of Charles himself, just as Gradiva is, in some ways, a mere figment of Hanold's unconscious. Ironically, this challenges Merk Ury's claims that human beings are 'able to tolerate others only in so far as they resemble themselves', for Charles is quite unable to tolerate this: 'I was thinking that someone standing a hundred yards away might say, at a casual glance, that it and I were of a similar species . . . but I felt too disgusted with it to stay there matching myself point by point (BDH, 71). But in what sense is this a vision of the self? Aside from reminding us of the ease with which the boundary between civilization and bestiality is broken down, it is perhaps through the manner in which both function as split subjects (indeed grotesque hybrid forms) that the mirror image is seen to exist. For even in Vasbinder's terms, Charles straddles an either/or divide between fictional discoverers who are either 'drawn from the scholarly community or else they are adventurers'.[26] Charles, of course, is simultaneously both as well as being simultaneously self and alien other.

This is important because, according to Roberta Rubenstein, Charles suffers from a profound nostalgia for a sense of union. She situates this reading within a Laingian analysis of the schizophrenic journey through 'inner space', regressing in time 'to recover something missed or lost'.[27] In this case, we unearth the realm of the lost mother (a subject of central importance to Lessing). Critics such as Jeanette King have argued that this entire text can be read as an allegorical exploration of the infant's journey through the mirror stage from the imaginary realm (which she suggests can be related to the womb-like space of the Crystal Disc and Charles's apparent desire to return to it) into the city as site of the symbolic order, for 'The traveler evidently accepts that order and the values and categories inscribed in it'.[28] But I am as reluctant to apply any single theoretical stance as a template over this complex and multi-layered narrative as I am to shackle it to the limitations of genre theory. And although King's reading does fit in with some of the narrative aspects, there are others with which it cannot come to terms. Returning to a comparison with Jensen's *Gradiva* we should remember that whereas the archeologist is fascinated by ancient artifacts, the classics professor is more specifically fascinated by ancient/lost languages. And the very fact that King reads this as an abandoned and 'primitive' site suggests that it has far more in common with Lacan's realm of the imaginary than it does with the symbolic. After all, not only is there no place for the adult human (or his/her language) within it, it is also a space driven and determined purely by bodily drives and functions. More useful is the Kristevan connection she goes on to draw between the relationship between the symbolic and Kristeva's semiotic, for we can see that the clashes between the poetic and the rational function in an analogous manner to this. Furthermore, returning to my reading of Charles as a subject severed from his desire for the mother, it does seem, as King rightly suggests, that it is what the symbolic order constructs as 'female' that is most consistently repressed in the context of the novel.[29] In this sense, the 'shadow of the third' that Lessing first adopts as a motif for personal relationships in *The Golden Notebook* (1962) and subsequently reworks in the triadic relationship central to *The Four-Gated City*, here emerges as the shadowy presence of a fantasized absence in the form of the mother. Represented collectively in the orgy scene by the three witch-like women who function as her decoy, ultimately the mother is revealed as that ancient site of loss to which Charles is, albeit 'unconsciously', drawn.

So here we find an alien who is, as much as any fantasy figure, well and truly a 'stranger to himself'. This explains why Charles's relationship with the Disc leaves him, not with a sense of terror (which we might expect in a science fiction context), but with one of fantastic 'foreignness' (BDH, 25). In that sense Bataille's words take on particular resonance when his word 'chrysalis' is replaced with that of Lessing's 'crystal': 'Man achieves his inner experience at the instant when bursting out of the chrysalis [crystal] he feels that he is tearing himself . . . this process, too, is linked with the turning topsy-turvey of his original mode of being.'[30] It is equally significant that Charles resents his inability to withstand the power of the pull of the moon (with its particular associations with the menstrual cycle), this explaining his compulsively reiterated horror of the 'strong sickly smell of blood' (BDH, 60) which fills the air. Two scenes resonate fully with this. The first accompanies the description of the protagonists in the aforementioned orgy scene:

> a terrible nauseating curiosity came over me – but that curiosity which is like digging one's fingers into a stinging wound. I knew quite well who they were . . . though there was a gulf in my memory, blotting out the exact knowledge of where these people fitted into my long-past life . . . their three faces, women's faces, all the same, or rather, all variations of the same face . . . blood was smeared around their stretched mouths, and ran trickling off their chins . . . Three women, all . . . bound to me by experience I could not remember at all. (BDH, 63)

Much has been made, not only of the fact that he names his seemingly demure wife Felicity as one of these women, but also that she is accompanied by two further possible doubles for the many characters with whom Charles is supposedly romantically connected. And yet where Jensen's protagonist turns away from the flesh and blood of real women towards cold, aestheticized images, so Charles turns to safely distanced dream images. Ironically, this and the following scene provide him with far more female flesh and blood than he can properly stomach:

> I saw a female Rat-dog, with its sleek brown hide all bloodied and gashed . . . she was giving birth. Puppies tumbled out of her scarlet slit in a spout of blood and tissue, while she fought for her life. The two round mounds on her chest . . . were swollen and had been torn, so that blood and milk poured out together . . . she became so crazed with fear and the need to help her puppies' birth, that even as she fought, she would give a deadly snap in front at an antagonist, and then snap downwards at her young . . . She died in a spasm that was as much a birth- as a death-spasm. (BDH, 85)

Birthing and female sexuality are, for Charles, inseparable from destruction and repulsive excess. Therefore what he is confronted by, in this horrifying image of the female rat-dog, is really the horror of his own maternal repressions. Like Vasbinder's lost civilization, Charles's city is also well and truly 'lost', both as an embodiment of the death of utopia and as a metaphor for the site of his birth. Irrespective of whether we read Charles's journeying adventures literally or metaphorically, what is clear is that he is on a voyage of often uncomfortable discovery and this, beyond all other themes and concerns, is perhaps the central fascination of all types of fantasy fictions.

## ***The Bridge*** **as Architectural Narrative**

Iain Banks's *The Bridge*[31] forms an interesting companion piece to *Briefing*. Like Lessing's text, Banks's hovers on that precarious point where psychological and fantasy narratives meet. As a writer who also feels the need to divide his work into compartmentalized sections (in his case between 'mainstream' and 'science fiction'), Banks places *The Bridge* in the former, since it lacks the 'big space ships' with which he associates 'SciFi with a capital S'.[32] Nevertheless, like Lessing's text, this novel does encompass within it a substantial section that can only be seen in speculative dystopian terms. Thus the central protagonist (named Orr by the hospital staff), projects himself into a futurist landscape within which the bridge is not only the central reference point but also the limits of existence, Orr beginning the text living 'close to the summit and not far from one angle of the squashed hexagon which the section resembles' (TB, 43). In addition, as Orr's use of the lift between storeys demonstrates, at times what begins as a fairly routine piece of technical equipment suddenly becomes defamiliarized, shifting into something far closer to a science fiction space/time travel machine: '[The attendant] opens the doors to a scene of utter chaos ... fire, fallen girders, mangled pipes and beams, collapsed brickwork and drooping cables ... The din and racket of jangling alarms and klaxons ... "doesn't look much like a library from this angle, does it?"'(TB, 56). Once again, it is not so much a question of whether this novel is or is not science fiction, for the terms of Fishburn's argument are as (in)applicable here as they were to *Briefing*; it is simply that Banks manipulates the genre issue in order to use the fantastic to disorientate both reader and protagonist in similar manner to Lessing.

There are striking similarities between these two novels. Once again we are plunged into the thought-processes of a 'disturbed' hospitalized patient whose psyche has become fractured between a number of superimposed levels of phantasy. Some of these even adopt similar manifest forms to those of Charles Watkins. This man, too, considers his memory to be a 'drowned landscape' (TB, 86) while the reader recognizes that connections between deep and surface layers are once again made in terms of mirroring, the double, and the utilization of wordplay. When Banks's character refers to a 'uniform surface' and the production of 'foldings' in the topographical imagery of his fantasy mode (TB, 86), we relate this immediately to the presence of nursing staff, attending to changing his bed around him on the level of mimesis, just as we did in the context of *Briefing*. Likewise, when Banks's protagonist tells us that 'waves of pain ... flood me, beating on the body's shore ... it is an ocean of burning oil I am cast adrift upon, no sea's repose' (TB, 142), or 'At my back lay the desert, ahead the sea ... Between the two, half submerged by each, the ruined city' (TB, 59), we are clearly reminded of the sea and city imagery which we have examined in detail in Lessing's novel. And once again the multi-layered narrative adopts two competing (if related) 'surface' layers of mimesis although, as we will see, the effect of these surfaces is rather different in this case. One of these mimetic strands covers a retrospective recounting of the protagonist's long-term romantic relationship with a woman called Andrea Cramond (a layer that in many ways offers us a genuine anchor-point throughout the text); while the second and more immediate element contextualizes Orr's hospitalization, revealing the details of a severe car accident that has sent him into a coma. Nevertheless, an important disparity manifests itself between the two novels in the choice of topographical imagery used to explore the symbolism of the psyche. Whereas, in Lessing's text, it is primarily the image of the lost city emerging out of the natural landscape that enables Charles to explore his relationship to repression and subjectivity, in Banks's the utilization of geological imagery as a central structuring feature is ironically in tension with the importance of the architecture that dominates this 'unnatural' world.

Quite obviously, the symbol of the bridge defines and structures everything in this book. Simultaneously a figure of home (in the mimetic sections) and terrifying estrangement (in the dystopian sections) its uncanny qualities are readily apparent. One of the most salient comments made about the image and its relationship to the narrative as a whole comes from Doctor Joyce, who in suggesting that 'Perhaps the dream is a bridge ... [and] Perhaps the bridge is a dream' (TB, 29) reminds us that this text self-consciously plays with the interconnection point between competing secondary elaborations, by means of anchoring them in this primary manifestation of latent phantasy content, the rootless aspect of which is made entirely clear. But it also reminds us that nothing exists outside this paranoid structure. Just as it gives its name to the text, so the bridge itself functions as a language on two levels. First, in structuralist terms, *The Bridge* as text is a *langue*, within which the bridge functions as an example of *parole*. But this particular *parole* is, in itself, structured as a language: 'In cross-section, at its thickest, the bridge closely resembles the letter A ... in elevation, the centre part of each section consists of an H superimposed over an X; spreading out on each side from this centre are six more Xs which gradually reduce in size until they meet the slender linking spans (which have nine smalls Xs each)' (TB, 34). Right from the start, then, it is as if a riddle is enmeshed within the very architecture, mirroring the riddling of the text which simultaneously pushes towards and away from a coherent unravelling. Another of these riddles surrounds the number three. Like Lessing's concept of the 'shadow of the third', threes recur in Banks's novel time and time again and on a multiplicity of narrative levels. These include: the 'three little asterisks' (TB, 284) that punctuate the central character's re-emergence into conscious reality; Andrea Cramond's superstitious fantasy that car accidents run in threes (TB, 107–8); and the 'Three big Xs one above the other' (TB, 284) which bridge the gap between strata by linking the bridge in the concluding consciousness sections with the ribboned fastenings on Abberlaine

Arrol's lingerie in the earlier fantasy/dream sections. Indeed, these games with shapes, numbers, structures and riddling wordplay are perpetuated throughout, always taking their direction from the bridge itself. This is clear right from the start when two geometrical patterns are shown to the protagonist by Dr Joyce:

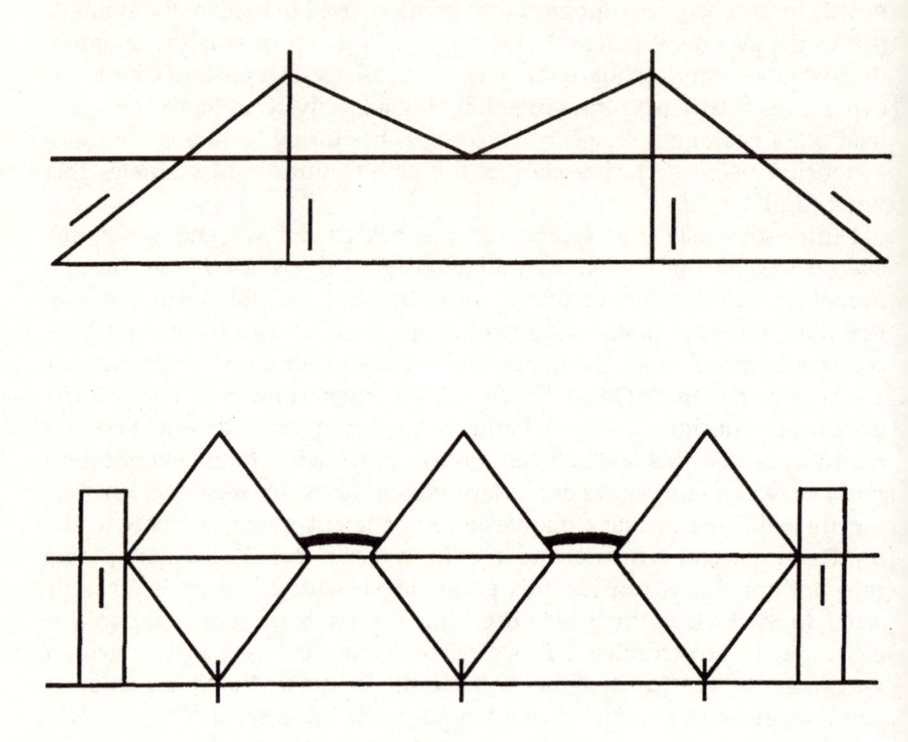

That the diagrams represent an architectural structure is indicated by the accompanying task that is set for the protagonist: 'You see those small lines . . . Complete those by making them into arrows so that they indicate the direction of force the structures shown are exerting at those points' (TB, 53). What makes this such a significant issue (although this is not rendered explicit by the narrative itself) is the symbolic comparison that we recognize to exist between the lower of the two diagrams and the overall structure of the novel. Quite aside from the fact that, when turned through a perpendicular axis the shape resembles the 'three of diamonds' playing card given to Orr at the end of the text (as a synecdochic replacement for the structure he is about to leave behind), one only has to look at the layout of the contents page to be struck by the intricate (almost architectural) patterning of the narrative and what we see to be another manifestation of this diagrammatic plan:

Coma

Metaphormosis: One<br>Two<br>Three<br>Four

Triassic

Metamorpheus: One<br>Two<br>Three<br>Four

Eocene

Metamorphosis: Oligocene<br>Miocene<br>Pliocene<br>Quaternary

Coda

So the diagram, comprising three diamond-like sectors connected by two linking spans and supported by two rectangular pillars, carefully mirrors the geometric design that actually parallels the narrative structure of the text. As we can see, this too comprises three main sections: 'Metaphormosis', 'Metamorpheus' and 'Metamorphosis', each of which is joined by two linking sections, 'Triassic' and 'Eocene', the entire structure being framed by two enclosure mechanisms, 'Coma' and 'Coda'. In each case the slightest of linguistic shifts functions to differentiate between various strata. And just before this, as the central character looks at a photograph of the bridge in construction, noting: 'three of the bridge sections . . . stand alone, unconnected except through their jagged, uncompleted similarity' (TB, 51), he seems to be articulating a cryptic encoding of the reader's own piecemeal reading position in relationship to this monumental structure that both upholds and undermines our orientation throughout. In line with this, it is not surprising that elsewhere in the narrative, gaps in textuality mirror semantic gaps in the reader's (and the protagonist's) awareness, both page- and line-breaks functioning in this way:

> No chance, of course but there
> you go. *Now* what? Good grief
> can't a fellow have a little talk with himself without
> being –
> *again*! What the fucking hell's going on here? What do you
> think I am you clumsy bastards? This part of the
> – will you *stop* that! No
> more bumping! It hurts! (TB, 188)

Progression through the narrative inevitably means a blurring of boundaries between levels, a process for which the bridge also provides a metaphor as Orr is relocated (similarly without warning) on differing levels mirroring the intersecting levels of consciousness. But ultimately such a 'sectioning off' is thrown into confusion as page-breaks become linked by intermeshing discourses 'properly' belonging to disparate levels:

> *She got*
> haud on, son; just doin the intro . . .
> *She got her*
> you'll get yours in a minute Jimmy if ye don't shut
> *She got her degree*
> is it me, eh? Is it? Does ma voice no carry or something?
> *She –*
> yeah . . . we know . . . Christ some people are just so fucking im
> (TB, 189)

Thus we should not overlook the role of the 'linking spans' at the centre, for they are a microcosm of the bridge in its overall entirety. Facilitating 'passage', closing obstructive gaps, we look to bridges to help us on our way. And yet Banks's bridge is a self-fulfilling structure; a linking piece severed (on all levels) from the land on either side. As Orr reluctantly asserts in true structuralist terms, the bridge itself 'has more than enough to offer the enquiring mind without recourse to anything outside it' (TB, 49). Stranded on a structure that refuses to span, we find ourselves, like Orr, driven by a journey with nowhere to go.

This is the paradox of what Hume has referred to as the literature of disillusion; that fictional form whereby a text strives to articulate the fact that we 'cannot know reality'. More concerned with naming the problem than finding a solution to it, such narratives function by drawing attention to the fallibility of our senses (and thus our experience of the 'real'), often by challenging the accepted relationship between dreams and reality by means of what seems, to the reader, to be the possible (but not definite) intervention of drugs, disorientation and hallucination. In Hume's terms then, our protagonist is cast as 'a stumblebum picaro' forced to negotiate 'skewed, hall-of-mirrors worlds'. Orr, like the reader, is forced into a reluctant journeying through a space and time that is at best disrupted and at worst chaotic, even if (as Hume's terminology implies) a cynical humour remains perceptible throughout. But where her argument starts to fall down is in her express belief that such fictions can and should be read as 'anti-form'.[33] As we have seen, few novels are as consciously and carefully crafted on a formal level as Banks's *The Bridge*. Far more useful, as I have consistently argued, is a reading of such literature as profoundly 'anti-genre'.

In some ways Orr resists this 'stumblebum' image. For although the 'clouded and formless' (TB, 58) nature of his sensory perceptions cannot be amalgamated into the integers and grid references by which the bridge is constructed, where Hume associates such fictions with a disorientating loss of the text's narrative frame, Orr consistently struggles against such disorientation precisely by struggling to regain the frame's dimensions. Although he occasionally lapses, referring to his social progress at one point as a 'coming down in the bridge' (TB, 154) as if the bridge were the 'world' (and thus the frame as well), for most of the narrative his interrogative stance is a consistent challenge to such assumptions. Once again we can read this as resistance to what is otherwise a structuralist stance:

> There are three possibilities:
> 1 The bridge is just that, a link between two land masses . . .
> 2 The bridge is, effectively, a pier . . .
> 3 The bridge has no connection with land whatsoever . . .
>
> There is an interesting sub-possibility in case 3. The bridge appears to be straight, but there is a horizon . . . So the bridge might eventually meet itself, form a closed circuit . . .
>
> (TB, 130)

Only the third of these would fall into line with a structuralist approach, for it is solely this that situates the bridge as a self-reflexive system without any boundaries. Orr's 'perspectivist' approach,[34] however, enables us to interpret him as the fictive embodiment of genre theory critiqued. In recognizing himself to be stifled by trappings that deter him from interrogating the relationship between the bridge and its surrounding topography and social context, he articulates the constraints of genre criticism. Determining to find out about possibilities one and two above, it is apparent why the authorities respond by relocating him deeper within the structures of the system, firstly as his living accommodation is moved to U7 306 and later when he finds himself in the prison/HQ (TB, 222). But of course, as Todorov reminds us, one of the ways in which such fictions succeed in their disorientating aims is by setting up an internal mechanism comprising a first-person narrative who is cast in the guise of 'an "average man", in whom (almost) every reader can recognize himself'.[35] The gender-imbalance of his remarks is unfortunate, but not preclusive of their application to female readers. Women learn early to fictively project themselves into a central male identification where the only alternative is the periphery and in texts such as this, readers of both sexes come to terms with the fact that we are all, in many ways 'stumblebum picaroes'. So we forge a path through chaos and conflict, turning it into that tunnel-visioned 'fiction' called linear progress. In this case then, the reader becomes conjoined with Orr in being 'determined to reach the end of the structure' (TB, 215), lured on by the hope that answers will be offered and that Orr will be wrong to suspect that 'there is no point trying to discover anything worthwhile about the bridge' (TB, 32).

It is also significant that Hume sees the image of the dream as a fictive anchor-point, a stable presence among otherwise ubiquitous instability,[36] for in many ways one could argue that it is the treatment of dream imagery in this text that consolidates its problematic status *vis-à-vis* structuralism and psychoanalysis. As Hume herself shows, it is not necessary to endorse a psychoanalytic perspective when analysing the utilization of dreams in fiction. Writing fictional dreams is simply writing fiction. Banks treads a fine line, at times, between seeming to uphold Freudian readings of dreamwork as a commentary on the interrelationship between levels of fantasy and those of mimesis and, at others, appearing to debunk what could be read as pretentious self-analysis on the part of the central character. But in essence he uses dreamwork primarily as a means of exploring the problematic dynamic between control and the lack of/loss of that control, a dynamic which ironically takes its application to the text from Kristeva's metaphorical reading of 'The space of the foreigner [as] a moving train'.[37] Here that space is literalized, turning against the ensnared protagonist to subject him to a multiplicity of vivid sequences spanning (like the bridge itself) both ends of the spectrum; from terrifying nightmares of being unremittingly pursued by a speeding train, to sexual wish-fulfilment (presumably wet-) dream narratives. In line with Freudian arguments, in all of these dreams his degree of control is only ever partial, the train 'easily negotiat[ing] the corners and kinks in the rails my stumbling, twisting progress has produced' (TB, 128) and his desires for sexual gratification simply resulting in him 'hold[ing] my prick like some stunted flagpole in front of me, running and shaking it and bellowing with frustrated desire' (TB, 144).

This is in conflict with Orr's role as first-person narrator, which we would expect to endow him with total textual autonomy. As analyst/teller of his own tale and subject/analysand into whose psyche we are immersed, he too straddles the divide between master and slave. This is a privileged position that he allows to be foregrounded in cynically playing tricks usually aimed at the foundational principles of psychoanalytic theory. Thus, in an explicit parody of the links we have seen Freud draw between creative writing and dreaming, Orr informs us that most of the dream sequences are nothing but 'a pack of lies' (TB, 26) fabricated for the very purpose of telling to his analyst. In psychoanalytic terms, the distinction Orr draws is to some extent a false one. Just as fictional dreams are simply fictions, so written narratives are as much secondary elaborations (and thus open to psychoanalytic insight) as genuine nightdreams. Only in terms of a non-psychoanalytic interpretation does this cynical reading of the fictional dream genuinely work to disconcert us. For what this reminds us of, is that our central protagonist is not simply unreliable (as first-person narrator) but also untrustworthy.

According to Hume, recognitions such as this risk the total alienation of readers who, in 'trying to protect themselves . . . cultivat[e] indifference, ironic distance . . . or allegiance to the "everyday"'.[38] Nevertheless, Banks ultimately negotiates this while still retaining our sympathies for the central character. And he does so via the most alluring technique of all: promising us the possibility of reader consolation by frequent recourse to a surface romance.

## The Technological Subject and the Fetishized Other

Hume is correct in her observation that readers of such texts find themselves pulled, simultaneously, in a variety of directions. And the most important of these vying concerns involves the textual battle between gratification and alienation on the part of the reader. Consequently, however much we may wish to claim otherwise, when we encounter comments such as 'I wake slowly, still immersed in the barbarian's rough thoughts' midway through the text (TB, 169), a substantial part of us longs for this to be the final waking to consciousness that will bring the protagonist back to surface reality. Banks, fully aware of this desire, teasingly perpetuates our very uncertainty by causing his character to waken in an environment that could, quite easily, be a hospital ward: 'The cold white sheets are twisted around me like ropes . . . I am trapped, tied down . . . and suddenly I am awake, cold and sweating and sitting up in the bed' (TB, 169). Part relieved and part disappointed, we soon recognize that he has awoken merely into another level of fantasy, several strata below the surface (in both senses of the term). And yet he has allowed us a glimpse of possible resolution, enough to keep us going for now and, more significantly, he is in a fictive space on the level of fantasy which turns out to be an encoded version of Andrea's Grandfather's house, a place where the two of them take a holiday from their studies. The path to the surface is starting to become navigable. The importance of this is that it pushes towards the most tempting element of narrative resolution: the presiding romantic structure that offers the final reading of the bridge's 'Three big Xs one above the other' (TB, 284), this time adding to their chain of representation the 'sealing' kisses of romantic fiction. However hard we struggle against it, part of us craves the very consolatory mechanisms that we recognise will threaten the text's creative impact. Banks himself veers dangerously close to such a capitulation, setting up an ending that is threaded through with wish-fulfilment devices, if ultimately it refuses fully to assert them.

So the reader is caught in a trap which threatens to stifle us even as we desire to remain ensnared within it. Again, this is part of our shared identification with the protagonist. It is only via Orr's physical entrapment within the bridge that the reader likewise becomes 'embedded' within it (as text). Furthermore, insofar as all the characters on the fantasy levels of the narrative are projections of his psyche, it is inevitable that they, too, will signify only insofar as they also take on meaning in terms of the bridge's architecture: 'Abberlaine Arrol's body is encased in blackness, strapped and ribbed ... another pattern of Xs form[ing] a cantilevered stripe from pubis to just below ... a separate brassiere ... Xs; that pattern within a pattern ... The zig-zagging lace of her camiknickers ... cantilevers and tubes, suspension ties ... the engineering of these soft materials' (TB, 174–5). This, in itself, is not surprising, for while in Lessing's narrative it is the boundaries which exist between the human and the elemental that are often thrown into confusion, here the connection is predominantly cybernetic. This is made clear right from the start: 'Trapped. Crushed. Weight coming from all directions ... Blood red. Red blood. See the man bleed, see the car leak; radiator red, blood red, blood like red oil. Pump still working – shit, I said shit this hurts – pump still working but the fluid leaking out all over the fucking place' (TB, 11). This is more than a description of his entanglement within the wreckage of his car. It is also, taken out of context, paralleled by his body being 'wired up' to a life-support system while unconscious in hospital. So bodily fluids are artificially pumped around his body, waste matter artificially excreted and brain-signals artificially monitored and mimicked. This is a war fought in the zone of abjection, a dynamic that derives its 'powers of horror' from the need for 'the expulsion or exclusion of the improper, the unclean, and the disorderly elements of its corporeal existence' in order to retain a clear and coherent relationship to the 'heart' of the self.[39] That Orr is losing his ability to protect self from not-self (as his very naming suggests) becomes clear when we pay detailed attention to the wording of this quotation. The word 'pump' could equally refer to his heart or the fuel pump of the car, while the word 'shit', rather than simply being an expletive voiced in response to pain and/or fear, could actually be indicating the presence of faeces, an 'automatic' bodily response to the extremity of the situation. It even seems likely that 'the fucking place' refers to his genitals as much as it refers to the vaguely structured 'everywhere' within his sight. But if my previous interpretation of the bridge as the structuring principle of the reading process is also applied here, then it comes as no surprise that, by the end of the text, the reader is also positioned in cybernetic terms. Orr, quizzing his own 'self as machine' on returning to consciousness, projects us into a similar identification as we realize that we share his own lack of self-knowledge: '"Hmm. And I suppose you don't know my name, do you?" "Correct"' (TB, 276).

This interface between subjectivity and technology brings us to the importance of screen imagery as it functions within the text. Here it provides us with a particularly interesting fictional boundary marker. In a novel such as this, where the liminal itself is a site of contention, we should remember that a television screen is both a boundary and a way of permeating a boundary (seeing into another world). When unused, it situates itself on 'our' side of the fantasy/reality divide as a piece of rather uninspiring household technology. When operational, however, it offers us a window into magical pleasures which are usually of the most gratuitous of kinds. Likewise, although the effect of the screen upon Banks's protagonist offers anything but gratuitous pleasure, it does straddle the divide set up in the narrative between the realms of realism and those of fantasy. Right from the start, looked at from 'within', it seems to offer a window between layers of consciousness, consistently revealing the embodiment of the 'unconscious' in the form of a comatose man lying in a hospital bed. But there is yet another riddle attached to this. In order for Orr to be able to witness this, he needs to be positioned within the very dream-layers of the text with which the unconscious is conventionally associated. From the other side of the screen, it is implied, the surface is entirely self-reflecting. As every other aspect of the text implies, there still seems little likelihood of a way 'out' into mimesis.

And yet this does not prevent the mimetic from impinging upon the dream-layers, even if they shatter and distort Orr's relationship with his own unconscious self. As Mary Ann Doane reminds us, 'The face is that bodily part not accessible to the subject's own gaze',[40] a realization foregrounded here by the face of his mimetic double being unidentifiable due to the angle and distance of the visual perspective offered. But that masked face is replaced on more than one occasion by the intervening presence of the image of a woman; be it a nurse (TB, 75) or, later, the close-up presence of Andrea (TB, 178). The effect of this disturbance is worth examining in more detail, for it relates to what Doane has perceived to be the 'veil-like' function of the cinema screen in its treatment of the fetishization of the face of the woman. Thus as the picture 'shakes, then settles on the man' (TB, 178) we see that the woman's presence, far from being a simple distraction, also functions as a decoy image threatening to take over the space where his own projected presence should be. So 'the gaze finds itself consistently displaced in relation to the horror of absence ... [and] aligns or misaligns itself with the body of a woman'.[41] Just as Doane remarks upon the frequency with which the close-up shot of the woman 'is masked, barred, shadowed, or veiled',[42] so Andrea's image here gradually emerges out of 'a textured blankness' worth comparing with the image of Abberlaine (her fantasy double), whose image we have seen to be 'encased in blackness' as she functions to embody the structure of the bridge. For this blankness/blackness is the site of the presence of Orr's own absence as he lies on the bed, substituting his self-image with versions of the fantasy other. Just as the woman replaces the central protagonist on-screen, there is a sense in which he, too, replaces her. Like the stage/screen actress, Orr has lost his status as flesh and blood, functioning simply as a 'body to be dressed, enfolded ... lined and laced' (TB, 176).

The utilization of the image of/on the screen forms an interesting 'bridge', in itself, between issues of genre and issues of subjectivity. For its presence in a paranoic novel of this kind, subsequent to its powerful usage in that canonical science fiction text George Orwell's *Nineteen Eighty-Four* (1949), immediately alerts the attuned reader to its possible fictional usage for the purposes of political espionage, particularly as its controls appear to function independently of him.[43] This returns us to the literature of disillusion, and the connections that psychoanalysis has drawn between the working of the screen and the duplicitous nature of its unconscious dynamics. As Doane informs us, although 'Psychoanalysis has consistently been suspicious of the realm of the visible, intimately bound as it would seem to be to the register of consciousness', it has had a profound influence upon our understanding of cinema.[44] Her adoption of the word 'suspicious' is important, for we have seen that it is precisely that manipulation of the cynical and the paranoic that Banks utilizes to create uncertainty. As psychoanalytic theorists observe, the false allure of the cinema screen is that it projects images that are, of necessity, not only distanced from us, but also 'in reality' inaccessible. In essence then, as we shall also see in the context of *The Passion of New Eve*, the screen bears a particularly privileged relationship with fantasy as phantasy or wish-fulfilment daydream.

As the aforementioned 'shaken' image implies, the screen does not have a fixed and finite frame. Rather, just like the play of the text itself, we are encouraged to 'see the pretty patterns form; watch it snow or rain, or blow, or shine' (TB, 211). And, if the bridge provides the fantasy frame for the narrative, the 'grainy' screen exists as the play of its surfaces, turning what we call vision into a series of free-floating optical illusions. This also impacts upon full subjectivity. In Lacanian terms, the screen obviously conceptualizes the splitting of the self; what Banks playfully refers to as 'not one i but two: i i. Or ii (well come on you can have a roman nose why not roman eyes . . . ). Aye-aye' (TB, 189). Just as Orr finds himself severed from self on either side of the screen, so the presence of the screen signifies the absence of the unified subject and the unattainable nature of our own unconscious: 'For that which is latent – the signifiable – is also always deferred, out of reach, subject to a metonymic displacement'.[45] In these terms Orr remains cybernetically '*Riveted* to an elsewhere as certain as it is inaccessible . . . seek[ing] that invisible and promised territory . . . that does not exist but that he bears in his dreams, and that must indeed be called a beyond.'[46] So this novel concludes by fetishizing Andrea as the object of desire who is there only in an unattainable form. Only present while he is mentally 'absent', re-emergence into full consciousness will make her disappear as she returns to her own fantasy 'other'; her French lover Gustave. In this sense, visual fetishizing denotes that she is like Orr in being only present in her absence as he is inexorably but reluctantly forced to choose between a living death with or a life without her: 'a sort of horror drew me on, made me walk towards this still not-quite-seen figure. It was as if some magnetic repulsion ... sucked me inexorably forward, drawing me towards something ... I feared – or should fear – utterly' (TB, 23).

Elsewhere in the text, Orr, wandering deserted and ruined streets, focuses upon his own ethereal presence as 'a white ghost billowing through the tumbled wreckage' (TB, 59), a scene that evokes the gothic 'dream' sequence Orr supposedly fabricates for his psychiatrist at the beginning. This scene is anomalous in the context of the narrative as a whole, for its fantasy aspects belong to the realm of the gothic rather than to the dystopian futurism which we find throughout. Indeed, its full significance is only retrospectively understood. What becomes clear is that it introduces us to the central image of the fantasy double and, more particularly, Otto Rank's reading of this motif as a shadowed existence and portent of death. As Rank informs us, the double negotiates an aesthetic manifestation of the manner in which 'a person's past inescapably clings to him and ... becomes his fate as soon as he tries to get rid of it'. Thus the double is a figure entrenched within time. And although chronology is undoubtedly disrupted in this text (as the temporal dimension of this rather archaic scene shows), it nevertheless does attribute Orr with a location in time that he cannot evade. All his dream sequences (fabricated or otherwise) connect him with a past that is simultaneously an ongoing present, and separation from time can only come with death. That Rank also reads the double as intrinsically related to 'catastrophe', and catastrophe to woman, is equally important. For Andrea (the woman in question) is, of course, the anchor-point via which retrospection is structured. She gives temporality its *raison d'être*, even in the sense that without her presentness he has no future. So, although this novel appears to follow that structure which Rank dismisses, whereby a double is constructed through 'the representation, by one and the same person, of two distinct beings separated by amnesia', the relevance of his work to our understanding of this scene is reason enough to justify its inclusion. Orr's depiction in the text aligns him closely with Rank's perspective: 'In the living human being ... there dwells, like an alien guest [ghost?], a *weaker double* ... whose realm is the world of dreams. When the other self is asleep, unconscious of itself, the double is awake and active.'[47] What renders this gothic dream sequence particularly significant is the relationship it bears to cultural taboos surrounding the double. Rank alerts us to the fact that staring in a mirror after dark is connected, for many cultures, with imminent death. In this scene it is only once night has fallen that the oncoming carriage appears and faces him. That this is a mirror image becomes gradually apparent:

> I reined the mares in, letting them amble slowly forward so that our two carriages would meet at the passing place. My counterpart appeared to anticipate

> me, and also slowed. It was at that instant that a strange, unnameable fear gripped me . . . I swerved to the right; the carriage facing me went to its left, so that our teams faced one another, each blocking the other's way . . . I waved at the shadowy figure on the other vehicle . . . We waved simultaneously. (TB, 20–1)

Only at the moment of utterance does this symmetry fracture. Though both figures speak at once, Orr informs us that 'he did not speak the words I spoke, and I was not even sure that he had spoken the same language' (TB, 21). Later he sees that they have different faces. This difference within similarity, along with the reflection's description as a 'shadowy' presence and a 'not-quite-seen figure' (TB, 23) marks it as the double, the shadow self who is both I and not-I. Importantly, then, though both figures contemplate and attempt to shoot the other as a means of resolution, such resolution is denied at this possible passing-place/place of possible 'passing'. Instead both move on, death having been denied by a very close call. This, of course, is our protagonist's dilemma for this 'double' who, like Orr, is poised on the brink of death, *is* his fantasy 'other' Gustave. Though positioned symmetrically to Orr, he speaks a different language and has a different face; one, moreover, that remains 'not quite seen'. Significantly, this not only sets up Andrea as the fetishized image of the screen/mirror; but also as the mirror itself which fractures 'Orr' from his own sense of self.

And yet as our first-person identification with Orr makes clear, it is the latter and not Gustave we situate as the 'foreigner' who 'tends to think he is the only one to have a biography, that is, a life made up of ordeals'. Of course, Orr is also a shifting signifier who fictionalizes himself through his multiple secondary elaborations, just as he fictionalizes/constructs the characters as 'others' with whom he interacts. This initial gothic encounter is therefore only the first of many strange and defamiliarized versions of the self which enable Orr to situate himself in terms of pretence and disavowal: 'Not belonging to any place, any time, any love. A lost origin . . . a rummaging memory . . . As to landmarks, there are none'.[48] Indeed, in both novels we have seen a variety of landmarks with apparent temporal or topographical significance fade away into disillusion and disorientation. Add to this the misleading landmark of genre identity and we are left with a chain of unstable coordinates typical of the literature of disillusion. This is a hybrid mode of representation. Seemingly anchored in the precepts of *sf*, once our expectations of these precepts are challenged, such texts (and their readers) are cast adrift upon a slipstream current at the meeting-point of fantasy, the fantastic, and the unconscious. Eventually bringing us face to face with that alien other who is the self, Banks's closing/opening scene is typical of the ways in which both narratives rethink the boundary demarcations of 'outer space' in terms of the frontiers of inner space. Now moving on to interrogate these further, Chapter 5 explores the uncanny effects of frontier negotiations once resituated in gothic terms.

## Notes

1 Doris Lessing, *Briefing For A Descent Into Hell* (London: Granada, 1972). All subsequent quotations are referenced within the main body of the text, the abbreviation BDH being used. The term 'border policing' is one taken from Roger Luckhurst, 'Border Policing: Postmodernism and Science Fiction', *Science Fiction Studies*, Vol. 18 (1991), pp. 358-66.
2 Patrick Parrinder, *The Failure of Theory: Essays on Criticism and Contemporary Fiction* (Brighton: Harvester, 1987), p. 135.
3 Katherine Fishburn, 'Doris Lessing's *Briefing For A Descent Into Hell*: Science Fiction or Psycho-Drama?', *Science Fiction Studies*, Vol. 15 (1988), pp. 48–60 (p. 54).
4 Fishburn, 'Lessing's *Briefing*', pp. 50–1 – my emphasis.
5 Fishburn, 'Lessing's *Briefing*', p. 51.
6 For a fuller discussion of this see Roland Barthes, *S/Z*, trans. R. Miller (London: Jonathan Cape, 1975). In brief, *lisible* texts require only a consuming/complicit/passive readerly stance, where *scriptible* texts require readers to be productive/interrogative/active. Not surprisingly, Barthes favours the latter over the former in creative terms.
7 Lucie Armitt, 'Introduction', in Lucie Armitt (ed.), *Where No Man Has Gone Before: Women and Science Fiction* (London: Routledge, 1991), pp. 1–12, (p. 9).
8 Fishburn, 'Lessing's *Briefing*', p. 55.
9 Fishburn, 'Lessing's *Briefing*', pp. 51–2 and p. 57.
10 Although there are a number of competing narrative voices which continually strive to undermine the autonomy of Charles's own, it is ultimately Lessing's prioritization of a destabilizing reader position that ensures that these are perpetually rendered subordinate to his.
11 Bruce Sterling, 'Slipstream', *Science Fiction Eye*, July (1989), pp. 77–80 (p. 78). Cited by Luckhurst, 'Policing', pp. 364–5.
12 These two five-volume series span the periods 1952–69 and 1979–83 respectively. Whereas 'Children of Violence' functions as an extended *bildungsroman* concerning the development of a character called Martha Quest, the 'Canopus in Argos' series is conceptually organized around the theme of outer space.
13 Claire Sprague, *Rereading Doris Lessing: Narrative Patterns of Doubling and Repetition* (Chapel Hill: University North Carolina Press, 1987), pp. 4–7 *passim*.
14 Rachel Blau DuPlessis, 'The Feminist Apologues of Lessing, Piercy, and Russ', *Frontiers*, Vol. 4 (1979), pp. 1–8 (p. 2).
15 Tzvetan Todorov, *The Fantastic: A Structural Approach to a Literary Genre*, trans. Richard Howard (Ithaca, NY: Cornell University Press, 1975), pp. 158 and 167.
16 Michel Foucault, 'A Preface to Transgression', trans. Donald F. Bouchard and Sherry Simon, in Donald F. Bouchard (ed.), Michel Foucault, *Language, Counter-Memory, Practice: Selected Essays and Interviews* (Ithaca, NY: Cornell University Press, 1977), pp. 29–52 (p. 42).
17 This being Foucault's definition. 'Preface', p. 39.
18 Foucault, 'Preface', p. 44.
19 See Todorov, *Fantastic*, p. 146.
20 Joan Didion, '*Briefing For A Descent Into Hell*', in Claire Sprague and Virginia Tiger (eds), *Critical Essays on Doris Lessing* (Boston: G.K. Hall, 1986), pp. 192–6 (p. 193).
21 See, for example, Jeanette King, *Doris Lessing* (London: Edward Arnold, 1989) pp. 65–6; Peter Malekin, '"What Dreams May Come": Relativity and Perception in Doris Lessing's *Briefing . . .*', in Donald E. Morse et al. (eds) *Celebrating the Fantastic: Selected Papers From the Tenth Anniversary International Conference on the Fantastic in the Arts* (Westport, Conn.:

Greenwood, 1992) pp. 73–9 (p. 76); Sprague, *Rereading*, p. 42; Ruth Whittaker, *Doris Lessing* (London: Macmillan, 1988), p. 82.

22 Samuel H. Vasbinder, 'Aspects of Fantasy in Literary Myths About Lost Civilizations', in Roger C. Schlobin (ed.), *The Aesthetics of Fantasy Literature and Art* (Brighton: Harvester, 1982), pp. 192–210 (p. 192).

23 Sigmund Freud, 'Delusions and Dreams in Jensen's "Gradiva"', trans. James Strachey, in Albert Dickson (ed.), *The Penguin Freud Library, Vol. 14, Art and Literature* (Harmondsworth: Penguin, 1990), pp. 27–118 (p. 65).

24 Freud, 'Delusions', p. 59.

25 Freud, 'Delusions', p. 42.

26 Vasbinder, 'Aspects', p. 197.

27 Roberta Rubenstein, *The Novelistic Vision of Doris Lessing: Breaking the Forms of Consciousness* (Urbana: University of Illinois Press, 1979), pp. 175–199 (p. 179).

28 King, *Lessing*, p. 57.

29 According to King, then, 'The sea on which Watkins begins his journey is a symbol of those bodily and unconscious rhythms which constantly disrupt the rigid chronological and spatial order into which the doctors attempt to insert him.' King, *Lessing*, p. 67.

30 Georges Bataille, *Eroticism*, trans. Mary Dalwood (London: Marion Boyars, 1987), p. 39.

31 Iain Banks, *The Bridge* (London: Abacus, 1990). All subsequent quotations are referenced within the main body of the text, the abbreviation TB being used.

32 See Robert Yates, 'A Wee Hard Kernel of Cynicism: Iain Banks Talks of Tories and Space Ships', *Observer*, 20 August 1995, p. 16.

33 Kathryn Hume, *Fantasy and Mimesis: Responses to Reality in Western Literature* (London: Methuen, 1984), pp. 124–5.

34 This is the term Hume applies to that type of fiction and its characters which deliberately renders us unsure of our senses and disorientates our relationship with what we think of as 'the real'.

35 Todorov, *Fantastic*, p. 84.

36 Hume, *Fantasy and Mimesis*, p. 129.

37 Julia Kristeva, *Strangers To Ourselves*, trans. Leon S. Roudiez (Hemel Hempstead: Harvester, 1991), p. 7.

38 Hume, *Fantasy and Mimesis*, p. 140.

39 For a fuller discussion of this see Elizabeth Gross, 'The Body of Signification', in John Fletcher and Andrew Benjamin (eds), *Abjection, Melancholia and Love in the Work of Julia Kristeva* (London: Routledge, 1990), pp. 80–103 (p. 86).

40 Mary Ann Doane, 'Veiling Over Desire: Close-ups of the Woman', in Richard Feldstein and Judith Roof (eds), *Feminism and Psychoanalysis* (Ithaca, NY: Cornell University Press, 1989), pp. 105–41 (p. 108).

41 Doane, 'Veiling', p. 120.

42 Doane, 'Veiling', p. 110.

43 Right from the beginning of Orwell's novel we are told, 'The telescreen received and transmitted simultaneously. Any sound . . . would be picked up by it . . . [and one] could be seen as well as heard. There was of course no way of knowing whether you were being watched at any given moment.' George Orwell, *Nineteen Eighty-Four* (Harmondsworth: Penguin, 1983), p. 8.

44 Doane, 'Veiling', p. 105.

45 As argued by Doane, 'Veiling', p. 129.

46 This being Kristeva's reading of the place of the alien. Kristeva, *Strangers*, p. 5 – my emphasis.

47 Otto Rank, *The Double: A Psychoanalytic Study* (Chapel Hill: University of North Carolina Press, 1971), pp. 6, 10, 20 and 60.

48 Again, this image of the foreigner is Kristeva's. See *Strangers*, pp. 7–8.

# 5

# The Body in the House of the Closeted Text: Stevenson's *Dr Jekyll and Mr Hyde* and Perkins Gilman's *The Yellow Wallpaper*

The obvious similarities between R.L. Stevenson's *The Strange Case of Dr Jekyll and Mr Hyde* and Charlotte Perkins Gilman's *The Yellow Wallpaper* make them particularly interesting texts to compare.[1] Published within six years of each other at the end of the nineteenth century, both are uneasily situated as liminal texts hovering between short-story and novella modes, while attracting the type of critical (and cinematic) interest more commonly bestowed upon full-length fictions. Retrospectively read as *fin-de-siècle* gothic narratives, both explore what was, at the time, a widespread cultural and aesthetic preoccupation with social metamorphosis and the problematization of individual identity in conjunction with this. Importantly, both prioritize the manner in which each of the central protagonists compulsively writes, only to be punished by/for their creativity in the end. And if we attend to Peter K. Garret's claim that 'the doubling of the subject . . . is always produced by telling one's story',[2] it will come as no surprise that in both of these texts it is primarily through the adoption of the uncanny motif of the double that such metafictional concerns are explored.

That it is mainly through the work of psychoanalysis that our understanding of the double has evolved, perhaps seems self-evident. As James B. Twitchell observes, 'a simple awareness of consciousness itself implies division . . . [it] means that there are at least two parties, the observed and the observing.'[3] Nevertheless, the double also has a particular application to Victorian fictions as a means of demonstrating the manner in which the notorious 'double standard' of morality can be literalized. In historical terms this can also be applied to the political context of the urban gothic of the time. As critics such as Spencer have argued, a clear distinction should be drawn between earlier gothic narratives and those which emerged towards the end of the nineteenth century, a distinction revolving around the representation of the urban landscape. Rather than being 'distanced somewhat from the world of their audience, set back in time and "away" in space',[4] during the *fin-de-siècle* period the unsettling effect of increased urbanization upon certain social groupings rendered the gothic admirably well suited to the exploration of cultural as well as individual *dis-ease.* In many ways this explains the manner in which Stevenson's depiction of the dark side of the 'capital' (London) is attributed with gothic significance. On the one hand, that Henry Jekyll is Edward Hyde's 'city of refuge' (JH, 92) reminds us that the nocturnal streets of late-Victorian London were anything but safe for the ordinary resident. Only for the likes of Hyde can sanctuary be sought in its dark, sinister and labyrinthine streets; sanctuary in this strange case being from 'the terrors of the scaffold' (and capital punishment) (JH, 91). The worst that befalls Hyde in these terms is that upper-class characters such as Mr Enfield threaten to 'make capital' (JH, 32) out of witnessing his misdemeanours, in response to which he is forced to make equally capital reparations in the form of the one-hundred-pound cheque paid out to the family of the girl that he needlessly tramples on in the street. In these socio-historical terms, the horror of Hyde is his bastardized existence as literate usurper of a class-ridden genealogy.

It is not just the urban landscape that contributes to the dark and sinister imagery of the text. Right at its centre stands the presiding motif of the gothic mansion. Ironically domesticated, the gothic remains centred around Freud's convoluted discussion of the *heimlich/unheimlich*, as discussed in full in Chapter 2. As Kate Ferguson Ellis observes, all too easily 'the literary use of the home as a place of security and concord' finds itself supplanted by images of the home 'as a place of danger and imprisonment'.[5] In this sense the text (like all gothic narratives) becomes intrinsically concerned with the dialectical interrelationship between inner and outer worlds, a point that makes the location of the mansion within the urban environment a particularly interesting combination. No longer is it possible to read the gothic mansion as an evil interior surrounded by the daylight world of order and reason. Instead, while the gothic continues to play on our knowledge that most victims of violent crime are attacked in their own homes (often, like Jekyll, by their so-called 'nearest and dearest'), in late-nineteenth-century London the only escape-route from domestic tyranny leads the victim out into streets haunted by monsters such as Jack the Ripper.[6] While Jekyll begins by retreating into domestic space for sanctuary, once he loses control over his ability to metamorphose into Hyde only at will (and therefore loses any relationship with his own anatomy as refuge) his level of control over the domestic interior likewise shifts. From being a safe haven, it is quickly transformed in its turn into a space of imprisonment. Ultimately, it is this breakdown of clear-cut demarcation lines that leaves Jekyll with no room, space or body of his own.

Few fictional domestic spaces encompass more clearly the problematic relationship between the gothic mansion and its own and others' limits than both the architecture and the atmosphere of Henry Jekyll's house. It is a strange and hybrid dwelling-place, part home and part 'laboratory or . . . dissecting-rooms' (JH, 51), as if severance and disunity are written into its very foundations. As the more homely portions of the interior are elaborated upon we find our narrator, Mr Utterson, standing in cosy fashion by the hearth of Jekyll's lamp-lit room, but only so that these *heimlich* elements can be shown to be in a state of dissolution. Here the sinister threat posed by the urban exterior starts to filter through into this haven of privacy, moral turbulence being symbolically suggested by the fact that 'even in the houses the fog began to lie thickly' (JH, 51). Very quickly, what began as homely cheer shifts into more claustrophic *dis-ease*, culminating in the image of the 'deadly sick' Jekyll who presides over the room.

But if the interior of Jekyll's house is a truly gothic space, then this is *doubly* implied by the facade of Hyde's: 'Two doors from one corner . . . a certain sinister block of building thrust forward its gable on the street. It . . . showed no window, nothing but . . . a blind forehead of discoloured wall . . . The door . . . was blistered and distained' (JH, 30). In this otherwise 'small . . . quiet, but . . . thriving' street (JH, 30) one needs precious little expertise in critical analysis to recognize that the description of this house will impinge, symbolically, upon the moral character of its inhabitant. Adjectives such as 'blistered' and 'distained' are particularly resonant, for here, as in so many gothic narratives, the body of the mansion represents the body of its owner. And while ownership of property implies a certain 'respectability' in social terms, a stained or delinquent frontage would also infer that its owner possesses not only a stained or delinquent character, but a body that will bear the physical imprint of its misdeneanours. No wonder, then, that images of the body in revolt combine with a conventional gothic motif in Utterson's speculations about the nature of the relationship between Jekyll and Hyde: 'Ah, it must be that; the ghost of some old sin, the cancer of some concealed disgrace . . .' (JH, 41). This is then combined with the symbolic significance of terms such as 'thrust', with its phallically aggressive connotations and the 'blind forehead' which prefigures the 'blind eye' that Enfield and even Utterson (for all his superficially exploratory role in the text) surely *choose* to turn to the exploitative bodily misdemeanours not only of Hyde (who, after all, is merely the 'rent-boy' tenant of the property), but more particularly of Jekyll, the real owner of the house and perpetrator of its 'ills'. This returns us to Jekyll's own house and the moment of 'revelation' when Utterson and Poole force their way into Jekyll's 'cabinet': 'Poole swung the axe over his shoulder ... the red baize door leaped against the lock and hinges. A dismal screech, as of mere animal terror, rang from the cabinet. Up went the axe again, and again the panels crashed and the frame bounded' (JH, 69). Once again, the structures of the house take on a hostile animation of their own, here going so far as to let out a scream. And once the two instigators discover that Jekyll's own body has disappeared, we are left with the impression that he has been not so much consumed, by the hand of Hyde as orally engulfed by the house itself.

## Anal and Oral: The 'In Here' and the 'Out There'

In Chapter 2, we saw Holland focusing upon the manner in which gothic narratives explore and problematize the fixity of the boundaries between 'in here' and 'out there' and that, as part of this dynamic, the mansion itself functions as an interrogative 'space between', a meeting point between these two worlds. The relationship already drawn above between the body of the house and the body of its inhabitant also returns us to Holland's belief that most literary texts are particularly affected by and expressive of a complex combination of anal and oral drives. Few texts make this more manifest than Stevenson's. Purely on the level of character construction, one can see that Utterson is a character driven by anal repressions. Thus, although he sets himself up as the purgative presence of the text he actually retains far more information than he gives away, a characteristic particularly suggestive of anal fixations. As a member of the legal profession he also fulfils Holland's association of such characters with 'laws and rules', whereas his general refusal to 'let himself go' (implied by his formal naming as 'Mr' Utterson throughout) also suggests the meticulous and petty precisions of this repressive patterning.[7]

But if Utterson is a representative of the anal drive, Hyde's function as a transgressive presence, forcing his way into this 'respectable' body of men and projecting them into disarray with his aggressive and implicitly libidinous urges and actions, obviously associates him with phallic repressions. According to Holland, one of the scenarios associated with this is a reiteration of primal scene fantasies, an issue that reveals itself here in Hyde's wilful trampling of the body of the girl in the opening chapter of the text. In Holland's terms, primal scenes translate themselves in the child's psyche into 'a struggle followed by a death-like sleep' in which the 'father's phallus [becomes] a weapon with which he wounds the mother'.[8] That Hyde re-enacts this is self-evident; but what this also reveals is the way in which, in doing so, he is shown to be unconsciously torn between the roles of adult and child in this respect. This is the boundary-problem at the heart of his Oedipal struggle with Jekyll. After all, that the phallic stage is intrinsically connected with the phase whereby the child 'learns through trial and error the powers and limitations of the body'[9] seems to summarize Hyde's behaviour throughout.

It is in the case of Jekyll that Holland's rather schematic appraisal is called upon to wrestle with more complex character construction. Somehow torn between Utterson's anal fixations and the temptations of the phallic Hyde, Jekyll is situated at that interactive limit between the 'in here' and the 'out there' as his recurrent oscillations between private and public realms imply. Perhaps it comes as no surprise then that Holland suggests that 'the single most common fantasy-structure in literature is phallic assertiveness balanced against oral engulfment',[10] for if Jekyll is swallowed whole by the body of the house, his struggle with Hyde also (as we shall examine in more detail later) situates itself within this dynamic.

Such repressions often manifest themselves, in a gothic context, as sicknesses of mind and body. This reminds us that through challenges to the purity of both, the gothic also offers an interrogation of the apparent fixity of social, cultural and generic limits. According to Gordon Hirsch, what we find in Stevenson's text is 'the corrosive presence of gothic passion'.[11] Such images of decay are intrinsically important to its exploration of the motif of the double. If even the solidity of the human anatomy can be called into question, how fixed can the fixtures of cultural, social and proprietorial norms be? This returns us to the cabinet scene and a consideration of the effect that Jekyll's disappearance has upon his relationship to his own and others' bodies. If Jekyll is swallowed whole by the hostilities of the 'closet', then surely this is making a socio-cultural statement in itself. After all, once the 'skeleton' has been removed, the house is permitted to return to 'normality': 'There lay the cabinet before their eyes in the quiet lamplight, a good fire glowing and chattering on the hearth, the kettle singing its thin strain . . . and nearer the fire, the things laid out for tea' (JH, 69–70). Stevenson's task, it seems, is to articulate a paradox. If one of its central themes revolves around the keeping of secrets, then how does he convey this without spilling their contents? Time and again he asks us to read between the lines of the text, and often such secrets are woven into characters' relationships with houses. As Utterson informs Enfield, 'if I don't ask you the name of the other party, it is because I know it already. You see, Richard, your tale has *gone home*' (JH, 34 – my emphasis). In a book preoccupied with strangers and the strange, Utterson's own strange choice of wording here inevitably draws our attention. Literally, of course, we understand what he means (even if we would more commonly adopt the phrase 'hit home'). Yet there is far more to it than this. What he gives us here is a new location for the uncanny space of the 'home': namely the mind of a character himself. No wonder then that elsewhere, in questioning the wisdom of Hyde being permitted access to Jekyll's apartment when the latter is away, Utterson refers to Jekyll as being 'from home' (JH, 41), for he implies here that Jekyll is not only 'out of doors', but also 'out of his mind'. But another playful presence lurks at the periphery of Utterson's phrase and it is one which underlies the whole meaning of the text. In Noel Carroll's terms, Jekyll and Hyde combine to produce one single 'fission' monster.[12] In other words, as two separate beings conjoined within the one body, the presence of either half of this coupling necessitates the reciprocal absence of the other. Time and again this present/absent dynamic manifests itself on a variety of levels. So we tend to find the presence of one term working to call attention to the equally articulate absence of another. In the case of the previous example, the chain of signification which takes us from the phrase 'from home' to 'out of doors' to 'out of his mind' also leads on to another allusion concerning 'out' and 'outing(s)'. For if it is clear that Jekyll is, like his friends, a 'man about town', what we are far less sure of, as William Veeder recognizes, is what, exactly, 'all these men *are* "about"'.[13]

The significance of Stevenson's frequent and playful usage of the presence of one word to call up the absent presence of another derives from its relationship with boundary problems. What is 'in' the text functions to indicate that which lurks 'out' on the periphery. Once again it is Holland who reminds us that wordplay unconsciously functions as a balancing act between defence and phantasy, and careful analysis of its function in this text clearly demonstrates such a dynamic to be at work. Perhaps the most expressive piece of 'poetic' encoding in the text communicates itself through alliteration. Just as mirror symbolism is conventionally used to encode homoerotic desire into texts (based on the symmetrical attraction of same to same), so here we see the mirroring presence of alliteration functioning as its linguistic double, magnetically pulling the words together, drawing them into clusters based upon sameness in difference. In Stevenson's text, particularly in the depiction of Utterson, alliterative techniques proliferate throughout. Two examples suffice as illustrations. First, as the omniscient narrator informs us, 'Hosts loved to detain the dry lawyer, when the light-hearted and the loose-tongued had already their foot on the threshold' (JH, 43). Here, the firm, 'common-sense' rhythm of the first few (predominantly) monosyllabic terms contrasts clearly with the rather more effeminate 'skipping' effect produced by the hyphenated, multi-syllabic words 'light-hearted' and 'loose-tongued'. It is through this combination that the hint regarding Utterson's implied sexuality is present right from the start of the text. And when one also takes into account that this very same alliterative patterning of the 'l' and the 'd' mirrors, in itself, the manner in which he is introduced at the beginning of the text, our suspicions begin to be reinforced. Here he is described as: 'lean, long, dusty, dreary, and yet somehow lovable' (JH, 29), the enclosure of the alliterative 'd's within a triad of alliterative 'l's (including the apparently misplaced 'lovable') inviting, not a skipping but a tripping of the tongue which renders present (again through absence) the terms 'lusty' and 'leary'. Only by negative inference can any suggestion of sexuality be firmly established. Finally, that 'play' is something that Utterson denies himself (even to the extent of avoiding the theatre (JH, 29) and apparently overreacting to Poole's reference to 'foul play' regarding Jekyll's death (JH, 62)), rather suggests that such repressions have inevitably erupted onto the surface of the text in other, more 'acceptable' ways.

The homoerotic content of Stevenson's narrative is by and large accepted by critics. Even the language use points towards this, Jekyll adopting the discourse of romance when confronted by the jealous Utterson asking questions about Hyde: 'I swear to God I will never set eyes on him again . . . I am done with him . . . It is all at an end' (JH, 52). But when Lanyon, just a few pages later, reassures Utterson in the same terms about his relationship with Jekyll – 'I am quite done with that person; and I beg that you will spare me any allusion to one whom I regard as dead' (JH, 57) – we suspect that it is not just Jekyll and Hyde who are bodily bonded. On a similar theme, frequent references to blood imagery serve to connect all four main protagonists, Utterson's friends being 'those of his own blood' (JH, 29) (presumably including his 'distant kinsman' Enfield (JH, 29)) and Jekyll recognizing that, when in the form of Hyde, 'a more generous tide of blood' courses around his body (JH, 88–9), this being obviously suggestive of sexual arousal. But these connections are structured by an equally shared discourse of disturbance that seems to invoke Elaine Showalter's work on syphilis as a central motif in *fin-de-siècle* texts. During the nineteenth century, though explicitly linked with female prostitution, Showalter claims that syphilis was culturally seen to be 'covertly linked with male homosexuality'.[14] And although the general absence of family relationships in this text might imply that there is no place here for what tended to exist as 'a family secret', the central theme of silence and lack of articulation that 'lies' at the centre of the text is seemingly mirrored by the stance of the syphilitic who, in iconographic terms, 'had a face, but no voice'.[15] No wonder then that, faced with the physical reality of Jekyll's stricken form at the window, the sight 'froze the very blood of the two gentleman [*down*] *below*' (JH, 61 – my emphasis). The role of Dr Lanyon is even more interesting in this respect. Despite his apparent ostracism of Jekyll, it seems as unlikely that Utterson is right to hope that 'They have only differed on some point of science' (JH, 36) as it is that the 'incurable' (JH, 58) cause of Lanyon's sudden death is really, as Jekyll asserts, the quarrel itself. After all, it is Lanyon who admits full knowledge of the manner in which 'Jekyll's private cabinet is most conveniently entered' (JH, 76) and, as we have seen, this closeted space bears a very intimate relationship with his body. Once again, this intimacy breaks through within the playful body of the closeted text. As Jerrold Hogle observes:

> Writing ... is one of the extensions of the body. It is a kind of birth process in which an emission from the body repositions a portion of the body outside the already amorphous boundaries of the self ... Writing is reconnected to the life of the body from which textualization works so hard to remove itself.[16]

Thus, as we also find, the cloistering of the text reveals the manner in which wordplay eventually *replaces* the body of Jekyll:

> Mr Utterson came home to his bachelor house ... opened his safe, took from the most private part of it a document endorsed on the envelope as Dr Jekyll's Will ... It offended him both as a lawyer and as a lover of the sane and customary sides of life, to whom the fanciful was the immodest. And [if] hitherto it was his ignorance of Mr Hyde that had swelled his indignation; now, by a sudden turn, it was his knowledge. (JH, 35)

When combined with the obsessively secret enclosures of a 'bachelor' house and the 'most private part' of a safe and a sealed envelope, the desire for revelation here is rendered all the more powerful by the obsessional combination of these prohibitive structures. But it is not so much the contents of the will that are revealed here as the nature of the relationship between the parties involved. In keeping with the symmetry of the conjunctions here ('*as a* lawyer and *as a* lover'), the alliterative effect of what are again two 'l' sounds reinforces the symmetry to draw these terms together and away from the ensuing 'vindication' of the phrase 'sane and customary sides of life'. When combined with references to 'the private part[s]' and words such as 'fanciful'[17] and 'immodest', all that is revealed here are Utterson's jealous suspicions about the sexual nature of Jekyll's liaison with Hyde. Thus, when Kelly Oliver argues that 'the pattern and logic of the language is already found within the body',[18] she is unwittingly articulating the manner in which the presence of absence functions in this scene. It is not just that the presence of certain words here playfully brings to life an absent echo of others, but that the presence of a written document inscribes within itself the absence of its author and the supplanting of him by one who is 'Hyde(n)'.

As if the terms of this 'final testimony' were not shifting and unreliable enough, they are profoundly augmented by the multiple additional testimonies that structure the rest of the text as a whole. Threaded throughout with hearsay evidence and partial and conflicting versions of the 'truth', even the so-called omniscient narrator comes under suspicion. Returning to the opening description of Utterson, by what evidence (for none is forthcoming) do we actually judge Utterson to be 'lovable'? If such an adjective were applied by another character, one would presume a level of intimacy shared between the two to which the reader had been denied access. But how can this be true of a third-person narrator who, by very definition, should have no connection with characters at all? It is such apparent partiality that casts immediate doubt on the fixity of the frame. It therefore comes as no surprise that similar untrustworthy strategies interweave themselves into every corner of the rest of the canvas. For quite aside from individual acts of character dishonesty (as when Jekyll is exposed as a liar in telling Utterson that he has received a hand-delivered letter from Hyde, despite Poole's assertion that 'nothing had come except by post; "and only circulars by that"' (JH, 53)) narrative 'revelations' usually reveil, reducing the 'truth' to nothing but rumours. Ironically, it is through this means (and the reader's desire for the sensations of gossip) that Twitchell sees us negotiating the text. In his opinion, 'we find ourselves led from one cul-de-sac into another . . . continually distanced from the horror until, too late, we . . . [are] taken level by level to the monster . . . from Utterson to Enfield to [Lanyon] to Jekyll to Hyde.'[19] This point is largely convincing. But he has omitted one significant additional layer and that is the account, offered by the maid-servant, of the murder of Sir Danvers Carew, an anecdote right at the structural heart of the text.

Like most of the narrative, this incident is reported by our frame narrator, a strategy that facilitates our trust in the account. Importantly, the maid-servant not only sees the incident, but apparently gives an account of it in her own words, a lone female voice in this androcentric text. But this is a perfect example of the manner in which Stevenson works to undermine the reader's trust in such 'eye-witness' accounts. By means of multiple narrative embedding, a series of careful manoeuvres conspires against her authority, even while seeming to underwrite her account. So, we are told, the maid-servant tells her story 'with streaming tears' (JH, 46), a detail that implies her to be partly hysterical if not deranged, due to her still suffering from shock. Once we consider the frame narrator's description of her, even prior to the incident, as 'romantically given' and taken with 'musing' (JH, 46), we become aware of the extent to which the narrator is determined to cast doubt upon the voice of a working-class woman prone to 'tell stories'. We are therefore left to unravel a paradox. For significance is nevertheless attributed to the tale, even while its teller is largely dismissed. Indeed, not only is she dismissed, she is ultimately silenced, because whatever our unreliable frame narrator may tell us, at no stage does she tell her own tale to *us*. Instead her words are further embedded within the voice of a male police officer, this being the final irony of the scene. Instead of the original combination of an unreliable witness giving a seemingly reliable account, once we read that 'his eyes lighted up with professional ambition' (JH, 47) at hearing the news, we find ourselves confronted by a so-called reliable witness telling us what is, to him at least, an unreliable tale. In his terms, it is the art of the telling that proves to be important, not its relationship with so-called 'truth-value'. And once we have realized this, we can fully reappraise the role of the maid-servant. In Freudian terms she becomes the creative writer/dreamer whose placement at the window, surrounded by the frame, clearly sets the boundaries of her own imaginative text. And insofar as this mimics the generic enclosure mechanism of all fantasy narratives this will inevitably invalidate the authority of all and any resisting voices, for in these terms we only too 'willingly suspend disbelief'.

Jekyll's main role also becomes that of the storyteller, rather than that of the narrative suspect. In collaboration with Hyde he produces the qualities Freud requires in the figure of the writer/dreamer. And if the ability to write 'arouses in us emotions of which, perhaps, we had not even thought ourselves capable',[20] Jekyll happily situates himself in this role: 'in my second character, my faculties seemed sharpened . . . [while] of my original character, one part remained to me: I could write my own hand' (JH, 93). It is ironic that in a narrative which foregrounds the significance of writing, being 'composed not of chapters but of ten disparate documents',[21] and which metonymically utilizes the 'hand' as a figurative representative of this, the otherwise ill-fitting halves of the Jekyll and Hyde double are seen to be interchangeable in their relationship with this bodily extremity. But in fact a closer reading reveals that, rather than sharing the self-same 'hand', the two together form an ambidextrous liaison. When Jekyll provides Hyde with a signature 'by sloping my own hand backwards' (JH, 87), it seems likely that this is achieved by writing with the other hand. When analysed a little closer, the full significance of this starts to become apparent. Earlier on in the narrative Jekyll implores Lanyon to help him, commenting (not unimportantly in a hand-written letter) that 'There was never a day . . . I would not have sacrificed . . . my left hand to help you' (JH, 74). It is never made clear whether Jekyll writes with the left or the right hand. But simply taking into account the fact that the gothic tends to employ every possible symbolic nuance for effect, it is likely that the left hand's traditional association with the sinister principle is sufficient to connect it with the writing of Hyde.[22] This suspicion is underlined by the fact that we have already seen Hyde's house, as version of his body, being described as a 'sinister block' (JH, 30). In these terms, of course, Jekyll's aforementioned plea to Lanyon implies a willingness to pay the price of 'divorcing' himself from Hyde if this is the 'help' that Lanyon requires. If, however, it is Jekyll who writes with the left hand, then the nature of the sacrifice would involve neglecting his own writing in order to attend to the needs of his friend.

But the nature of the distinction between these choices is false, Hyde being as much a secondary elaboration of Jekyll's phantasy as the full statement with which the latter unsuccessfully tries to tie up the text. Enfield, giving shape and form to his own fears, actually makes manifest the role Hyde plays in Jekyll's unconscious:

> [his] tale went by before his mind in a scroll of lighted pictures . . . his friend lay asleep, dreaming and smiling at his dreams; and then . . . there would stand by his side a figure to whom power was given, and . . . he must rise and

> do its bidding . . . And still the figure had no face, or one that baffle melted before his eyes . . . If he could but once set eyes on him, he thoug mystery would lighten . . . as was the habit of mysterious things when w examined. (JH, 37–8)

Hyde, then, like a fearful spectre, intervenes into this wish-fulfilment fantasy, embodying the means by which night-dreaming lowers the wish-fulfilment closure mechanism to turn pleasurable fantasies into such spectres, straddling the limit between presence and absence like the apochryphal ghost of the gothic night-text. Ultimately it is this ability to straddle the divide between worlds that projects Hyde into the key role of gothic interloper who, in making an untimely entrance into the work of inner secrets, causes disruption on every level.

As we have seen, houses, bodies, and workings of the unconscious are identically positioned with regard to Hyde and, as Stephen Heath has demonstrated, this is even encoded into the word-play of his name: '*ey/ye* . . . giv[ing] the *yd* in the middle of the *he*'.[23] But of course, if Hyde lies at the centre of the text, all of the main characters who radiate from this centre become initiated into his transgressive desires. So it is Enfield who first projects us into the world of the gothic by raising the issue of the door to Hyde's lodgings (JH, 30), while Jekyll ironically interposes himself amid an area of bachelor flats by taking up residence in a 'family house' (JH, 40). But it is the mysterious Utterson whose gothic function means that this connection with 'chambers' and closets carries far more than legal connotations. The Victorian obsession with outsiders as symbols of bodily contamination[24] also manifests itself here in the presence of those chemical exchanges which, located on the surface 'skin' of the text, mask the absent presence of 'natural' fluid exchanges. By the end of the text, all of these bodies become seemingly drawn into a final metamorphosis of Hyde as corpse. For although we are aware that Hyde's body is also Jekyll's (and are thus unsurprised by the latter's 'disappearance'), we are rather more surprised by the attendant disappearance of Utterson. Nevertheless, like his own faceless double (the third-person frame narrator), we hear no more of him after this event. Instead, like Jekyll, he is replaced by a final testimony within which he merely appears as the parenthetical 'you' to whom it is addressed by Dr Lanyon (JH, 76). Heath may be correct to observe that 'Writing . . . needs enclosures, something that must . . . have protections in the telling',[25] but that here *only* the enclosures are left seems to be taking safety a little too far. Even Enfield seems to have deserted us, last seen 'walk[ing] on once more in silence' [JH, 61] after the earlier sighting of Jekyll at the window. In summary, the anal drives ultimately win out; for the final ascendency of the enclosures returns us to the invisibility and silence with which we began, resealing the closet in the process once more.

## Gothic as a Family Narrative

f child development and its intrinsic effect upon the ning of *Dr Jekyll and Mr Hyde* inevitably situates this as And, just as deep and surface layers seem to conspire an reveal, so the inarticulated desire that underlies this (and surprisingly) functions to recentre the mother. murder of Sir Danvers Carew, Veeder resituates this in Oedipal terms:

> With the woman up at the second floor window, the two men approach . . . The three figures form a triangle . . . it is the classic Oedipal configuration. Set in the place of the mother, the maid belongs to a patriarch . . . and yet she is available to filial fantasy since she lives 'alone' . . . Positioning her 'upon her box' (46) at the open window emphasizes her sexuality and availability.[26]

In this context the maid-servant functions as the maternal presence, Sir Danvers Carew the 'superior' father and Hyde the son who must avenge, to the death, his overwhelming jealousy at the father's supposed intimacy with the mother. However, while Veeder's reappraisal of this scene may be alluring (even entertaining), it bears precious little resemblance to the actualities of the text. On the contrary, as Stevenson makes abundantly clear, Carew's interest (which may well be sexual) is completely and utterly restricted to Hyde. Hyde's interest (though seemingly of a different kind) is similarly completely and utterly restricted to Carew. Neither seems remotely interested in the maid-servant, or even aware of her presence. Admittedly the maid-servant can be defined in relation to a more affluent 'master' who functions in this sense as a surrogate father, but this patriarch is certainly neither Carew nor Hyde and, in this sense, remains irrelevant to this particular Oedipal struggle. Nor, indeed, is Veeder right in his belief that her position at the window implies that she is 'for sale'. As I have already implied, far from being an object of desire, the maid is the subject who elaborates upon the scene. Veeder, it seems, will not be deterred. As seemingly Oedipally driven as Hyde, he determines to replace Utterson by taking over the role of 'Mr Seek'. So he unearths the most cryptic of clues, clinging to the hope that they *just might* imply that sexual relations in this text derive from latent urges centring around, not simply the body of the generically absent mother, but more specifically of *Jekyll's* absent mother. This, he argues, both explains Stevenson's choice of the surname 'Maw' for the name of Jekyll's chemist and the fact that Hyde is said to 'maul' Carew. In addition, 'The basically regressive nature of Jekyll's orality is expressed agonizingly in his cry, "find me some of the old" (66). Jekyll yearns to return to the old source of oral satisfaction.'[27] To cut a long story short, Veeder's argument finds its most illogical conclusion in the belief that the very fact that Jekyll's mother plays no part whatsoever in the text ('There is neither a picture of mother nor saved letters from her') shows that she is really what the whole thing is about.

Veeder may well be correct in arguing that the absence of heterosexual identification could derive from the recognition that 'Against the attraction of maternal security, woman as wife cannot prevail'.[28] Where he goes wrong is in believing that this offers an explanation for Jekyll's inferred homosexual orientation. For it is more likely to be Hyde's maltreatment of women and/or avoidance of female encounters that results from a desire for 'maternal security', and it is therefore not so much Jekyll's mother that is the 'lost territory' of this text, but rather Jekyll *as Hyde's* 'mother'. Seeing Hyde 'licking the chops of memory' (JH, 92), we witness a man who is far more significantly driven by a sense of oral loss than is ever indicated in Stevenson's depiction of Jekyll. It is via the application of object-relations theory that this interrogation of the limits between inner and outer, oral and anal can best be understood. Jekyll the mother and Hyde the offspring fall entirely into line with Winnicott's theories on motherhood and pregnancy and the implications of these for what he has notoriously referred to as the presence of the 'good enough' mother.[29] For instance, his belief that the mother's fantasies about and prior to pregnancy and birth play a crucial part in the resulting relationship, is reflected in this text. Hyde is the fulfilment of Jekyll's desires, a point that derives its major symbolic significance from what Utterson and Poole perceive to be the mysterious presence of Jekyll's cheval glass. As his 'Full Statement' later confirms, only by using the mirror can Jekyll proudly witness the birth of his own offspring (JH, 84). Still in control at this stage, Jekyll then voluntarily undergoes a period of identification with his 'child' which requires, according to Winnicott, the mother's 'protect[ion] from external reality'. Thus Jekyll gradually withdraws from his friends and retreats into the domestic arena. And perhaps we should not overlook the fact that Winnicott claims impregnation fantasies to be commonly held by male homosexuals, for this shows that a Winnicottian reading need not conspire against the rest of my argument.[30] But control gradually gives way to loss of control, Jekyll's newly discovered position as irrevocably split subject ultimately casting him as a substitute phallic mother whose bodily limits are shown to be *reluctantly* thrown into question by the presence of the love/hate parasite 'Hydden' within. Like the gothic narrative itself, Winnicott's theories privilege the role played by ambivalence in the mother/child dyad, and the simple substitution of Winnicott's original terms 'children' and 'baby' with the word 'Hyde' here immediately alerts us to the application his ideas have to the workings of this text: 'Probably you won't find anything worse than the way [Hyde] invade[s] your innermost reserve . . . At the very beginning there is no difficulty, because [Hyde] is in you and part of you . . . The secret becomes [Hyde]. [But when the time comes . . . ] there starts a tremendous struggle – [Hyde], no longer being the secret, makes a claim on all your secrets.'[31]

This is experienced as a power dynamic, an imbalance seemingly endemic to all psychoanalytic interactions. But just as Marilyn Edelstein claims that, in the family narrative, the impact of genealogies means that 'far more voices . . . are at play in the dialogue' than simply belong to the immediate participants,[32] so the many conflicting narrative voices which continually destabilize this particular dyad inevitably conspire against a fixed political imbalance. As part of this, Jekyll as mother becomes 'neither subject nor object but a function'[33] and this is the real nature of his attempt to re-identify himself in the terms of boundary demarcation:

> I saw that, of the two natures that contended in the field of my consciousness, even if I could rightly be said to be either, it was only because I was radically both . . . If each, I told myself, could but be housed in separate identities, life would be relieved of all that was unbearable . . . It was the curse of mankind that these incongruous faggots were thus bound together – that in the agonised womb of consciousness these polar twins should be continuously struggling. How, then, were they dissociated? (JH, 82)

Thus Jekyll's excessive need to identify with Hyde causes the shift in the metamorphic structure that alters the self-willed bodily changes of the planned pregnancy into a series of unwanted and unwilling maternal transformations. Importantly, this inability to separate off also creates, in line with Winnicott's theory, a 'False Self' which is seen to have 'one positive and very important function: to hide the True Self'.[34] Obviously the use of the word 'hide' could not be more appropriate. But is it that Hyde hides the true self who is Jekyll or, more likely, that Hyde is the true self that Jekyll hides? By the time Jekyll sufficiently separates himself from Hyde to assert their distinct and total separation – 'He, I say – I cannot say, I' (JH, 94) – the point of no return has well and truly been reached. At this stage Jekyll's retreat into the domestic arena has culminated in the aforementioned oral engulfment. Carrying this mutual destruction to its poisonous conclusions, Hyde chooses an oral form of self/(m)other destruction in imbibing what can only be read as bad mother's milk. Hyde, like all of us, can only ever define himself through a negative identification in terms of the body of the mother. He may well succeed in being the death of 'her'; but 'her' death inevitably results in his own. It is this anatomical dependency, among other things, that restrains Hyde within the limits of the newly born child; his rebellious and enraged behaviour consistently following those patterns that Winnicott associates with 'I AM moments' during the first year of life.[35] So Hyde is repeatedly being reborn, ever renewing his infantile status at the same time that he seems to follow an adolescent rebellion. This returns us to the work of Twitchell, who, in arguing that 'Hyde only does what Jekyll wants', appears to be guilty of a textual inaccuracy.[36] After all, Hyde does many things that Jekyll claims to despise. But on the other hand, when read as 'Hyde only does what Jekyll wants [to do]', the full significance of the statement emerges. In terms of physical stature, Hyde's presence in clothes that are 'enormously too large for him . . . the trousers hanging on his legs and rolled up to keep them from the ground, the waist of the coat below his haunches, and the collar sprawling wide upon his shoulders' (JH, 77–8) clearly reveals him to be a child dressed up in adult's clothing. Or, to put it metaphorically, he embodies an adolescent psyche uncomfortably positioned on the inconsistently demarcated boundary-divides between childhood and adult maturity. On this basis, Twitchell reads Hyde as a manifestation of Jekyll's past self projected into the present in order to continue to enact the rebellious fantasies which Jekyll has been forced to leave behind on entering the 'respectable' circles of Victorian society.[37]

It is this that takes us on to the final feature of the gothic as a family narrative: namely its connection with issues of inheritance and the compulsive repetition of Oedipal repressions through biological/familial reproductions. Often such inheritances are profoundly intertextual, for, almost in mimickry of family relations themselves, gothic texts tend to rework each other. According to Twitchell, this compulsive reminiscence almost accounts for the uncanny aspect of the gothic, for 'Some otherstory beneath . . . must coalesce with the surface story for the terror images to become horrible'.[38] In the case of *The Yellow Wallpaper*, the apparent intertextual connections function simultaneously to disturb (through the extent to which they are seen to proliferate) and to offer hope in the sense of creative and affirmative female solidarity in the face of adversity. Reflecting a number of nineteenth-century cultural concerns, *The Yellow Wallpaper* is a narrative account of a supposedly monstrous, supposedly 'mad' woman who is incarcerated in an attic by a husband who seems to be 'fully occupied' elsewhere. In this sense it is typical of those 'dramatizations of imprisonment and escape' that Gilbert and Gubar have seen to be 'all-pervasive' in the literature written by women of this period.[39] It is this that causes so many of these female-authored texts to be read as gothic narratives, for in them we find a number of women who are consistently wronged, abused and walled-up within the limits of a world inscribed by patriarchy. In such cases, it is not simply that the woman's place is seen to be in the home, but that the home has become the limits of her world. As Eugenia C. Delamotte puts it: 'Woman in these nocturnal spaces is really woman in her everyday relations.'[40]

What becomes clear is that this particular narrative bears a specific relationship to Charlotte Brontë's *Jane Eyre* (1847). Like Rochester, Perkins Gilman's male protagonist John shelters, not only behind an appealing facade, but also behind his wife's so-called 'madness', enabling him to use it to his own advantage. But the narrative, like Bronte's, is careful to retain a sense of ambivalence as far as this husband's motivations are concerned, for uncertainty can always be put to *our* literary advantage. So even our protagonist oscillates in her opinion, at times asserting that 'He is very careful and loving' (YW, 12) and at others admitting that 'I am getting a little afraid of John' (YW, 26). On the whole, though, her stance is encapsulated by the playful ambiguity of the following remark: 'I have found out another funny thing, but I shan't tell it this time! It does not do to trust people too much' (YW, 31). The nature of the uncertainty here derives from the question of to whom the term 'people' refers. If it simply refers to the presence of the direct addressee (the reader) then it is a simple suspense mechanism used to withhold information that we desire to have. But 'people' (particularly as a plural term) is far more likely to refer to other characters in the narrative who have done something (as yet unrevealed) which has demonstrated to the protagonist that they cannot be trusted. After all, if nothing else provokes our disturbance in this regard, that John is increasingly away at nights 'when his cases are serious' (YW, 13) suggests that he is, like Stevenson's protagonists, engaged in noctural pastimes of a potentially untrustworthy nature: 'No wonder the subject of Gothic romance is fear. Women Gothicists were desperately afraid of their real subject, which is anger.'[41]

*The Yellow Wallpaper* has further connections with *Jane Eyre*. Both concern themselves with an irreconcilable duality at the centre of Victorian womanhood for, if this protagonist and Brontë's Bertha Mason are considered to be madwomen in the attic, they fit this description only in contradistinction to the valorized figure of the 'angel of the house'. When the protagonist articulates her final words of defiance – 'I've got out at last . . . in spite of you and Jane' (YW, 36) – a number of critics express bewilderment at what is the only mention of this name in the entire text. One of the more useful readings of this is articulated by Conrad Shumaker, who identifies the mysterious Jane as simultaneously self and not-self to the protagonist or, as he puts it, 'the wife she once was' (in other words before she became 'ill').[42] My reading of this as evidence of an intertextual liaison with *Jane Eyre* feeds into Shumaker's quite well. For Jane is simply a prototype for Bertha Mason, the next angel of the house to be 'kicked upstairs' when a further, more alluring, angel comes along. In this sense, it may even be Jane's presence that gives meaning to the husband's aforementioned 'wanderings'. And there are rather more positive possibilities which start to erupt through this gothic despair. For the highly unsatisfactory 'happy ever after' ending that Brontë forces over her own unresolved text does little more than 'wallpaper over' the gaps that start to break open at the end. Few female readers (perhaps even few readers) can genuinely feel 'consoled' by Jane's uncharacteristic decision, not only to marry the unrepentant adulterer, but also to rejoice in the untimely and violent death of an abused wife. How much more satisfactory it would have been if Bertha and Jane had conspired together to dispense with the duplicitous Rochester. And, in an otherwise bleak and horrifying narrative, this is exactly what Perkins Gilman's protagonist does. First of all she rips up the wallpaper (the intertextual manifestation of Brontë's patriarchal masquerade) and thereby frees her madwoman double. Secondly, like Bertha, having 'thought seriously of burning the house' (YW, 29), she thinks again and realizes that her violent retributions must engulf the body of her husband, not just the body of his house: 'Now why should that man have fainted? But he did, and right across my path . . . so that I had to creep over him every time!' (YW, 36).

This is not to render the body of the house entirely insignificant, for, as we have seen, it is the presiding motif of all gothic texts which, according to Judith Fetterley, 'are haunted by the ghosts of women buried alive within them'.[43] In the case of *The Yellow Wallpaper*, the central protagonist and her husband rent out a colonial mansion that has come available to them due to 'some legal trouble . . . something about the heirs and coheirs' (YW, 11). Importantly, then, family connections are shown to be threaded through, right from the start, with discord and disruption. Inheritance is a patrilinear power structure intrinsically connected with naming, appropriation and the ownership of property. Perkins Gilman's protagonist holds a peripheral relationship with all of these connections. On the one hand (like Hyde) she is merely a tenant whose rent is paid for by her 'respectable' male partner. But she is also a character without a name, a position that marginalizes her from the patrilinear code. Inevitably, though not able to behave appropriat(iv)ely, she is, herself, appropriated in the sense of being named 'mad'. Paradoxically, of course, it is this act of naming that denies her identity and, in this sense, it becomes inevitable that what she is left with is an endlessly shifting series of 'I's. Homonymically, this returns us to the walls of the mansion and the common motif of the ancestral portrait, whose own shifting eyes are once again expressive of the rebellion against entrapment which the family provokes. But in this text it is as if such entrapment has imprinted itself within the very walls, for it is not the eyes of portraits that tyrannize the protagonist, but the shifting outlines of the chamber's cladding: 'Up and down and sideways they crawl' (YW, 16), just as we will find the central 'I' doing later on in the text. And it is this which reminds us that, like all characters of the female gothic, her real source of entrapment derives from: 'the nightmare of trying to speak "I" in a world where the "I" in question is uncomprehending of and incomprehensible to the dominant power structure'.[44] In apparent contradiction to this, there are moments in the text where this protagonist fully asserts her first-person presence. As Catherine Golden remarks of the scene in which the woman behind the wallpaper first starts to emerge, 'Appearing a total of seven times in this sequence, "I" introduces each of four consecutive sentences, three of which begin a new paragraph . . . The positioning and four-fold use of "I" most noticeably recalls the four-fold repetition of John on the opening page.'[45] In asserting herself here she suggests that her marital relationship is at last ceasing to be her first point of self/other identification. This is important, for it is easy to read the fracturing of the subject as an inevitable dissolving into futile hysteria, rather than a deliberate challenge to what feminist critics have read as the artificially coherent determining presence of the unified voice of the patriarchal text.

That the wallpaper is a manifestation of this patriarchal text is, by now, a commonly accepted reading. After all, it not only surrounds and intimidates the central protagonist, but also walls up another woman behind it. Instead of being named on their own terms, then, both women are defined by its inescapable parameters, forced to identify themselves in line with its form, even as they struggle to wrestle against its constraints. In a gothic context this is unsurprising, for the paper's relationship to the Freudian uncanny derives from the creative images the protagonist herself works into its surface design: 'I never saw so much expression in an inanimate thing before . . . I used to lie awake as a child and get more entertainment and terror out of blank walls and plain furniture than most children could find in a toy-store' (YW, 16–17). We have seen that, according to Freud, the ability of fantasy to blur the boundaries between the animate and the inanimate leads children to endow it with pure and simple wish-fulfilment pleasures. This child-like protagonist shows him to be wrong, for although she does cast this activity in retrospectively positive terms, its present effect upon her is far more ambivalent. According to Janice Haney-Peritz, what she refers to as the 'unheard of contradictions' (YW, 13) of the paper's pattern are actually the unarticulated fantasies that the narrator herself has of defying and disagreeing with her husband's cruel and reductive diagnosis.[46] This makes mirror imagery as important in this text as in Stevenson's.

## Mirroring and Maternal Identification

Ironically, the first mirror image of the text reinforces the structures of patriarchy: 'My brother is also a physician, and also of high standing, and he says the same thing [as my husband]' (YW, 10). But almost immediately the protagonist retaliates by using a piece of lexical mirroring of her own:

> Personally, I disagree with their ideas.
> Personally, I believe that congenial work, with excitement and change will do me good.
>
> (YW, 10)

This repetition of 'Personally', each time starting a new paragraph and 'spelled' with a capital 'P' suggests an incantatory patterning which is also reiterated later on in the text:

I don't know why I should write this.
I don't want to.
I don't feel able.
And I know John would think it absurd.
(YW, 21)

Psychoanalysis, of course, is a discourse that places tremendous emphasis on the importance of verbal articulation as a means of revealing the compulsive repetitions that lurk within and drive our unconscious. Here, what this textual reiteration also successfully encodes is the effect that reproduction (as repetition) has upon her sense of self-worth. For in this particular gothic mansion, with all its paranoic enclosures and its constricting definitions, the most powerful of all the uncanny presences is that spectral one of the woman 'within'. As Clare Kahane observes, 'Beneath the crumbling shell of paternal authority, lies the maternal blackness, imagined by the gothic writer as a prison, a torture chamber.'[47] So, while the ancestral hall, with its patrilinear associations, appears to be a realm of the symbolic, the protagonist's relationship with the wallpaper (within which her own distorted mirror image appears) takes her back into the imaginary realm. Thus its seemingly opaque designs require her to search for the features she finds there in order to make out a familiar image. As she does so she starts, like Lacan's infant, to see a sense of her real self emerging from behind the facade: 'I didn't realize for a long time ... but now I am quite sure it is a woman' (YW, 26). Simultaneously reflected self and 'shadow-self ... of the past',[48] these all-too-familiar features gradually reveal that she is staring into our very first mirror: a one-to-one encounter with the face of the mother.

That, in Freudian terms, repressed intimacy with the mother's body functions as the most uncanny of all concepts, manifests itself here as a central concern. Ostensibly suffering from post-partum depression, this protagonist is at war with her own body, rebelling against a family relationship which ties her both to a house and a husband that deny her autonomy. And it is in this sense that her dilemma is best understood. For the manner in which house and body interrelate in the gothic inevitably means that her incarceration within a nursery will impact upon her anatomical form. This of course mirrors her social expectations, since under the terms of nineteenth-century marriage, a woman is faced with one of only two undesirable choices. Having refused the role of the maternal angel, her only socially acceptable alternative is to be treated, instead, just like a child. In this text Perkins Gilman, like Winnicott, demonstrates the effect that a combination of unconscious drives and environmental/societal influences can have upon the development of a character, this protagonist (like Jekyll and Hyde) becoming engaged in a battle between true and false selves: 'In typical cases the imprisoned true self is unable to function, and by being protected its opportunity for living experience is limited. Life is lived through the compliant false self, and the result clinically is a sense of unreality.'[49] Perpetually constrained by things that 'one expects . . . in marriage' (YW, 9), she learns to accept her own infantalization and, in turn, to transform her 'true' desires into 'false' fantasies. Her bodily response to this infantile state belies the awareness, despite herself, that the fantasized mother does, indeed, lie at the crux of this text. In voluntarily choosing to 'creep smoothly on the floor' (YW, 35), she positions her own body in intimate proximity to Kahane's positioning of 'maternal blackness'. But of course the floor is only one application of the preposition 'beneath' and the structures of this particular 'crumbling shell' are primarily explored in their perpendicular situation. It is 'beneath' the face of 'paternal authority', in the form of the yellow wallpaper itself, that the real realm of the mother is to be found. And this is the woman with whom this child desperately longs to be reconciled – 'I pulled and she shook, I shook and she pulled, and before morning we had peeled off yards of that paper' (YW, 32) – at the same time that she embraces her with great trepidation. For this ghostly double seems to attribute the only possible meaning to the otherwise inexplicable and rather frightening 'common centre' at 'one end of the room'. And that this is the focus for 'interminable grotesques' (YW, 20) reminds us that it is not an easy identification.

The presence of the bed reminds the reader that interior fixtures are the protagonist's most significant site of bodily interaction. Here the oral pleasures of sucking are aggressively transformed into self-destructive and futile excess: 'This bedstead is fairly gnawed! . . . I tried to lift and push it until I was lame, and then I got so angry I bit off a little piece at one corner – but it hurt my teeth' (YW, 34). According to Veeder, it is in the protagonist's relationship with the furniture itself that the extent of both her positive and negative feelings for the absent mother become apparent. In these terms, the 'bureau with its . . . breast-like "knobs"' is an image of the maternal ideal who can only exist in fantasy. By far his most interesting observation, however, concerns his reading of the colour yellow itself. For whereas most of the voluminous criticism which exists on this text focuses compulsively upon the image of the wallpaper, precious little has been said about the choice of its shade. As Veeder very convincingly argues, once we situate the observation that: 'The color is repellent, almost revolting; a smouldering unclean yellow' (YW, 13) within the discourse of object-relations theory, an obvious interpretation starts to take shape. This is clearly not only a contaminating, but also a familiar presence: 'It makes me think of all the yellow things I ever saw – not beautiful ones like buttercups, but old foul, bad yellow things' (YW, 28). When combined with an 'enduring' and a 'peculiar' odour, we quickly realize that this is the evocation of the absent presence of urethral drives, which turn the 'permeated wallpaper' into a 'saturated diaper' and the mother a reminder of bodily shame.[50]

Just as the paper demarcates the boundaries between the good mother 'within' and the bad mother 'without', so it plays a role in the manifestation of monstrous maternal fantasies. In the following detail, we find fantastic forms taking on shape in terms of a horrifying, even torturous vision of birth: 'They get through, and then the pattern strangles them off and turns them upside down . . . If those heads were covered or taken off it would not be half so bad' (YW, 30). Imprinted upon this double-sided paper, then, are a number of familial nightmares which begin to cohere as 'All those strangled heads and bulbous eyes and waddling fungus growths just shriek with derision!' (YW, 34). Encapsulated within this sick gothic eruption of the grotesque body are a combination of the distorted physical dimensions of the 'waddling' infant she has rejected; the 'derisive' shrieks of laughter from John and Jennie; and the monstrous 'fungus growths' that the paper's design seems to mimic as it shifts from being a *heimlich* to an *unheimlich* presence. The protagonist's writing seems to mirror such horrifying forms, 'loll[ing] like a broken neck' in places (YW, 16), reminding us that the role of the maternal is also interwoven into literary creativity. Usually, of course, this is understood in positive terms, just as her stance of writer/dreamer of her own text may seem positively to recontextualize this gothic imprisonment as an empowering space of play. But in some ways it may cause it to close in upon her as, rather than a nursery, its confines are further tightened, and the infantalized dreamer finds her freedom limited to the restrictive dimensions of her own *play(ing)-pen*. Unlike in Stevenson's text, then, where we witness for ourselves the 'death of the author', here we have an author who 'turns an ancestral hall into a haunted house and then encrypts herself therein as a fantasy figure'.[51] As the palimpsestic shadow that undercuts her writing implies, society permits this woman to be nothing more than a mere 'ghost-writer'.

That *The Yellow Wallpaper* was originally read as a ghost story may seem anomalous to a late-twentieth-century reader. Although Freud rather overstates the case in claiming that 'All supposedly educated people have ceased to believe officially that the dead can become visible as spirits', there is a sense in which psychoanalysis (at least in its application to the reading of literature) has functioned to render obsolete the traditional image of the frightful phantom.[52] Thus we reconceptualize our understanding of it in terms of the all too 'explicable' haunting presence of familial repressions. But, as we have seen, the world of the gothic mansion is the realm of the 'between' and this, according to Cixous, is where the site of ghosting is found: 'neither alive nor dead . . . the relationship of presence to absence is in itself an immense system of "death", a fabric riddled by the real and a phantomization of the present.'[53] The protagonist's lack of confidence in her writing implies this oscillating dialectic between presence and absence to be a basic structuring device here. When she notes, '*I* would say [this is] a haunted house and reach the height of romantic felicity – but that would be asking too much' (YW, 9 – my emphasis), she implies her own lack of belief in her ability to write, albeit in the guise of asserting belief in the supernatural. Indeed, the two are found to be inseparable. In striving to re-animate what she perceives (or wants us to perceive) to be 'dead paper' (YW, 10), she is explicitly connecting writing with the ability to bring ghosts back to life. And if society forces the protagonist into the situation of the ghost (locked up in the space 'in between', a silenced voice and an invisible presence), so the space of writing which she circumscribes around herself also draws her into a narrative of death. What immediately strikes us about this narrative within a narrative is the extreme and idiosyncratic manner in which it is described. So, we read, the 'lame uncertain curves' of the writing 'suddenly commit suicide . . . destroy[ing] themselves in unheard of contradictions' (YW, 13). More in keeping with *Dr Jekyll and Mr Hyde*, one wonders precisely what could merit such a violent analogy. And yet it functions to mirror the writer/protagonist's relationship with her own body and identity as 'undead' and 'unnamed'. If, as Fetterley claims, the adjectives by which her 'text' is described – 'Sprawling, flamboyant, sinful, irritating, provoking, outrageous, unheard of' – equally apply to her own mind, body and situation,[54] then her creation can only mimic a suicidal dynamic in existing as nothing more than a living death 'by her own hand'.

And yet, of course, as the aforementioned positive possibilities suggest, once we look beyond these surface hieroglyphics we may well find an ancient and buried subtext which exorcizes both past and present. In dispelling the 'spirit' of Victorian motherhood from her own body she sets free that part of herself which gives birth to texts. Nevertheless, despite using the first-person narrative voice throughout, the protagonist begins by denying her own position, implying that her own writing career is at an end. Her husband derides her creativity, laughing at her and her paper-bound 'fancies'. In this respect we should note that he only abstains from covering over her own creative traces by repapering the room because he believes she is 'letting it get the better of [her]' (YW, 14) anyway. And yet, despite him, the writer gradually faces her task: 'I'm getting really fond of the room in spite of the wall-paper. Perhaps because of the wall-paper. It dwells in my mind so!' (YW, 19). The significance of this final phrase derives from the choice of the word 'in' as opposed to 'on'. This is neither a statement about reflection (although the mirroring of the double carries connected associations), nor one of compulsive repetition (although the strips of wallpaper metonymically embody this too). This is an assertion of her chosen role as dreamer/writer of her own fantastic text. But we should not forget that this is first encountered 'stripped off . . . in great patches' (YW, 12), for these are the hesitant gaps that our reading must fill. Annette Kolodny may be right to locate a shift in the text which could be described as 'the narrator progressively giv[ing] up the attempt to record her reality and instead begin[ing] to read it,'[55] and yet, even here, Perkins Gilman is alert to the irony. While Kolodny perceives this protagonist's desire as a search for coherence among the creative excesses of the wallpaper's design, this does not accord with the protagonist's fully acknowledged awareness of contradiction. She may, at one stage, articulate a determination that 'nobody shall find [that pattern] out but myself!' (YW, 27), but she has already appraised us of her recognition that such aims are 'pointless' (YW, 19). Richard Felstein goes so far as to argue that multiple interpretations are encoded from the start within the very structure of 'both' (inner and outer) texts. Offering a detailed account of the various spellings of the term 'wallpaper' ('wall paper', 'wall-paper') as they are employed in both present and past (including original) editions, he concludes that the very 'word(s) wall(-)paper' deliberately function(s) to circumscribe ambiguity into the surface of the text.[56] As the protagonist herself acknowledges, interpretations must be partial, incomplete and perhaps even contradictory: 'Looked at in one way each breadth stands alone . . . But, on the other hand, [the curves and flourishes] connect diagonally, and the sprawling outlines run off in great slanting waves of optic horror . . . The whole thing goes horizontally, too, at least it seems so . . . [the frieze] adds wonderfully to the confusion' (YW, 20).

No wonder, then, that one of the most interesting motifs of this gothic design are the windows 'that look all ways' (YW, 12) at once. For, as could only happen in a fantastic narrative, out of every one of them she simultaneously sees 'the same woman . . . always creeping' (YW, 30). At first, it is tempting to read this woman outside as the same one that she frees from the paper within. But this is actually not the case. Once the woman within the wallpaper starts to emerge, the protagonist turns her back on this woman beyond. And although, like the paper, the window generally functions as a positive distraction from the world of her prison (as implied by her husband's insistence on closing it (YW, 11)), by the end of the text she has come to fear the possibilities it offers: 'I don't like to *look* out of the windows even – there are so many of those creeping women, and they creep so fast' (YW, 35). What the women inside and outside undoubtedly share is their function as projections of the protagonist's own self. But the relationship she holds towards each is different. On one level the women outside are more threatening to the protagonist simply because they are plural, always escaping the gaze and, in the rapidity of their movements, seemingly unstoppable. They are not simply split, but fractured in myriad ways. Conventionally, of course, this mirrors her social situation. In contrast to the unified masculine self of the time (which, as we have seen, was rarely questioned except through 'perversion'), nineteenth-century patriarchy forced women into a fragmentary existence which required them to function simultaneously (and in all directions at once) as wives, mothers, daughters, but never autonomously as the singular (or even the single) self. In that respect her fear may derive (in true uncanny tradition) from the very familiarity of the paralysis involved.

A second source of fear may, on the other hand, derive from the very fact that these women (in being 'out') *have* managed to free themselves from patriarchal confines. As Gilbert and Gubar demonstrate, the self-willed choice of 'monstrosity' may be an exit, but that is not an easy choice either.[57] This appears to set up a rather dismal competition between constraint via capitulation or rejection via non-conformity. This protagonist is typical in her thoroughly exhausting and dispiriting tug-of-war with herself. At times (particularly early on in the narrative), the angel of the house within her own mind takes on a dominant role. So, in the words of the 'good enough' mother, she exclaims: 'It is fortunate Mary is so good with the baby. Such a dear baby!' (YW, 14). Yet when she asserts, 'Why, I wouldn't have a child of mine, an impressionable little thing, live in such a room for worlds' (YW, 22), the words are unconvincing as being her own. After all, in many ways her only genuine sense of a 'child of mine' is her own self, as her infantile regression fundamentally illustrates. This has importance for the nature of her relationship with play and/as desire. Returning briefly to Winnicott, we remember that, for him, the spatial domain between mother and child becomes reconceived as the type of transitional space that we have equated with the world of the gothic. But in his terms, wish-fulfilment lies at the heart of this space, which he redefines as 'the child's area of play, creativity and fantasy. [It is] suffused with the mother's protection and one's own freedom to create and imagine and discover.'[58]

Certainly, in the context of *The Yellow Wallpaper*, the main protagonist tries to become this child, not only turning her prison into Woolf's 'Room of One's Own' (a positive space of writing used to kill off the angel in the house), but also discovering what Jessica Benjamin has more recently referred to as 'A Desire of One's Own': 'It seems to me that what is experientially female is the association of desire with a space, a place within the self . . . This space is in turn connected to the space between self and the other.'[59] It is here that the most intriguing piece of textual encoding starts to take on shape and form in terms of Freud's reading of female narcissism: 'Women, especially if they grow up with good looks, develop a certain self-contentment which compensates them for the social restrictions that are imposed upon them . . . Strictly speaking, it is only themselves that such women love.'[60] Although the protagonist's physical attractiveness is never raised as an issue in this text, we have witnessed the significance she attributes to the 'good looks' that she takes from every face of the building. And, as we know, what these reveal to her are the images of numerous women (all of whom are both self and not-self) that she simultaneously desires and fears (to be). Her social restrictions are obvious to all; but her self-contentment tends to express itself in terms of a self-*containment* which allows her to free her mirrored double. In these terms it seems that she largely conforms to Freud's image of the narcissistic woman. And yet there is one facet of his theory that seems inapplicable: 'Even for narcissistic women, whose attitude towards men remains cool, there is a road which leads to complete object-love. In the child which they bear, a part of their own body confronts them like an extraneous object, to which . . . they can then give complete object-love.'[61] Undoubtedly cool towards her husband, her relationship with her estranged child is far from being 'complete object-love'. But the connection once again falls into place when we realize that the child-mother bond is implicitly reworked here in terms of the very homoerotic bonding that Freud himself associates with a narcissistic identification. That she sees herself mirrored by the women beyond the window is made clear in her speculations about their own 'birthing' and origins: 'I wonder if they all come out of that wall-paper as I did?' (YW, 35). This is important, of course, because a shared relationship to origins is the basis of ancestral inheritance and nothing subverts this patriarchal structure more effectively than the presence of a powerful sisterhood (the one familial relationship deliberately devalued by patrilinear inheritance). Furthermore, as we saw in Stevenson's text, same-sex relations as expressed through the double are usually communicative of a homoerotic dimension and this woman, like Stevenson's 'servant-maid', is a 'romantically-given' storyteller/writer/day-dreamer. While Veeder incorrectly ascribes the former with a sexual dimension, in this case such a reading is far more convincing.

## Narcissism and the Clandestine Self

We have situated this woman as the marginalized 'other' of nineteenth-century patriarchy and, in the true style of the female gothic, her imprisonment within the home functions to mirror her imprisonment within the structures of heterosexual marriage. This need not function as a negative paradigm. As Delamotte claims, 'the "mysteries" heroines try so desperately to decipher while immured in gothic space are only a disguise of the real mystery, woman herself.'[62] Few mysteries, it seems, are more mysterious to patriarchy than those concerning female sexuality. Whereas the immense outer structure of the house, with its associations of wealth and privilege, takes on the masculine connotations of its 'rightful' male owner, the soft furnishings, alluring secret corridors and beckoning keyholes of the interior relate to the young heroine's budding libido. If we put these two demarcations together, we immediately recognize that such structural and decorative symbolism very clearly places the masculine in the position of total control. The images of the woman's body are encased within and constrained by those relating to the man's, while the supposed softness and allure of her sexuality is dominated by the physical power of his. In *The Yellow Wallpaper*, what we discover is that walled up behind the structures of the mansion and within the patriarchal text of the wallpaper is an alternative sexual identity not just concerned with 'breaking out' but also, more significantly, with 'coming out'. As Twitchell rightly observes, 'What characterizes Victorian schizophrenia is not that the nasty shadow gets loose . . . but that, once outside, the second self is often rather appealing.'[63]

Much hangs upon the nature of the relationship between the protagonist 'who dare not speak her name' and this closeted mirror image.[64] Right from the start, despite the fact that the protagonist appears to call up gothic elements only to dismiss them, she nevertheless asserts that 'there is something strange about the house – I can feel it' (YW, 11). One cannot help but wonder, therefore, if what is (not) 'strange' here proves to be precisely the same as what is (not) strange about Jekyll and Hyde's so-called 'strange case': in other words the subversive (absent) presence of a deviance which erupts from behind the mask of social acceptability. No wonder, as Perkins Gilman's protagonist observes, 'There are things in that paper that nobody knows but me, or ever will' (YW, 22). Like its own eponymous motif, *The Yellow Wallpaper* is obviously a complexly patterned, double-sided text. And like the rest of its gothic devices, it has implications in this sense for sexual identity. The presence of a palimpsest is a conventional means by which lesbian writers have encoded their sexuality between the lines and behind the facade of textual and social literary conformity. How ironic, then, that it is by means of using this uncanny 'space between' of the gothic mansion that what lesbian theorists have referred to as the finding of 'freedom by enlarging *spaces-in-between*, including the spaces between cracks' starts to come out into the open.[65] Quite aside from their obvious vaginal significance, such 'cracks' relate not only to the gaps existing between lengths of wallpaper, but also to those aforementioned gaps riven into *Jane Eyre* through Brontë's dispiriting capitulation to the consolationist gratifications of heterosexual romance. Stuart Kellogg, defining the place of the homosexual, effectively describes this protagonist's place: 'removed from the rest of society . . . forced to keep their homosexuality secret . . . The condition of being a stranger makes [them] keen observers of the world around them.'[66] Once we consider that this protagonist only ever uses mirror imagery to reconcile self with self by projecting names onto others, it comes as no surprise that it is her husband to whom she refers as being 'very queer sometimes' (YW, 26) and Jennie whom she tells us 'wanted to sleep with me – the sly thing!' (YW, 32). Neither is it any wonder that she 'proudly declare[s]' that there is a 'queer' presence in the house at the start of the text (YW, 9), for this is the closest she ever comes to asserting her identity.

As in the context of Stevenson's text, then, mirroring and wordplay are once again the means by which covert references to sexuality are made.

Of course this also impacts upon our understanding of her so-called 'madness' in the text. In exploring desire through the mode of the fantastic, much hinges on the usage of the term 'fancies'. Thus, as John's de(f/v)iant wife confesses that her newly emergent self feels/has caused her to feel 'better in body', his response is one of dismay rather than of pleasure: 'I beg of you, for my sake and for our child's sake, as well as for your own, that you will never for one instant let that idea enter your mind! There is nothing so dangerous, so fascinating, to a temperament like yours. It is a false and foolish fancy' (YW, 24). Frequently, this retort is taken to be the anticipation of a subsequent negative response regarding her own mental health. But this is not the only possibility that reveals itself here, particularly when attending, again, to the connotations of the term 'fancy'. Another interpretation implies that John is not so much desperate as furious at the suggestion that she is suddenly, and because of the presence of 'the other woman', enjoying a more 'healthy' physicality than she has ever done with him. In these terms, his reference to his own and the child's position is a clear-cut recognition of the implications of her actions for heterosexual marriage, motherhood and the position of the family, in so-called 'respectable' Victorian society.

What we need to address now is how to reconcile this homoerotic reading of the text with the simultaneous presence of the double as the mother. Concentrating, for a moment, upon Kristevan readings of the intrinsically homoerotic dimensions of the female child's relationship with the maternal body, a further intriguing interpretation comes to light. In Kristevan terms, poetic/figurative language is intrinsically connected with the semiotic chora, a point embedded in this text by the protagonist's awareness of the way in which, beneath the surface layer of the wallpaper, a creative and disruptive but inarticulable drive exists: 'I know a little of the principle of design, and I know this thing was not arranged on any laws of radiation, or alternation, or repetition, or symmetry, or anything else that I ever heard of' (YW, 20). Here we also need to understand the relationship that exists between the semiotic and the thetic. Functioning analogously with the recurrent and ongoing space of interaction between the two palimpsestic layers of the text, the thetic is that 'break in the signifying process' caused by the eruption of the semiotic.[67] And in that sense it seems to take on lexical form in the place of that endlessly shifting absent presence of Felstein's hyphen which comes (one should note) between the 'wall' and the 'paper' or, in other words, between the structural principle of the mansion as signifying space and the text within which it finds its voice. Like the thetic and the semiotic, the yellow wallpaper within the text and *The Yellow Wallpaper* that is the text are as mutually dependent upon each other as the two sides of the palimpsest itself: '[I] lay there for hours trying to decide whether that front pattern and the back pattern really did move together or separately' (YW, 25). Just as the thetic finds its embodiment in the shape-shifting hyphen, so the ongoing struggle between front and back pattern is also the ongoing struggle between the protagonist's relationship to self as mother and her subsequent embracing of the homoerotic other as mother. And, if it is true that 'Depression is the *hidden* face of Narcissus',[68] then it is only by artificially severing the latter from the former that it will remain in place as a site of loss.

One of the great achievements of Kristeva's work is her reinstatement of the maternal as a presiding and legitimate academic motif. Perkins Gilman likewise reinstated it as a legitimate symbol for feminist protest. This is facilitated by the protagonist's eventual willingness to plunge herself into that 'world beyond' which is the space, place, or moment of the maternal, Kristeva's notion of the semiotic chora. Here, with her fungoid growths and bulbous forms, she becomes an embodiment of the semiotic itself, 'indifferent to language, enigmatic and feminine . . . rhythmic, unfettered, irreducible'.[69] And yet it is in these terms that Kristeva distinguishes between the 'good' and 'bad' mother/daughter bond. For although her reading of the maternal lacks the judgmental sense of 'adequacy' that underlies the work of Winnicott, she is far less forgiving about lesbian desire. So the lesbian 'bad daughter', in wilfully turning her back upon the symbolic, pays the price of eternal estrangement from the dominant ideology and its attendant power in the form of a psychosis that seems dangerously close to the patriarchal diagnosis imposed upon this protagonist by her nineteenth-century clinician/husband. Therefore, although Kristeva sees the pre-Oedipal connection between the female subject and maternal identification as intrinsically homoerotic, she remains convinced of the need to sever ourselves from this in order to enter fully into social relations. In that respect she is far less positive about its transformative potential than the aforementioned identification would seem to imply.

In the context of *The Yellow Wallpaper*, this ambivalence is largely borne out by narrative events. Despite the existence of many celebratory feminist re-readings of the text, one cannot escape the sad recognition that, at the end, having reconceived her identity, the protagonist is still trapped by the same social constraints. Having turned her back upon her Winnicottian 'true self', her subsequent decision to 'crawl' or 'creep' is simply a manifestation of the means by which she will continue to 'plot' her way around and around that endless spiral of lack and desire that is the realm of the symbolic order: 'I love him/her . . . but even more, I hate him/her; because I love him/her, in order not to lose him/her, I install him/her in myself; but because I hate him/her, this other in myself is a bad ego, I am bad, I am worthless, I am destroying myself.'[70] Like *Dr Jekyll and Mr Hyde*, *The Yellow Wallpaper* deals with boundary problems. Trapped in a social system whereby her only opportunity of becoming a 'speaking subject' lies within conformity to the marital 'norm', there is no way she can join those women who are 'out' in the world that she sees beyond the window. Instead, homoerotic desire is playfully revealed only in order to be firmly reveiled as the gothic replaces the lid upon its own *unheimlich* desires. Inhabiting the realm of the 'space-in-between', what the protagonists of both narratives find, is a mirroring double of silent articulation in the guise of 'the love that dare not speak its name'.

## Notes

1 R.L. Stevenson, *The Strange Case of Dr Jekyll and Mr Hyde and Other Stories* (Harmondsworth: Penguin, 1979); Charlotte Perkins Gilman, *The Yellow Wallpaper* (London: Virago, 1981). All subsequent quotations are referenced within the main body of the text, the abbreviations JH and YW being used respectively.

2 Peter K. Garret, 'Cries and Voices: Reading Jekyll and Hyde', in William Veeder and Gordon Hirsch (eds), *Dr Jekyll and Mr Hyde After One Hundred Years* (Chicago: University of Chicago Press, 1988), pp. 63–7 (p. 63).

3 James B. Twitchell, *Dreadful Pleasures: An Anthology of Modern Horror* (New York: Oxford University Press, 1985), p. 231.

4 Kathleen L. Spencer, 'Purity and Danger: *Dracula*, the Urban Gothic and the Late Victorian Degeneracy Crisis', *ELH*, No. 1 (1992), pp. 197–225 (p. 200).

5 Kate Ferguson Ellis, *The Contested Castle: Gothic Novels and Subversion of Domestic Ideology* (Urbana: University of Illinois Press, 1989), p. x.

6 As Elaine Showalter comments 'the strange case of Jack the Ripper . . . was a myth of warning to women of the dangers of lives outside the home . . . [the] moral message is clear: the city is a dangerous place for women'. Elaine Showalter, *Sexual Anarchy: Gender and Culture at the Fin de Siècle* (London: Bloomsbury , 1991), p. 127.

7 For a fuller discussion of this see Norman N. Holland, *The Dynamics of Literary Response* (New York: Oxford University Press, 1968), p. 40.

8 Holland, *Dynamics*, p. 45.

9 As argued by Kathryn Hume, *Fantasy and Mimesis: Responses to Reality in Western Literature* (London: Methuen, 1984), p. 175.

10 Holland, *Dynamics*, p. 43.

11 Gordon Hirsch, '*Frankenstein*, Detective Fiction and *Jekyll and Hyde*', in Veeder and Hirsch (eds), *Dr Jekyll and Mr Hyde After One Hundred Years*, pp. 223–41 (p. 241).

12 Noel Carroll differentiates between monsters of fusion and fission in the following manner: 'In fusion, categorically contradictory elements are fused or condensed or superimposed in one unified spatio-temporal being whose identity is homogeneous. But with fission, the contradictory elements are, so to speak, distributed over *different*, though metaphysically related, identities.' Noel Carroll, *The Philosophy of Horror or, Paradoxes of the Heart* (New York: Routledge, 1990), p. 46.

13 William Veeder, 'Children of the Night: Stevenson and Patriarchy', in Veeder and Hirsch (eds), *Dr Jekyll and Mr Hyde After One Hundred Years*, pp. 108–55 (p. 119 – my emphasis).

14 Showalter, *Anarchy*, p. 195.

15 As Showalter explains, 'In the Victorian home, handbooks of popular medicine made terrifying images of the syphilitic wages of sin readily available for the instruction of the young boy', and yet sufferers were given no sanctioned cultural voice. *Anarchy*, pp. 191–3 .

16 Jerrold E. Hogle, 'The Struggle for a Dichotomy: Abjection in Jekyll and his Interpreters', in Veeder and Hirsch (eds), *Dr Jekyll and Mr Hyde After One Hundred Years*, pp. 161–202 (p. 188).

17 The play inherent in the use of the word 'fanciful' (imaginative) and 'fanciful' (fanciable) becomes particularly clear in this context when we compare it with the observation Dr Lanyon makes to Utterson on the following page: 'it is more than ten years since Henry Jekyll became too fanciful for me' (JH, 36).

18 Kelly Oliver, 'Introduction: Julia Kristeva's Outlaw Ethics', in Kelly Oliver (ed.), *Ethics, Politics, and Difference in Julia Kristeva's Writing* (New York: Routledge, 1993), pp. 1–22 (p. 13).
19 Twitchell, *Pleasures*, p. 235.
20 As argued by Sigmund Freud, 'Creative Writers and Day-Dreaming', trans. I.F. Grant, in Albert Dickson (ed.), *The Penguin Freud Library, Vol. 14, Art and Literature* (Harmondsworth: Penguin, 1990), pp. 129–41, (p. 131).
21 As noted by R.R. Thomas, 'The Strange Voices in the *Strange Case*: Dr Jekyll, Mr Hyde and the Voices of Modern Fiction', in Veeder and Hirsch (eds), *Dr Jekyll and Mr Hyde After One Hundred Years*, pp. 73–90 (p. 75).
22 As a 'left-hander' myself, I am fully aware of the potentially offensive connections being drawn upon here. My employment of them is purely observational and should not, in any way, be seen as evaluative.
23 Stephen Heath, '*Psychopathia Sexualis*: Stevenson's *Strange Case*', *Critical Quarterly*, Vol. 28 (1986), pp. 93–108 (pp. 96–7).
24 For more on this see Spencer, 'Purity', p. 207.
25 Heath, '*Psychopathia*', p. 96.
26 Veeder, 'Children', p. 128 .
27 Veeder, 'Children', pp. 128–9.
28 Veeder, 'Children', p. 148.
29 See, for example, Chapter 2, 'The Accumulation of Experience in the Mother and in the Parents', in Madeleine Davis and David Wallbridge (eds), *Boundary And Space: An Introduction to the Work of D.W. Winnicott* (New York: Brunner/Mazel, 1987).
30 Clare Winnicott et al. (eds), *D.W. Winnicott: Psycho-Analytic Explorations* (London: Karnac Books, 1989), pp. 44 and 79.
31 D.W. Winnicott, 'What Irks' (1960), cited in Davis and Wallbridge, *Boundary*, p. 123.
32 Marilyn Edelstein, 'Toward a Feminist Postmodern Poléthique: Kristeva on Ethics and Politics', in Oliver (ed.), *Ethics, Politics, and Difference in Julia Kristeva's Writing*, pp. 196–214 (p. 202).
33 This being a phrase Kelly Oliver adopts in her Kristevan reading of the maternal. See Oliver, 'Introduction', p. 7.
34 D.W. Winnicott, 'Ego Distortion in Terms of the True and False Self' (1960), cited in Davis and Wallbridge, *Boundary*, p. 48.
35 D.W. Winnicott, 'The First Year of Life: Modern Views on Emotional Development' (1958), cited in Davis and Wallbridge, *Boundary*, p. 34.
36 Twitchell, *Pleasures*, p. 220.
37 Twitchell, *Pleasures*, p. 237.
38 Twitchell, *Pleasures*, p. 15.
39 Sandra Gilbert and Susan Gubar, *The Madwoman in the Attic: The Woman Writer and the Nineteenth-Century Literary Imagination* (New Haven: Yale University Press, 1984), p. 85.
40 Eugenia C. Delamotte, 'Male and Female Mysteries in *The Yellow Wallpaper*', *Legacy*, Vol. 5 (1988), pp. 3–14 (p. 4).
41 For a fuller discussion of this see Delamotte, 'Mysteries', p. 11.
42 Conrad Shumaker, '"Too Terribly Good to be Printed": Charlotte Gilman's *The Yellow Wallpaper*', *American Literature*, Vol. 57 (1985), pp. 588–99 (p. 597).
43 Judith Fetterley, From 'Reading about Reading: "A Jury of Her Peers", "The Murders in the Rue Morgue", and "The Yellow Wallpaper"', in Catherine Golden (ed.), *The Captive Imagination: A Casebook on the Yellow Wallpaper* (New York: Feminist Press, City University of New York, 1992), pp. 253–75 (p. 253).
44 As argued by Delamotte, 'Mysteries', p. 8.
45 Catherine Golden, 'The Writing of *The Yellow Wallpaper*: A Double Palimpsest', in Golden (ed.), *Captive*, pp. 296–305 (pp. 299–300).
46 Janice Haney-Peritz, 'Monumental Feminism and Literature's Ancestral House: Another Look at *The Yellow Wallpaper*', *Women's Studies*, Vol. 12 (1986), pp. 113–28 (p. 117).

47 Clare Kahane, 'Gothic Mirrors and Feminine Identity', in *Centennial Review*, Vol. 24 (1980), pp. 43–64 (p. 47).
48 For a fuller exploration of this concept see Harold Fisch, *A Remembered Future: A Study of Literary Mythology* (Bloomington: Indiana University Press, 1984), p. 43.
49 Clare Winnicott et al., *Winnicott*, p. 43.
50 William Veeder, 'Who Is Jane? The Intricate Feminism of Charlotte Perkins Gilman', *Arizona Quarterly*, Vol. 44 (1988), pp. 40–79 (pp. 45–51 *passim*). Note, also, that according to Winnicott et al., 'In psycho-analytic writings there are copious references to the mother's conscious and unconscious fantasies about her child. Often we find the expression "baby" equated with ... articles of furniture, pillows, etc. etc.'. Winnicott et al., *Winnicott*, p. 161.
51 As argued by Haney-Peritz, 'Monumental', p. 123.
52 Sigmund Freud, 'The 'Uncanny', trans. Alix Strachey, in Dickson (ed.), *The Penguin Freud Library*, p. 365.
53 Hélène Cixous, 'Fiction and Its Phantoms: A Reading of Freud's *Das Unheimliche* (The "Uncanny")', *New Literary History*, Vol. 7 (1976), pp. 525–48 (p. 543).
54 Fetterley, 'Reading', pp. 257–8.
55 Annette Kolodny, 'A Map for Rereading: Or, Gender and the Interpretation of Literary Texts', in Golden (ed.), *Captive*, pp. 151–65 (p. 156).
56 Richard Felstein, 'Reader, Text and Ambiguous Referentiality in *The Yellow Wallpaper*', in Golden (ed.), *Captive*, pp. 306–17 (p. 308).
57 'Unlike her male counterpart ... the female artist must first struggle against the effects of a socialization which makes conflict with the will of her (male) precursors seem inexpressibly absurd, futile or even ... self-annihiliating.' Gilbert and Gubar, *Madwoman*, p. 49.
58 This is Jessica Benjamin's reading of Winnicott. See 'A Desire of One's Own: Psychoanalytic Feminism and Intersubjective Space', in Teresa de Lauretis (ed.), *Feminist Studies/Critical Studies* (London: Macmillan, 1986), pp. 78–101 (p. 94).
59 The first image derives from that symbol of liberation that Virginia Woolf situates at the centre of the plight of the woman writer: 'a woman must have money and a room of her own if she is to write fiction'. *A Room Of One's Own* (London: Grafton, 1977), p. 6. The second is from Benjamin, 'Desire', p. 97.
60 Sigmund Freud, 'On Narcissism: An Introduction', trans. C.M. Baines, in Angela Richards (ed.), *The Penguin Freud Library, Vol. 11, On Metapsychology* (Harmondsworth: Penguin, 1991), pp. 59–97 (p. 82).
61 Freud, 'Narcissism', p. 83.
62 Delamotte, 'Mysteries', p. 11.
63 Twitchell, *Pleasures*, p. 232.
64 The phrase 'the love that dare not speak its name', coined by Oscar Wilde, became a code for homosexuality in the *fin-de-siècle* period.
65 For a fuller discussion of this see Mary Meigs, 'Falling Between the Cracks', in Karla Jay and Joanne Glasgow (eds), *Lesbian Texts and Contexts: Radical Revisions* (New York: New York University Press, 1990), pp. 28–38 (p. 37).
66 Stuart Kellogg, 'Introduction: The Uses of Homosexuality in Literature', in *Essays on Gay Literature* (New York: Harrington Park Press, 1985), pp. 1–17 (pp. 6–7).
67 For a fuller explanation of this see Julia Kristeva, 'Revolution in Poetic Language', trans. Margaret Waller, in Toril Moi (ed.), *The Kristeva Reader* (Oxford: Basil Blackwell, 1986), pp. 89–136, (p. 98).
68 As argued by Julia Kristeva, 'On the Melancholic Imaginary', trans. Louise Burchill, in Shlomith Rimmon-Kenan (ed.), *Discourse in Psychoanalysis and Literature* (London: Methuen, 1987), pp. 104–23 (p. 104) – my emphasis.
69 As defined by Julia Kristeva. See Kristeva, 'Revolution', p. 97.
70 This being a Kristevan paradigm. See Kristeva, 'Melancholic', p. 106.

# 6

# Changing the Narrative Subject: Carroll's *Alices and* Carter's *The Passion of New Eve*

In this chapter, we shall be comparing texts which, on the face of it, seem to have little in common. Lewis Carroll's *Alice* texts are frequently thought of as charming, if accomplished, nineteenth-century children's stories, while Angela Carter's *The Passion of New Eve* is a violent, often shocking, contemporary novel.[1] Yet simply by scratching the surface we discover similarities. In each case we are encouraged to identify with a central protagonist who finds him/herself unwittingly embarked upon a literal journey through space and time.[2] As is so often the case, this ultimately becomes a metaphorical journey involving a profound (and in Carter's case irreversible) reassessment of the character's subjectivity. In both narratives this reassessment impacts centrally upon the importance of the body as a mainstay for identity and the resulting effect when the limits of that body are called into question by a confrontation with metamorphosis. The *Alice* texts are an archetypal example of such fictional exploration and for that reason form our starting-point.

Commencing here with a brief summary of some of the more obviously applicable psychoanalytic readings, the discussion quickly moves to a more sustained exploration of the implications of game-playing and ideology, using the many Bakhtinian tropes of these texts. Wheareas, in *The Passion of New Eve*, life is lived in the desperate game-playing space of simulation, in the *Alice*s games are structured in line with the carnivalesque. This is a point crucial to our understanding of their bourgeois protagonist who nevertheless defines herself in contradistinction to the many 'adult' authority figures she meets. Figuratively positioned as a Victorian reincarnation of the biblical Eve, Alice ultimately transgresses in a way that is entirely related to an overstepping of limits that brings the acquisition of knowledge into a contiguous relation with a newly emergent feminine consciousness. This forms the most obvious bridging-point with Carter's novel. As implied by the centrality given to the metamorphic in both fictional works, the respective protagonists' journey into knowledge is paid for by acquiring an awareness of origins conceptualized through what is perceived as inevitable loss. In each case this loss takes on anatomical inference in line with pubescent female development. In Carter's text this is more fully explored in terms of postmodern theories of cybernetics and the application of these hybrid forms to Carter's retheorising of binary gender divides. The ideological difficulties of Carter's work have always, paradoxically, been one of its strengths. Perhaps this also explains Alice's ongoing cultural currency. In Chapter 2 we saw Bettelheim's analysis of the child reader's relationship with the fairy tale to be one of false (even dangerous) optimism. From this perspective Alice's own assertion 'I used to read fairy tales . . . now here I am in the middle of one!' (W, 59) does little to deflect my prevailing interest in the ideological difficulties of Carroll's texts.

Reading the *Alice* texts alongside *The Passion of New Eve* provides a further advantageous position, for it conspires against the conventional stance of situating the former as simple canonical examples of children's literature at its best. It is not that this is an incorrect or invalid perspective, it is merely that it tends to coerce critical readings into a restrictive concentration upon those aspects of the texts which shore up the child's celebratory sense of her own worth, autonomy, resiliance and affirmation. Typical of this is Ann Donovan's claim that 'in chapter after chapter, incident after incident, [Alice] extricate[s] herself from nightmare-like situations with complete aplomb'.[3] Certainly Alice *is* a positive role model for young female readers, being intelligent, adventurous, 'canny' and assertive. But it is a mistake to reduce the whole text to pure gratification. On the contrary, it is Alice's flirtation with danger, mutilation and the allure of intriguing but potentially untrustworthy strangers that makes it such an exciting book. Not only are a number of the characters taken from the motifs of nightmare (a severed head that talks by itself, a female dictator with a predilection for ritualized death and giant insects 'about the size of a chicken' (LG, 221)) but, to use an appropriately anatomical image, Alice frequently escapes substantial danger only by the 'skin of her teeth'. For a child reader in particular, it is the *presence* of such danger, not merely her escape from it, that provides the thrill of this extraordinary book.

As far as 'adult' readings of these narratives are concerned, it is undoubtedly the psychoanalytic that has provided the most sustained appreciation of the internal workings of the *Alice*s. But this is inevitable, for their very narrative content (being dream-texts about the bodily changes of a young girl approaching adolescence) makes psychoanalysis an obvious choice. In *Looking Glass*, Carroll even draws an implicit analogy between the world of the unconscious night-dreamer and that of the unconscious as he separates out various strata of the psyche in terms of sleeping and waking. In this manner the reader journeys with Alice from the world of the 'unconscious' in chapters 1 to 9, into the midway 'shaking' state of chapter 10, in which the dream-screen images start to shift and blur, while, turning over in sleep/turning the page, we gradually 'wake up' in chapter 11. In terms of Freud's views on the creative writer as day-dreamer, on the other hand, that Alice situates herself as such a dreamer/writer is made as clear as could be when her movement into the world of the magic mirror is accompanied by what we are told is her favourite phrase, 'Let's pretend' (LG, 181). Once we add to all of this the obvious sexual implications of disappearing into rabbit-holes and discovering that parts of the body have suddenly, and without warning, turned into 'an immense length ... ris[ing] like a stalk' (W, 74), we see that we are dealing with an all-too-tempting text for any would-be Freudian. The only problem facing such a critic lies with finding symbolism that is sufficiently encoded to make it worth the effort of fully unravelling.

Perhaps for this reason the *Alice* texts are also fiercely defended by *anti*-Freudians, although such voices often end up unwittingly asserting the importance of the psychoanalytic in preference to the alternatives they can offer. So Martin Gardner, the current editor of *The Annotated Alice*, offers little more instead than a series of rather strange biographical speculations: 'In appearance Carroll was handsome and asymmetric – two facts that may have contributed to his interest in mirror reflections'.[4] Accordingly, his interest in the text (and other critics' readings of it) revolves solely around what they might be able to tell us about that mysterious man who 'lies' behind the pseudonym Lewis Carroll. This, in itself, is not without interest, but it does little to facilitate our reading of the text. If anything, it reduces these endlessly creative and imaginative books to nothing short of a monodimensional narrative. For example, referring to the preponderance of oral images, instead of addressing orality in terms of Holland's work, object-relations theories, connections with the excesses of the carnivalesque, implications for feminist theory, the body politics of bulimia, or any other of the many possible and interesting critical readings of it, Gardner reduces it to the lowest common denominator: 'Are the many references to eating in ALICE a sign of Carroll's "oral aggression", or did Carroll recognize that small children are obsessed by eating . . .?'[5]

Undoubtedly it is the case that an adult reader of the *Alice* texts (in common with an adult reader of any text generally perceived to have been written for children) will relate to it in a rather different way to the child who encounters it for the first time. But, as Sarah Gilead suggests, this may in fact facilitate, rather than problematize, the level of identification with the central protagonist. In this sense, Alice's journeys into

Wonderland and the Looking Glass parallel what the text sets up as our return to what *only* an adult can perceive as that idealized world we inhabited as children. So, she claims, we 'recuperate the familiar ... link[ing] slippery modern culture to the lost wholeness and stability of an imagined (and largely *imaginary*) past'.[6] As her fortuitous usage of the word 'imaginary' demonstrates here, this has immediate relevance for psychoanalytic interpretations. One has only to take the most cursory of glances at *Looking Glass* in particular, to see the ease with which Lacanian readings of the mirror stage have application. Alice's journey is, like that of Perkins Gilman's protagonist, a regressive one back into the realm of the imaginary. That this is the realm of *jouissance*, with its combined meanings of play and pleasure, also makes it entirely appropriate that what we find here is an immense game-playing structure with language as a series of free-playing 'slips' of the tongue: '"Things flow about so here!" [Alice] said at last ... after she had spent a minute or so in vainly pursuing a large bright thing, that looked sometimes like a doll and sometimes like a work-box, and was always in the shelf next above the one she was looking at' (LG, 253). But it is Alice's stance with regard to this that sets her firmly apart from the protagonist of *The Yellow Wallpaper*. Alice remains, at all times, a child of the symbolic (hence her dislocation and disturbance at being thus positioned and her frustration at what is always the free-play of the signifier). As with all of us, it is only her *displacement* with regard to the imaginary that determines the fact that she is ultimately estranged from her own 'self'. And it is in this way that she becomes, simultaneously, the subject of the enunciating and the subject of the enunciation. For, as Mark Conroy observes, 'the dreamed Alice can always be quite properly appalled at the grotesque spectacle which Alice the dreamer is busily producing.'[7]

In Kristevan terms, Alice is the archetypal 'foreigner', for not only does she find herself far from home and surrounded by strangers, she is also alienated by other characters' usage of language. But, as narrative point of view requires the reader to identify with Alice, we share her place as textual foreigner, if not the manner in which it is most clearly articulated. For although we know from our first glance at the title of *Alice in Wonderland* that Alice is this character's name, this is a source of knowledge not apparently shared by the creatures she meets. Variously named (if at all) as 'child', 'monster', 'dear old thing' or simply 'you', the word 'Alice!', when it is uttered by the White Rabbit in the Wonderland court, not only comes as a shock to us, but also to Alice herself (W, 152). Placed as the final word of the penultimate chapter of the book, it signals a move (as does the court itself) away from Wonderland (anti-)logic and imaginary riddles and an initiation into that law of the father that heralds (in the form of the White Rabbit) the boundary crossing which accompanies Alice's return to the symbolic order. In this sense, the chapter title 'Alice's Evidence' does not just refer to the evidence she gives, but also to the evidence that she (unlike the Cheshire Cat) exists in a 'corroborative' sense. Ultimately Alice's journey shows that it is not, as Jane Flax claims, merely other people whom we can know only in terms of how we project our own 'fantasies and libidinal investments' upon them.[8] Through her extraordinary encounters with foreignness in all its various and fantastic guises Alice demonstrates that this is also true of ourselves. And yet, it is important to realize that it is not only the psychoanalytic that can inform our readings of bodies, naming and their relationship to power. Via the work of theorists such as Massey, Bakhtin and even Baudrillard, we now consider some of the other ways in which the *Alice* texts can be opened up by theoretical means.

## Game-Playing and the Carnivalesque

As we saw in Chapter 3, Massey's work offers an interesting perspective on the nature of the interrelationship between bodies and language as they are encoded within textual metamorphoses. And, as he acknowledges, the *Alice* texts are particularly useful illustrations of this. Such evidence can be found in Alice's recitals of poetry, which never quite mirror their 'original' form, even as they trace its outline through a metamorphic mimickry. As part of this resistance to closure, whereas the usage of unfinished sentences in *Looking Glass* sets up a deliberate tension between page- and chapter-breaks that mirrors the presiding structure of these two texts when taken together, in *Wonderland* it is an 'unfinished sentence' with which the text ends. In this case the term 'sentence' implies a court sentence, unfinished due to a playful 'stay' of execution which requires, paradoxically, a departure for another world. Thus, as the Queen utters the command 'Off with her head!' (W, 161), Alice (following the example of the Cheshire Cat) dissolves into thin air and back to 'reality'.[9] Taking into account the grammatical fact that a sentence is the basic syntactic unit, we rightly expect that the rest of language will 'follow suit' in this respect. But, like the shape-shifting form of Alice herself, words consistently deny us security here, slipping away at the contact of our gaze to enter into a new 'touching' relationship with yet another shifting signifier. Just as Carroll offers us a world of child's play, so Massey transforms language into a children's game, within the terms of which: 'certain letters of the alphabet are peep-holes, or chinks through which one can slip into the world beyond language . . . as if they were swinging doors, which while pertaining superficially to language were really meant to lead the way into the world within.'[10]

That, particularly in *Looking Glass*, Carroll encodes the free-play of the text into a game which is the text also encapsulates Massey's ideas. While existing as two separate texts published six years apart, *Looking Glass* and its sister text, *Wonderland*, also enter into an internal game structure. Like

Alice herself, the two are fractured selves, frequently (as here) read largely as one narrative riven down the middle. But this splitting, far from irrevocably separating the two, coerces them into an internal folding that conjoins them, even in the process of their division. And, in that respect like two players of a game, these texts collaborate in forging their own rules which, while being clearly distinct from the rules of the outside world, are understood and referred to in and by both. This is best illustrated by an example taken from *Looking Glass*. Alice, entering the wood 'where things have no name', articulates her fear of losing her own name by referring to the following metamorphic doubling structure: 'they'd have to give me another, and it would be almost certain to be an ugly one. But then the fun would be, trying to find the creature that had got my old name!' (LG, 225). Not only, then, is it apparent that a shifting of the signifier results in a bodily metamorphosis (as is found to be the case when Alice encounters Tweedledum and Tweedledee in these very woods), but also a shifting of the signifier results in a profound metamorphosis from within the body of the text. For the use of the term 'ugly' here resoundingly echoes the playful *Wonderland* coinage 'uglification'. The latter, referred to by the Mock Turtle as one of the four branches of Arithmetic, the other three being 'Ambition, Distraction ... and Derision' (W, 129), clearly reveals that, as we saw in the previous chapter, to multiply is intrinsically to uglify (and vice versa).

Such intertextual play also manifests itself through a number of actual character doubles who are split across the demarcations between texts. So the *Wonderland* Duchess with her baby/pig remanifests herself in *Looking Glass* as the White Queen with the baby kitten; and Hatta, a peripheral character in *Looking Glass*, stands watching the fight between the Lion and the Unicorn 'with a cup of tea in one hand and a piece of bread and butter in the other' (LG, 284), just like the pivotal figure of the Mad Hatter who presides over the tea-party in *Wonderland*. U.C. Knoepflmacher takes this further, suggesting that Hatta's companion Haigha can also be read as a homonymic double for the (March) Hare.[11] The important issue is not simply to recognize the presence of such game-playing, but to consider its application to the narrative treatment of power, rank and social hierarchies. Just as 'Jack and the Beanstalk' is far more than a simple children's story, so John Batchelor is incorrect in believing that the textual centrality of metamorphosis in the *Alice* texts is nothing more than 'one of the simplest child-fantasies in which one *becomes big enough to get one's own way*'.[12] Instead, a very clear political back-drop underscores the play of these texts, as the very choice of their respective games (cards in *Wonderland* and chess in *Looking Glass*) suggests. Both games are aristocratic in orientation and depend upon the motifs of battle and military domination for effect, despite the fact that (in the true spirit of the carnivalesque) they couch their politics in the discourse of jest. And in this sense, these seemingly 'meaningless' playful manoeuvres have a genuine external referent.

To continue with the analogy outside the text, while it may appear that there is no reason behind the rules governing the movement of any particular chess piece, in fact we find that they largely replicate the ranking of the power hierarchy from which they derive. So the pawns are obvious 'canon-fodder', making most of the running and shielding the rather more 'valuable' pieces, whereas the King is relatively sheltered, static, no more than a presiding figurehead or trophy. Alice is fully appraised about hierarchies even as she chooses to subvert their structure. After all, at the end of *Wonderland* it is she who has the last laugh as the pack of cards which 'rose up into the air' (W, 161) around her is transformed into the joke game '52 card pick-up'.[13]

It is surprising that critics such as Batchelor can see nothing more in this than 'spectacular nursery naughtiness',[14] for of course it is crucial to our understanding of the ideologies of these texts that both culminate in carnival chaos: an excess clearly expressive of the gluttonies of adult indulgence. So, when we read that the bottles 'each took a pair of plates, which they hastily fitted on as wings, and . . . went fluttering about in all directions' (LG, 335), we are conscious not just of the usage of hybridized forms here, but also of the possible hallucinatory implications of an image produced through drunken excess. Such transgressive motifs find their pinnacle in the carnival mascot of the gluttonous pig. Better still, in transgressive terms, in *Looking Glass* we have a pig which is always in the process of metamorphosing into something else. Importantly, it is in chapter 6 of *Wonderland* (the same chapter within which the pig is introduced) that the boundaries of the narrative open up to their full limits. For we know that the carnival pig always embodies that attempt to push back the fixity of boundaries of all kinds. Thus, as Allon White asserts, 'the pig was to be slaughtered and eaten . . . but it was also a king, a gigantic eater . . . a procreator symbolizing fertility'.[15] Like Alice herself, the pig is always defined in bodily terms, even as those terms shift and blur. And here, just as the play of the signifier reduces the pigeon to a pig and then transforms it into a fig (W, 90), so this gradual reduction in both linguistic size and, ultimately, in terms of the food chain, mirrors a parallel socio-political lowering. So it begins the text as the Duchess's baby, only to be transformed into what culture perceives as the lowest of the low. In this sense both pig and Alice become textual doubles, simultaneously children and creatures of excess.

Nevertheless, we must beware of placing too much emphasis upon genuine political subversion, particularly in the context of Alice herself. The *Alice* texts are in no way manifestos for political subterfuge. On the contrary, what subversion there is functions in clearly demarcated terms. Alice's overthrowing of more powerful forces derives solely from her identity as a child overturning a pseudo-aristocratic hierarchy comprising a king, and in particular a queen, who are an obvious fantasy manifestation of father and mother. Other than this, there is relatively little deconstruction of her own position as a privileged member of the polite middle classes and even when such a suggestion occurs (as it does in chapter 2 of *Wonderland*), it is suggested in the 'nicest' possible way. Thus Alice, whose own sense of subjectivity has become disorientated because, no longer capable of correctly reciting poetry, she presumes herself to be somebody else, muses upon whether this particular metamorphosis has resulted in her transformation into Mabel instead. Even to Alice, this is an anatomical shift with clear political consequences: 'I shall have to go and live in that poky little house, and have next to no toys to play with, and oh, ever so many lessons to learn!' (W, 38). That this is one of very few occasions upon which the narrator invites the reader's displeasure with Alice is, of course, a positive sign, for it implies a critique of those bourgeois assumptions linking relative poverty with relative intelligence. Once we discover, two chapters later, that Alice finds herself in precisely this situation, trapped in the 'poky little house' of the White Rabbit, 'one arm out of the window, and one foot up the chimney' (W, 58) we recognize, with pleasure, the irony of this. In fact, not only does she have precious few toys to play with in this text, more significantly she is turned into a plaything herself, as characters toy with both her emotions and her all-too-precocious intellect. Nevertheless, having 'many lessons to learn' during the course of the text hardly operates as a political statement. This is merely the reprimand given to a privileged child taught not to make fun of those less fortunate than herself.

Indeed, as Donald Rackin argues, Alice's sense of the 'topsy turvey' carnival motif derives primarily from finding herself in two topsy-turvey, 'Backwards' places 'where the sensible child of the master class acts as servant, and the crazy servants act as masters'.[16] Again, this is hardly a radical socialist critique and such elitist complacency is threaded throughout. Thus, when the Dormouse begins to recount the story of three sisters who lived in a well, Alice interrupts by asking 'What did they live on?' (W, 100). We take this, surely, as an enquiry concerning their means to exist without capital. But the narrator hastily introjects at this point to steer us away from such an uncomfortable subject by inserting an important point of clarification, namely that Alice 'always took a great interest in questions of eating and drinking' (W, 100). Hence this becomes a question concerning sustenance, rather than one concerning subsistence. On one level this is a legitimate child's-eye view; for children (at least in Alice's 'well-to-do' social circles) food is neither grown nor bought, it simply appears on the table 'as if by magic'. But in the political game-playing of this text, this is really no answer at all. On the contrary, money, far from being absent altogether, is present in a number of playful guises. So we remember the anomalous presence of the sales ticket on the Mad Hatter's hat and the extraordinary shop in *Looking-Glass*. Just as Alice herself rather coyly refrains from asking Humpty Dumpty about the nature of the wages that he gives to his words (LG, 270), so these other images actually function to avoid the mention of 'filthy lucre'. The shop is particularly interesting in this respect, for it highlights the way in which the relationship between linguistic free-play and textual metamorphosis can actually work to suppress the political. Behind the sales-counter sits a sheep. This choice (ridiculous in most other literary contexts) is a little surprising, even here, for we are as bemused as Alice about how a boat on a river can (as it does) suddenly and without warning metamorphose into a shop, even if we accept the unlikely figure of the sheep. For William Empson, this can be put down to pure personal sentiment on Carroll's part, the author circumscribing this scene with visions of Oxford: 'Everyone recognizes the local shop . . . the rowing, the academic old sheep'.[17] But such cosy analyses of playful eccentricity mask a rather more significant point. Bearing in mind Massey's preoccupation with the relationship between metamorphic structures and linguistic play, the relationship between the sheep and the shop suggests two further playful associations of intrinsic relevance to issues of capital. First, of course, the word 'sheep' rhymes with 'cheap' (in precisely the same way that Carroll presumably places a 'sheep' here because it phonetically relates to 'shop'). In addition, the application of music-hall humour to this linguistic choice reminds us that, in a shop run by a sheep, we run the risk of being 'fleeced'. Carroll carefully (almost wilfully) avoids any allusion to either – resulting, paradoxically, in the presence of this shop affirming the *absence* of money as textual currency.

To some extent this issue is raised by Rackin, who resituates Carroll's usage of the fantasy world in terms of the socio-historical phenomena of Victorian industrial society. Thus, he confidently asserts that 'what often seems a glorious escape from time and place – from historical context itself . . . depend[s] on tangible connections to [a] specific historical milieu', the temporal dislocations set up in the text being mirrored by a political anxiety that 'time itself will no longer "behave" its erstwhile governors so that in the Mad Tea-Party it is always six-o'clock (quitting time for many factory workers)'.[18] Empson and Rackin also share an interest in the apparent significance of the advent of Darwinism on the text. Empson, referring to the pool of tears, compares it to the sea (out of which Darwin thought all forms of life to have evolved). Thus the assorted creatures who join Alice become 'a whole Noah's Ark' of evolutionary species. The importance of this (aside from its obvious connection to Victorian thought), is that it returns us to Carroll's preoccupation with hybrid and mutant forms and their transgressive function as a means of destabilizing what we think of as the Victorian obsession with cultural and moral order: 'Thus, *Wonderland* is paradoxically both a denial and an affirmation of constructed order – a kind of comically disguised catharsis of what can never be truly purged but what must, for sanity's sake, be periodically purged in jest, fantasy, and dream.'[19]

This inevitably raises, once again, the extent to which such generically enclosed forms can ever radically reassess (or even fully interrogate) cultural norms, without capitulating to a consolatory reading of the present as that place to which we always desire to return. Ultimately, Rackin perceives this to be the problem with the *Alices*, for '*Wonderland* enfolds Alice's disturbing dreams in circular, idyllic peace, in a narrative frame that turns back on itself and ends where it begins – with a stable tableau of a sheltered mother-child dyad nestled within a structurally static, centripetal frame story.'[20] This obsession with circles as security mechanisms is also present in *Looking Glass* where, as Nina Auerbach observes, we find Alice 'in a snug, semi-foetal position, encircled by a protective armchair and encircling a plump kitten'. But it remains Rackin who takes this furthest, perceiving in this preponderance of circular images, a clear unconscious link with 'the rich, passive, static, undifferentiated and fluid world of the nurturing womb; the concentric id logic of fetal desire: "Beautiful Soup"',[21] Of course we are not shackled by such consolatory readings. Taking into account the aforementioned carnival structures, Alice's encounter with (and fears of drowning in) a pool of her own tears (W, 40–1) can also be read as the fate of the drunk who, finding herself submerged in a pool of bodily excrescence, is likely to drown, not in her own tears, but in her own vomit. And it is also possible, as Gilead argues, for the frame to refuse us narrative consolation. In these terms, our very removal into the alternative world of the fantasy narrative will inevitably undermine the 'return frame' also, reducing it to an equal or even deeper fictionality whereby what turns out to be no more than a mere *simulation* of closure actually 'disrupts rather than smoothly concludes [the] linear socialization plot'.[22]

What is often undervalued, in this sense, is the extent to which the 'loss of a comprehensible space-time frame'[23] in the *Alice* texts opens them up to postmodernist discourses. For in these texts 'truth' (insofar as it has any place here) becomes divorced from its usual partner, 'authority'. Unlike Bakhtinian readings of carnival, which transgress the limits (but therefore accept the power) of authority, here authority is foregrounded as having only the power with which we choose to endow it. In this sense, truth becomes part of the Carrollian game, whose rules are entirely self-generating and thus self-legitimating. But again, this is the very essence of all games, for we have already seen that playing, playing up and playing about are all means of really playing with the rules themselves. In terms of the political issues that we having been addressing, this takes on a cynical (perhaps even a sinister) perspective which Carroll shrugs off through jesting and riddles. Nevertheless, there are very important issues at stake. Even in the context of warfare we construct games in which 'friend and foe [are] indistinguishable . . . the goals seemingly impossible to articulate . . . heroic acts and base behavior hard to differentiate.'[24] This is the irony of Carroll's own military manoeuvres. In a book where guards double up as croquet hoops (W, 111), where a Lion and a Unicorn fight for a crown they cannot win (LG, 283) and where soldiers charge out of a wood only in order that they will fall over each other and land in an entangled heap of bodies (LG, 277–8), we see a prophetic manifestation of Baudrillard's perceptions of culture as an embodiment of the play of simulacra. In this respect these futile battles and conquests are precisely of the same order as Alice's memories of 'trying to box her own ears for having cheated herself in a game of croquet she was playing against herself' (W, 32–3). In both *Alice* texts the game is all there is and only the frame narrative functions to suggest anything else.

## The Child, Knowledge and Inevitable Loss

According to Beverly Clark, although the Victorian age tended to idealize childhood, intrinsically connecting it with innocence and goodness, it was nevertheless also the case that children were perceived to be inherently 'tainted' by original sin and thus, like society, requiring restraint in order to civilize and humanize them.[25] Whatever else one says about Carroll's work, it is evident that he valorized and celebrated the erotic dimensions of childhood in a manner that, while acknowledging and exploring Victorian perspectives, nevertheless transcended them in order to push back the limit(ation)s of children's fiction. Perhaps it is not surprising, then, that one of the central motifs that connects these two texts is simultaneously taken from traditional sources and manipulatively adapted to a more complex exploration of the nature of female identity. This, of course, is the motif of Eve, which though explicitly pivotal to Carter's novel is also implicitly important to *Wonderland* and, towards the end of *Looking-Glass*, is alluded to in the shape of the repeated falls from grace suffered by the White Knight and his attempt to rectify some aspects of loss (in this case hair loss) by means of the invention of a tree (of knowledge): 'First you take an upright stick . . . Then you make your hair creep up it, like a fruit-tree . . . things never fall *upwards*, you know' (LG, 299). That Alice, by the end of this scene, becomes queen and finds herself in the flower-garden is clearly significant. For in *Wonderland* it is primarily her relationship to that beautiful but unattainable garden from which she is banished because of her bodily transgressions, that the Edenic references are fully explored. In some ways, in fact, it is the garden, rather than the tea-party (as some critics claim) that functions as the presiding metaphor for this text. So Alice's desire to gain access to this becomes the primary motivation for her narrative journey and the only motivation she has for self-willed metamorphosis. But it is not merely its utopian qualities that render it Edenic here. According to Anita Moss, we can also read the garden as being 'chaotic' and as a metaphorical statement of the child's false view of adulthood as a libertarian if carefully controlled world.[26] In that sense these narratives are a similarly Edenic journey into knowledge, and Carroll insists on this being represented in the most extreme of empirical terms, namely 'what could be reported, observed, measured and classified'.[27] This is undoubtedly borne out by the manner in which Alice addresses many of the characters she encounters on her travels, from the caterpillar who is 'exactly three inches high' (W, 72) to the previously mentioned 'four thousand two hundred and seven' soldiers (LG, 276–7). But it is in her encounter with the Cheshire Cat that she ultimately learns the postmodern belief that knowledge defies (indeed evades) empirical precepts and laws. Perhaps, then, Alice is one of the first truly postmodern fictional constructs, for her real journey involves tracing a route out of empirical fact into one of complete narrative uncertainty. And in this sense it shares a clear boundary with Carter's novel, both locating such secular interrogations within an ill-fitting backdrop of Christian originary mythology.

In *Wonderland*, this centres around a temptation to partake suggested by the aforementioned caterpillar who, sitting on his mushroom, encourages Alice to take a bite, not exactly of forbidden fruit, but certainly of a magic mushroom. Alice, the first bite giving her an unpleasant sense of shrinking, quickly bites again and, as a result, finds herself 'high as a kite' in the tree-tops. Here, Alice comes face to face with a bird and its nest, the eggs themselves reminding us that this is a book that pushes simultaneously in two directions: forwards into maturation and backwards into origins (hence the number of allusions to growing, shrinking or fading away into nothing). But a number of additional reversals also become clear. Despite Alice and the bird's shared belief that the former has, as well as being the Eve substitute, become serpent-like in form, it is the bird that makes the hissing noise (W, 75). This appears to be the final textual metamorphosis, as Alice's rebelling body becomes oppressor and victim, knowing and unknowing. And yet if Alice's simultaneous identification as Eve and Serpent appears anomalous and mythically inaccurate, a closer reading reveals its political legitimacy. For not only, in biblical terms, are woman and serpent paired up through 'enmity',[28] but also, for the Victorian moralist at least, woman metamorphoses into seducer and serpent at will and, by extension, transforms man into Eve (as is more imaginatively reworked in Carter's novel).

I began this chapter by arguing that Carter's and Carroll's texts both share a pivotal concern with the notion of female subjectivity. In Carter's case this is, of course, depicted in a hard-hitting, graphic manner whereas, as one would expect, Carroll's texts are far more cautious in their treatment of gender issues. But interesting points still come to light here, perhaps because of the careful encoding of desire that takes place within both. This is vociferously (even defensively) resisted by Batchelor, who repeatedly clings to Alice's textually specified age of seven years in order to assert '[Alice] is *not* "adolescent". The *Alice* books are . . . not about sexual growth'.[29] Nevertheless, in referring above to the structural patterning of these two texts as both a splitting and an internal folding, I am also tracing the outline of Irigaray's reading of female sexuality as a pair of lips placed in a continually contiguous relationship of the flesh: 'within herself, she is already two – but not divisible into one(s) – that caress each other'.[30] Batchelor has more to say on such issues. Referring to another remark by Auerbach, he retorts: '"Does it go too far to connect the mouth that presides over Alice's story to a looking-glass vagina?" Yes, it does, it is a crass and loathsome idea.'[31] But it is less the vagina that is of significance and more the pervasive orality which Irigaray recognizes to be encoded/enfolded within the suggested presence of vaginal lips. As Auerbach asserts, that Carroll persistently returns to such imagery implies that it is via this preoccupation, above all, that he 'probe[s] in all its complexity the underground world within the little girl's pinafore'.[32] Ironically, it is also this that enables the *Alice* texts to speak out against a Victorian culture that 'leave[s] room neither for women's sexuality, nor for women's imaginary, nor for women's language'.[33]

This is even implied from the start of *Looking Glass* as Alice intercepts the White King's writing. In Gilbert and Gubar's terms, this scene depicts the White King as the epitome of the literary patriarch, who: 'precisely because a writer "fathers" his text, his literary creations . . . are his possession, his property. Having defined them in language and thus generated them, he owns them, controls them, and encloses them on the printed page.'[34] That Alice is anxious about being brought under the 'spell' of a paternal writer/dreamer is made clear towards the end of the text, when she comments, 'I do hope it's my dream, and not the *Red* King's!' (LG, 293 – my emphasis). Wisely choosing to hit back at patriarchy via the rather more impotent White King, Alice, at this point invisible, usurps the 'father's' creativity by means of undermining his textual author/ity:

> she took hold of the end of the pencil, which came some way over his shoulder, and began writing for him. The poor King looked puzzled and unhappy, and struggled with the pencil for some time . . . but Alice was too strong for him, and at last he panted out 'My dear! I really must get a thinner pencil. I can't manage this one a bit'. (LG, 190)

Here, rather than Alice being 'penned up' or 'penned in', her castrating action seems to reinforce the validity of Gilbert and Gubar's opening questions: 'Is a pen a metaphorical penis?'.[35] For although Gardiner may characteristically dismiss such readings with the remark 'it is only by accident that a pencil in this scene is shaped the way it is',[36] his very choice of the phrase 'only an accident' here demonstrates his misunderstanding of the unconscious as well as the conscious influence that symbols have upon our reading of these texts.

Just as the wider socio-political concerns of the text should not be read as entirely subversive, so Carroll's resistance to female autonomy, even as he encodes it, comes to the forefront of the narrative. Indeed, it is this that leads Batchelor to argue against himself. Although extremely defensive about gender and, in particular, Alice's depiction as a sexualized being, he nevertheless correctly recognizes the predominance of female violence, aggression and matriarchal domination as a negative response to female subversiveness in these texts. What he misses is what this tells us about Alice herself. For Batchelor, this safely constrains Alice within the world of innocent childhood, separate from the type of 'shrieking sisterhood' we saw referred to in Chapter 3. But on the contrary, Alice's relationship to femininity is one that locates her *precisely* in adult terms, not because adult women *are* monsters, but because patriarchs such as Carroll feel them to be so. U.C. Knoepflmacher agrees that it is this that contextualizes Alice's own sexuality and the hostility she faces from so many of the male creatures.[37] And in these terms it is perfectly appropriate for this sexuality to be buried 'underground', for the real root of the female (as) grotesque is precisely that *'horror of nothing to see'*.[38] No wonder, then, that in a text which prioritizes the politics of naming and the playful slippages inherent in language, Alice is informed that there are no names for what are to be found in the murky depths of the forest 'down there' (LG, 222). In these terms we recognize a fearful rejoinder to the invisible threat of an approaching female sexuality which must be persuaded of the 'unspeakable' nature of its own nether regions.

Ironically, this results in an almost ubiquitous repression. By the time we reach the end of *Looking Glass* we have been consistently confronted by a panoply of impotent males: the White Knight, the fragile Humpty Dumpty and the 'whisker-less' White King (LG, 189), all of whom Knoepflmacher reads as inscribed versions of Carroll. Not inconsequentially, of course, these come to the fore only in contrast with '[a] determined girl who induces her own dreams of domination as crowned ruler of the matriarchal chessboard'.[39] But this is not to unproblematically assert Alice's dominance (even if she does find herself crowned Queen by the end). Her reign as 'mistress' comes at a price, and this turns out to be a very high one indeed. As we near the end and, by inference, Alice's puberty becomes imminent, she learns easily and 'naturally' to adapt to being named 'monster' by a Lion and a Unicorn (LG, 288), whilst simultaneously taking upon herself the servile role of the angel of the house, who 'very obediently got up, and carried the dish round, and the cake divided itself into three pieces as she did so' (LG, 290). As we have seen, woman can never be anything but monstrous to a patriarchal society petrified by her power. This is also the message of *The Passion of New Eve* where Eve/lyn the central protagonist and Tristessa, his/her idealised 'other', come together as mirrored doubles. Thus we find a multiple hybridisation of the female grotesque trapped like Alice, within the structures of a fantastic monstrosity, this being the inevitable price paid for full initiation into the realm of the adult world of the female erotic.

## Dystopian Landscapes and Dehumanized Forms

Conflicting geographies form the backdrop to Carter's mythological redefinitions in her tortured novel, *The Passion of New Eve.* In tension with the solidly factual landscape of the known (but foreign) continent of North America reside the futurist, dystopian speculations of cybernetic experimentation. Alongside the decentring of the fully gendered subject is a parallel decentring of spatial territory, where the desert becomes a place of rebirth and the city becomes a desert of death. Switching places with the fully developed body, the fully developed city of/after postmodernism becomes, in itself, a cybernetic structure within which 'the only tissue ... is that of the freeways ... an incessant transurbanistic, tissue' and the corpuscules within this tapestry of veins and arteries comprise 'thousands of cars ... coming from nowhere, going nowhere: an immense collective act ... without objectives'.[40] Of course, as Carter's earlier novel *The Magic Toyshop* (1967) tells us, woman herself is an 'America ... [a] new found land', where received and enclosing mythologies of the body can be reconceptualized in new and fantastic forms.[41] In this sense Carter's relocation of the historical past as dystopian future transforms itself into a topographical landscape upon which the power-games of virtual maternal omnipotence play out their sadistic fantasies in a defamiliarized gangland state. Iain Chambers, in his postmodern reading of cultural identity, refers to the act of journeying to the United States as 'life lived in the third person, as myth, as dream, as cinema'.[42] And, in *The Passion of New Eve,* mythology does indeed combine with the cinematic and the fantastic, but here it produces a first-person narrator split into a singular third person within him/herself. In this respect, like so many others, Eve/lyn is not dissimilar to Tristessa him/herself: 'She had been the dream itself made flesh though the flesh I knew her in was not flesh itself but only a moving picture of flesh, real but not substantial' (PNE, 7–8).

For Chambers, the city functions as a computer interface, information highways carrying traffic on the Internet. But Carter returns to the image of the grotesque, restructuring the urban jungle as mounds of rotting flesh. In true Bakhtinian tradition, in *The Passion of New Eve* we read that 'by the time the winter was over, [Zero and his wives] believed the cities would all have broken open like boils' (PNE, 98). Living off and as rubbish, their bodies have become the city displaced. That Evelyn also perceives Leilah to be a gift from the city (PNE, 36) implies that women and the city are of the same essence: 'she seemed to manufacture about herself an inviolable space ... So she led me deep into the geometric labyrinth of the heart of the city, into an arid world of ruins and abandoned construction sites, the megapolitan heart that did not beat any more' (PNE, 21). This connection between the body of the woman and the body of the city is significant for two reasons. First, it reverses the usual association between the phallic erections of urban architecture and its ability to intimidate its female inhabitants. Secondly, if we combine Chambers's reading of it with Carter's we find that the close connection between the two exists, in part, from their shared sense of cybernetic construction. Nevertheless, for Chambers, material existence bows out in the face of a metaphorical discourse of city-limit, for, as he puts it, 'The metropolis no longer orders space but time ... Here sense is connected to speed.'[43] Undoubtedly the culturally constructed horrors of the city are uncontainable by its limits, and fleeing the city merely brings Evelyn to Beulah where images of the city (like a 3-D cinema screen) pursue him, transform him and ultimately overpower him. Thus are we coerced into fictional explorations of 'a world we have made but have not yet recognized'.[44] Consequently, whereas the *Alice* texts can be read in terms of the politics of the body, *The Passion of New Eve* opens up the debate far more explicitly in terms of the body politic. As Chambers comments, 'our bodies – dressed, undressed, disguised, accentuated ... are moulded and transformed' only through cultural means.[45] Certainly, most of the characters we encounter in this narrative comply, in one way or another, with Bakhtinian readings of the 'extraordinary' human being: 'Some of them are half human, half animal ... This is an entire gallery of images with bodies of mixed parts ... All this constitutes a wild anatomical fantasy.'[46] So Tristessa is only half human while Mother, with her 'bull-like pillar' of a neck and tiers of nipples like a sow (PNE, 59), is a grand hybrid of human and animal. In addition, as we follow Eve/lyn's tortuous journey through his anatomical transition s/he, in his/her totality, becomes a mixture of body parts and the entire novel, indeed, 'a wild anatomical fantasy'.

We have seen that Bakhtin's work on carnival and the grotesque adds an ideological dimension to the type of transgression theories that Bataille and Foucault have expanded upon. This particular combination is especially well suited to the exploration of overtly politicized fantastic fictions. During the first five chapters of *The Passion of New Eve* Carter gradually immerses us in a realm of defamiliarization and reader disturbance which illustrates this in graphic detail. Gradually coerced through realism, surrealism, mythology and science fiction, only by the time we reach chapter 5 have we been fully initiated into the realms of the fantastic. This is just part of the narrative journey. Employing the typical conventions of the picaresque novel, Eve/lyn is a presiding anti-hero of fleshly excess. Shifting between one physical location into a second of vast contrast, Eve/lyn is forced to encounter and question his/her own identity and radically reassess his/her situation in the first world: 'There is no safe place here; there are, however, many maps of possibility.'[47] Indeed, the moment that Evelyn sets foot in 'the New World', this 'primitive society of the future',[48] we find him confronted with a visual feast of the flesh in all its most corrupt and grotesque manifestations. Graphic embodiment of the dark side of a Bakhtinian carnival, murder, rape, prostitution and pornography provide the sinister cultural geography of this dark urban space where even hotel-life is carnivalesque: 'The lobby filled with firemen, policemen and disaster-loving night-walkers who drifted in . . . while the roused guests in their pyjamas wandered about like somnambulists, wringing their hands. Beneath a crystal chandelier, a woman vomited into a paper bag' (PNE, 11). As part of this, populating the sulphurous miasma of this sick cityscape are a plague of black rats and a plague of black whores whose function and form seem frequently interchangeable: 'I could not slip down to the corner to buy a pack of cigarettes from the kiosk without kicking aside half a dozen of the sleek, black monsters as they came snapping round my ankles. They would line the staircase like a guard of honour to greet me when I came home to the walk-up, cold-water apartment I soon rented' (PNE, 12). These 'rats', 'fat as piglets and vicious as hyenas' (PNE, 17), begin the shape-shifting theme of monstrosity that structures this book. Thus Evelyn, tracking Leilah as 'fully-furred' prey, becomes, in true carnivalesque tradition, a violent hybrid of the masculine and the bestial: 'nothing but cock . . . My full-fleshed and voracious beak tore open the poisoned wound of love between her thighs' (PNE, 25).

Few novels more clearly demonstrate the disturbing political possibilities of supposedly liberating carnival excess. And here it perpetually victimizes women. While both male oppressors (Evelyn and Zero) are clearly dismissed for their bestial practices, the women exist as their mirroring double. Like Lessing's city rat-dogs, the rat-pigs of Carter's urban sewer function as an anthropomorphic image of the woman as filth. Thus Zero, the 'pig lover', 'only honoured them because they were gross' (PNE, 94), much the same being true of his motivations for dis-honouring his seven wives. Faced with the pigs as emotional and perhaps even erotic competition, the women's only choice is to compete for his attention on bestial terms: 'Some of the girls chose their favourite method of desecration, pulled down their dungarees and pissed copiously on the floor, while others tore off every stitch of clothing and danced obscene naked dances . . . contemptuously flourishing their ringed holes at him and brandishing mocking buttocks. The clamour and gesticulations were those of the monkey house' (PNE, 128). Throughout the ages, of course, western philosophy and religion have drawn a distinction between the soul and the body, the spirit and the flesh, always assigning women to the body/flesh side of the coupling, and preferencing the soul/mind half of the equation as morally superior. Despite the aforementioned scenes, Carter's choice of title for this novel immediately signals her intention to deconstruct such clearly defined cultural polarities, the word 'passion' being one of the few Christian terms that articulates the very taboo that spirituality vehemently strives to suppress. Like Freud's term *unheimlich*, 'passion' simultaneously embodies two seemingly irreconcilable meanings: 'the sufferings and death of a Christian martyr' and 'intense sexual love'. This, in itself, transgresses the prohibitive limitations of the words of St Paul: 'if you live according to the flesh, you will die; but if by the Spirit you put to death the misdeeds of the body, you will live.'[49] So, in the true spirit of Bataille, Carter plays with the sacred in order to explore sacrilege. But also in keeping with transgressive approaches, Carter does not simply manipulate the contradictions of biblical doctrine in order to dismiss them. More interestingly, she creatively employs those contradictions, drawing upon the terminology of both Old and New Testaments in order to set up a new creation myth: the myth of the New Eve (a fallen man who finds himself a new woman, a new mother and, in the process, the new oppressive church of Zero and the fundamentalist 'souldiers' of Christ). For Tetel, carnival maintains a rather more rejuvenating trajectory than Bakhtin acknowledges. In his terms: 'From chaos and utopian freedom is meant to emerge a new order, a different spiritual and intellectual structure of society.'[50] Certainly, in these terms, Carter's narrative functions to challenge received ideas about women, spirituality, and female sexuality (and in the process becomes a means of exploring the relationship between the fantastic, the mythological and phallocentric reality). What is less certain is the extent to which we *can* read Carter's bleak, dystopian vision as unproblematically renewing.

Chapters 1 and 2 of Carter's novel deal at some length with two of the most common types of fantasy held by men about women as flesh (or more accurately, about constructed images of women as flesh): the idolization of the screen and stage actress and the obsessive allure of the eroticized woman. This returns us to the concept of passion. Quite apart from the doctrinal issue, secular readings also set up the spirit and flesh as two parts of an antithesis. The fleshly is that which is tangible, material and 'real', whereas the spirit suggests ephemera, the intangible, and thus the 'unreal'. By exploring the complexities of the relationship between desire and the body Carter offers, instead of binary oppositions, a plurality of possibilities. The primary means via which she does this is through the metaphor of cinema, which, as Carter herself admits, is to her a powerful church: 'I'm not in the least a religious person, as I think is very well known. But there is something sacred about the cinema, which is to do with it being public; to do with people going together, with the intention of visualising, experiencing the same experience, having the same revelation.'[51] If, as Baudrillard suggests, America is interested in '*one single passion only: the passion for images*',[52] then what better way to secularize worship than through the image of the stage/screen goddess? Like Baudrillard, Carter depicts life in America as life on the giant screen: 'All manner of movies ran through my head when I first heard I'd got the job there – hadn't Tristessa herself conquered New York in *The Lights of Broadway* before she died of, that time, leukaemia?' (PNE, 10). Evelyn's confusion of screen and 'real-life' scenarios here results in an ironic commentary upon the mortality of the body. Tristessa, in these terms, is born (as image) perpetually to die, but only in order to give a truly cinematic lie to 'the total certainty of [the body's] non- resurrection'.[53] Consequently, if, as Baudrillard suggests elsewhere, religious iconography paradoxically points to the non-existence of God in 'enact[ing] his death and his disappearance in the epiphany of his representations',[54] then celluloid provides another iconographic substitute in the paradoxical form of flesh as spiritual simulacrum.

Carter, it seems, has an answer for those theorists of cyberspace who argue that 'The real problem is the skin . . . Skin as an organ is just very, very limited.'[55] She retaliates by turning it from a porous film into an impermeable screen. But the idolization of the female screen body involves, in itself, a difficult paradox. The mediation of celluloid necessitates the subject's complete dehumanization into an objectified other by turning living, fully rounded, three-dimensional flesh and blood into a two-dimensional projected screen image. Tristessa is a particularly poignant example of this, because if an essential part of this dehumanization process involves the concealment or removal of all kinds of unpleasant bodily characteristics, Tristessa takes this to obvious extremes, concealing his penis within his own anal opening 'so that my mound was as smooth as a young girl's' (PNE, 141). Only as an extension of Bakhtin's concept of the fleshless classical body can Tristessa as screen image be any kind of human form: 'That which protrudes, bulges, sprouts, or branches off . . . is eliminated, hidden, or moderated. All orifices of the body are closed . . . The opaque surface and the body's "valleys" acquire an essential meaning as the border of a closed individuality that does not merge with other bodies and with the world.'[56] Where, according to psychoanalysis, sexuality remains the mainstay of the self – our site of repression or the framework for the unconscious, the source of our pleasures and also our fears – for the postmodernist (as for Tristessa), sexuality has become something to be 'into' or something to 'display' rather than something to perform or to share or even to have. Instead of repressions, 'Things fade into the distance faster and faster in the rear-view mirror', an inevitability, perhaps, in a simulated 'skin-deep' society with no room for the psyche. So narcissism is replaced by a 'frantic self-referentiality . . . which [simply] hooks up like with like',[57] and Eve/lyn, seemingly driven by his libido, is in fact simply magnetically/cybernetically drawn towards the only being who could, in these terms, provide him with precisely the same 'endless sequence of reflections . . . [which produce] a double drag' (PNE, 132). So this man who masquerades as a woman, confronted by an adoring man who has been transformed into a woman, responds by donning a layer of masculinity in order to permit sexuality to echo biology and effect (in the most anti-conventional of ways) a fully heterosexual coupling.

But the mirror that lies at the heart of this trickery is a central image throughout Carter's work. Central, indeed, to women's writing as a whole and fantasy fiction in particular, this symbol derives versatility from its ability to permit or deny entry into alternative realities, to function as an interrogation marker for identity and its particularly oppressive potential for women under patriarchy. These applications come together in this novel, most particularly in the architecture of Tristessa's palace: 'Grand transparencies lodged there – swollen, tear-shaped forms of solid glass with dimples and navels and blind depressions in their sides, the abortions of expressive surfaces' (PNE, 111). These 'transparencies' (the filmic analogy is not inconsequential) suddenly shift into flashing mirrors as light deflects off them, taking on the image of the absent body that inhabits their structure. Ironic inverse of that evanescent form, these 'swollen' shapes parody Tristessa's lack of corporeality, just as the 'navels' they possess come to supplant the originary form that s/he lacks. But if we have been trained to think that the mirror is lack, here, in another ironic reversal, it is via 'parted strands of silver' (PNE, 127) that we see a presence where we expect an absence of Lacan's transcendent signifier. Only Tristessa as self disappears into a shower of shards: 'you had become nothing, a wraith that left only traces of a silver powder on the hands that clutched helplessly at your perpetual vanishings' (PNE, 110). So Tristessa's palace, the novel's centrepiece, sits like a presiding gothic mansion, its necrophiliac exhibition of corpse-like mannequins functioning as an ironic commentary on the cybernetic surgery of flesh-turned-plastic that haunts our television, video and cinema screens. Chief inhabitant of this simulated mausoleum, Tristessa presides as ghost not only over his/her own mansion, but over the span of the narrative itself. In a novel whose only destination seems to be the death of the flesh, it is with this absent presence that Eve/lyn leaves us: 'He himself often comes to me in the night . . . after many, many embraces, he vanishes when I open my eyes' (PNE, 191).

The ghost analogy is not unimportant, for, as Baudrillard reminds us, 'In America the spectral does not refer to phantoms or to dancing ghosts, but to the spectrum into which light disperses.'[58] In this sense, Carter's usage of the screen as skin has obvious implications for cinema imagery. Quite aside from the fact that Tristessa's existence resides only in beams of projected light, his/her own skin mimics this pattern, becoming 'so insubstantial only the phenomenon of persistence of vision could account for his presence' (PNE, 147). In addition, like its biological poor substitute, synthesized skin has multiple layers and projected on to the epidermal screen like a technological tattoo is the imprint of the celluloid image, the 'made-up' complexion of Tristessa the simulacrum. This is important to our reading of the end of the narrative. For the block of amber retrieved in the cave scene seems, on the face of it, a commentary upon time and evolution as linear and progressive. And yet earlier in the narrative, amber is used as a metaphorical comparison with the 'innumerable spools of celluloid from which [Tristessa's] being could be extracted and endlessly recycled in a technological eternity' (PNE, 119). Fittingly, we have to return to the opening page to remember that only once 'the desolating passage of time [is] made visible in the rain upon the screen, audible in the sound track' (PNE, 5) will the face of Tristessa begin to decay.

For postmodernists such as Scott Bukatman, the cinema screen operates as 'a space without centre . . . an eye suddenly distinct from its corporality . . . in other words, from its subjectivity'.[59] But such a belief can only exist where the relationship between body, self and subjectivity can easily be taken for granted. As feminist research into both the gaze and body politics makes clear, only patriarchal readings of the female anatomy can inscribe its form as a space without centre, and it is usually the female who is the object of the gaze. An early scene detailing Evelyn's memories of a visit to a London cinema admirably illustrates the point. Obsessed with the fleshless eroticism of the waif-like Tristessa, he turns the powers of memory into a pornographic fantasy:

> When she perceived how Tristessa's crucifiction by brain fever moved me, the girl who was with me got to her knees in the dark on the dirty floor of the cinema, among the cigarette ends and empty potato crisp bags and trodden orangeade containers and sucked me off. My gasps were drowned by the cheers and applause of the unruly section of the audience as Tyrone Power, in too much hair-cream for a convincing Heathcliff, roared his grief over the cardboard moor in a torrent of studio rain. (PNE, 9)

The absurdist humour of this unlikely anecdote is nevertheless compromised by its disturbing dynamics. So we have the perfect wish-fulfilment combination: the fantasy vision of an untouchable other combined with a faceless, bodiless 'sucker' who pleasures his flesh without making demands. Just as his gaze is literally unobstructed so, more significantly, its politics are uncomplicated. The fantasy necessitates his position as looker, Tristessa's as the 'looked-at' and the depersonalized vessel of the unnamed accomplice as the competitor for the attentions of his flesh. The fact that this reads as a wish-fulfilment day-dream matches the location of the body as a whole. For this, too, is no more than an endlessly evasive and shape-shifting illusion, only fixable through the spotlight of the mind's eye.

This is only part of the significance of the gaze in this text. In addition, Alan Dundes's essay on the 'evil eye' can help us understand precisely how the linkage between mythology, the fantastic and ideological concepts of the gaze starts to become fully formulated in this novel. At the opening of his argument, Dundes defines the evil eye as 'the idea that an individual ... has the power ... to cause harm to another individual ... merely by looking at ... that person'. But let us then consider the motivation for its usage. According to Dundes, among those circumstances that might 'invite or provoke' such an attack are 'good fortune, good health, or good looks'.[60] It would seem, therefore, that the three characteristics said to incite such attention are due to a perceived imbalance of attributes between parties which leads, in turn, to envy and revenge. Dundes is careful, throughout, to describe both possessor and victim in strictly gender-neutral terms. But although envy does seem to be the only logical explanation for assault in the case of fortune and health, another possibility exists in the case of 'good looks'. As even Dundes acknowledges, there is a presiding cultural association linking eye and evil-eye imagery with the masculine perspective, partly through its association with the symbol of the sun and partly because many of the cultural artifacts used in such rituals have 'unmistakable phallic elements' inscribed upon them. This is not surprising, for we know that the holder of the gaze (in cultural terms) is usually male and heterosexual and the objectified 'other' a female generally considered to be in possession of 'good looks'. Yet this makes the relationship between beholder and beheld unlikely to be one based upon envy alone. Perhaps, instead, it is actually one of fear. For it is not unimportant that Dundes, alluding to the relationship between 'attacker' and 'victim', uses the ambiguous phrase 'invite or provoke'. In his terms, it seems, having something that the beholder desires and/or fears at least partly excuses the actions of the latter. The analogy is clear. Women provoke the attentions of men, not because men resent women's good looks, but because they simultaneously desire and fear engulfment by the power of their bodies: 'Of course psychoanalysts have also argued that the eye could be a female symbol with 'the pupil representing the vagina, the lids the labia, and the lashes the pubic hair'.[61] In the context of *The Passion of New Eve*, one need look no further than the symbol of the *vagina dentata* adopted as the insignia of the freedom fighters known as 'The Women' to find that Evelyn's own evil eye is more than avenged in these terms. How ironic that Dundes argues it to be envy over *having* something that is the issue, for, as Freud makes clear, women have no-'thing' at all and, quite neatly, Eve/lyn's wishes, in this respect, really do come true. He looks for so long that he ends up with that very same no-thing, given to/taken from him by the ultimate 'female symbol', Mother herself. In embodying the *vagina dentata*, she forms the epitome of that oral aggression which Dundes perceives at the root of all motivations behind the evil eye. No wonder that, just as Dundes's victim suffers from 'loss of appetite ... vomiting and fever',[62] so Eve/lyn is 'spat out', his 'appetite' reduced to a dangling appendage, for the real feverishness of passionate heat belongs to her, the most oppressive presence of all.

## Birthing, Mythologies and Nowhere to Call Home

This eroticized heat drags us inexorably back to the wide open spaces of desert terrain. For Baudrillard, the function of the American desert is to 'denote the emptiness, the radical nudity that is the background to every human institution' whilst also embodying 'culture as a mirage and as the perpetuity of the simulacrum'.[63] In Carter's work it is almost as if the function of the desert is to provide a type of blank canvas against which a variety of graphic horrors and nightmares can play out their part. For postmodernists in general, 'no staging of bodies, no performance can be without its control screen',[64] and, in a novel structured via cinematic motifs, the desert becomes the ultimate stage/screen backdrop to a variety of bodily performances. Indeed, although in many ways a 'road-movie' novel (within which Eve/lyn is not simply a questor, but for much of the narrative on the run), it is almost as if the vast panorama of the landscape provides a static spatio-temporality in which a variety of antagonists come into focus only in order to move away again. Eve/lyn, on the other hand, though desperately struggling to make progress, actually remains stuck in his/her tracks (as is epitomized by him/her running out of fuel not once but four times). Indeed, Eve/lyn is the simulated embodiment of the postmodern crisis: 'Perhaps, after . . . wandering in the metropolis, and then almost getting lost in the desert, it is now time to go home. But then, again, it may be that there is no home, no fixed abode waiting for us.'[65] It is this aspect of Carter's novel which tends to challenge Csicsery-Ronay, Jr.'s reading of science/speculative fiction as intrinsically redemptive.[66] Far more interested in demythologizing than in resolving, Carter denies the apocalypse which might pave the way for renewal. Instead she provides us with what Haraway refers to as 'not a "happy ending" . . . but a non-ending . . . [in which] none of the narratives of masculinist, patriarchal apocalypse will do. The System is not closed; the sacred image of the same is not coming.'[67] In consequence, not only is Mother shown to be artificial, spurious and ultimately absent, but the birth and death that are inscribed in her body take up an equally futile position in cultural terms. Thus the 'grotto-esque' space of the dissecting room is simply reproduced in what we might refer to as Mother's grotto of impotence at the end of the text. In real terms, Eve/lyn's defining geography turns out to be the topography of his/her body and his search only superficially a search for Mother: 'The earth has been scalped, flayed; it is peopled only with echoes. The world shines and glistens, reeks and swelters till its skin peels, flakes, cracks, blisters. I have found a landscape that matches the landscape of my heart' (PNE, 41).

Baudrillard's *America*, first published in 1986, could almost have been based upon Carter's fictional narrative. As a novel intrinsically concerned with theoretically eclectic explorations, *The Passion of New Eve* brilliantly prefigures the work that Baudrillard and Haraway have subsequently accomplished in the related areas of the philosophy of simulation and cyborgian politics. For Baudrillard, America (more specifically the United States of America) epitomizes and embodies the postmodern preoccupation with the processes and order of the simulacra: 'The Americans ... have no sense of simulation. They are themselves simulation in its most developed state.' Like Carter, Baudrillard also juxtaposes city and desert, structuring his text around the motif of travel – a travelling that seeks a geography of time, space and cultural essence. But there is another important characteristic that they share, and this is their refusal to situate themselves safely within an 'acceptable' political framework. Solipsistically drawn into the pleasures of the game, Baudrillard calmly asserts that 'Politics frees itself in the spectacle, in the all-out advertising effect' of society.[68] In many ways this is written into the spectacular topography of *The Passion of New Eve*, its endlessly cinematic preoccupations tending to aestheticize the horrific violence they portray:

> The first thing I saw ... was, in a shop window, an obese plaster gnome squatly perched on a plaster toadstool ... The next thing I saw were rats, black as buboes, gnawing at a heap of garbage. And the third thing I saw was a black man running down the middle of the road as fast as he could go, screaming and clutching his throat, an unstoppable cravat, red in colour and sticky, mortal, flowed out from beneath his fingers. (PNE, 10)

As if the third of these images is not horrific enough in itself, Carter transforms it into something inhumanly chilling through this precise collocation of visual fragments. What is so profoundly disturbing is the way in which it contextualizes racial violence as both kitsch (the presiding artwork of the postmodern), through its association with the squat gnome, and then as 'ethnic cleansing', through the implied paralleling of the man with the rats which are 'black as buboes'. Of course Carter, like Baudrillard, is pointing out the horror of this, but she does so in a manner that remains highly unresolved. For these images are only very slightly defamiliarized by situating their dystopian application within a televisual realism that is far too close for comfort to the world of today. This also returns us to the postmodern. While such scenes clearly come under Carter's own definition of the surreal – 'looking at the world as though it were strange' – they fit Baudrillard's definition of the hyperreal even better. In these terms such images can *only* be understood as being '"obscenely" on display, moving endlessly ... across a surface where there is no control or stabilising depth'.[69] Undoubtedly, then, this novel shares Baudrillard's desperate cynicism. And yet at times it is only through such cynicism that we find genuinely illuminating insights into twentieth-century life: 'Driving is a spectacular form of amnesia. Everything is to be discovered, everything to be obliterated.' For our purposes the most significant impact of this derives from the effect it has upon our understanding of the fantastic. In a landscape that has *become* a science-fiction backdrop, where is the place in which fantasy is to be found? What role might wish-fulfilment play in a country in which 'among the ... monotony of the human species, lies the tragedy of a utopian dream made reality'? Here, even the very notion of the dream, that very basis of our inner phantasy, has been supplanted by its technological simulacrum, the hologram: 'Everything [being] destined to reappear as simulation. Landscape as photography, women as the sexual scenario ... terrorism as fashion.'[70] Without its wish-fulfilment content, the dream structure is simply a cultural bombardment of clashing motifs, its inheritance a mere set of anarchic displacements. This is the culture that Carter takes on.

Of course this issue of inheritance returns us to origins, an issue again embedded within the conflicting landscapes of the text. So the desert becomes the place of Eve/lyn's first communion, Sophia giving him 'a few brackish mouthfuls' of water and 'a few wafers of a synthetic ... bread or biscuit-like substance' (PNE, 46), while, according to Bukatman, 'that there should be something beyond the city, is as heretical as imagining a time before time began'.[71] Nevertheless, in striving to replace god, language, biology and the body with a series of endlessly free-floating and competing counter-structures, it is this that renders Baudrillard's *America* the obvious illustration of the postmodern condition: 'America ducks the question of origins; it cultivates no origin or mythical authenticity; it has no past ... it lives in a perceptual present.'[72] Even this, of course, relies upon a fabricated artifice, a wilful and precarious sleight of hand which banishes its own 'native' history in order to call up endlessly replicating celluloid simulations of it. As Baudrillard himself admits, America is actually obsessed with the nature of origins, even as it tries to render them absent. This is precisely what happens in *The Passion of New Eve*, where one of the central issues revolves around what happens to our identity when our origins (and the organs that produced them) are irreversibly excised. Thus, although a number of these characters appear to be cut adrift from personal time and space, their own histories are clearly recalled. Leilah, we discover, herself a version of that culturally suppressed originary mother Lilith, 'was seventeen; and her mother ... somewhere in California' (PNE, 26); Betty Boop 'had been a hairdresser's apprentice in ... Kansas City' (PNE, 133) and even Mother, dressing in a white coat, gives Eve/lyn 'a vague glimpse of her past self ... the surgeon ... the medical student; before that?' (PNE, 75). The point is, of course, that there *is* a 'before that', despite the precariousness of present and future time in the text. Consequently, although Evelyn may refabricate a fictional autobiography about a 'cruel mother who kept me locked in the coal-shed, and a lustful step-father' (PNE, 87), the chosen fairy-tale structure belies a need for compensation for its own lack of textual author/ity by compulsively searching out Oedipal connections (an awareness fully demonstrated through Eve/lyn's embarrassment on being confronted by the Snow White-like Tristessa in the guise of psychoanalyst: '"Tell me about your childhood," he said to me, comfortably enough . . . [But] how could I reply?' (PNE, 143)).

In this respect, Haraway's critique of conventional readings of 'natural birthing' actually functions as a critique of Lacanian psychoanalysis:

> This productionism is about man the tool-maker and -user, whose highest technical production is himself . . . He gains access to this wondrous technology with a subject-constituting, self-deferring, and self-splitting entry into language, light, and law. Blinded by the sun, in thrall to the father, reproduced in the sacred image of the same, his reward is that he is self-born, an autotelic copy.[73]

Here, the patriarchal analyst (tool-maker and -user) masquerades (with the help of mirrors) as the magician/conjuror who, in the guise of healing and revealing, simply produces narcissistic reflections of his own projected image. Instead of this Carter, seemingly before her time, challenges in the clearest of postmodern terms those Enlightenment beliefs in 'the sacred image of the same' perpetuated by mythological versions of 'masculinist self-birthing'.[74] Ironically, her chosen means for this lies in depicting a mother goddess who produces a being which, while of the same sex, is most certainly not made in her own monstrous image. So, although we might accept that mythology, postmodernism and the psychoanalytic share a fundamental belief that 'A past that is not yet known is a form of the future',[75] this does not reconcile the tensions inherent within them. Carter, in line with postmodern theory, depicts Eve/lyn's journey not as an abandonment of the present, but as an extension of our *dialogue* with it. This is also what Rackin, from a very different perspective, refers to as 'a voyage into [our] own hearts of darkness, without the old maps, without even a reasonable hope of replacing them'. The implied reference to Conrad's *Heart of Darkness* (1902) is by no means inappropriate here.[76] Intrinsic to Carter's journey is an exploration of cultural identity through the discourse of the self as irrevocably 'foreign', at the same time that she also refuses to trace a path which would completely negate the past. Indeed, part of this temporal concern to extend a dialogue with the future *necessitates*, alongside it, a re-evaluation of the past. Symbolic almost to the point of being laboured, then, Carter's own cave scene is quite obviously the landscape of Eve/lyn's return 'home': 'I edged my way forward, flat as a flounder. Every movement necessitated the most extreme exertion: I was soon drenched with sweat. The passage was choked, airless, dank, and a faint reek of rotten eggs hovered above . . . I was making progress, pressed as I was like a cheese, oozing forward' (PNE, 179–80). Right down to the reference to rotten eggs and cheese (produced from sour milk), this is the body of the redundant mother and Eve the prodigal son turned daughter, forced to return. Home, then, exists on a number of levels: bodily (the cave as birth canal), geologically (the rockface as map of human civilization), and environmentally (from the buzz of the city as human construct to the peace of the cave as natural refuge).

If we take Tetel's utopian line of argument regarding the carnivalesque, we might be tempted to read this as an 'emergence of the pristine' (for surely that, at least, describes New Eve) 'from a necessary passage through the old' and 'the forbidden' (such being the taboo surrounding this intimate contact with the body of the mother).[77] But Carter is as resistant to simple utopianism as she is to the redundancy of *cliché*, and this scene poses far more questions than it offers answers. As Eve herself acknowledges, 'My return to the world only confirms my permanent exile' (PNE, 180). Mother is not where we might expect to find her and Eve can no more return to a mother she never had than we, like Alice, can return through the Lacanian looking-glass: 'There was a mirror propped against the rugged wall, a fine mirror in a curly, gilt frame; but the glass was broken, cracked right across many times so it reflected nothing, was a bewilderment of splinters and I could not see myself nor any portion of myself in it' (PNE, 181). Seemingly in keeping with its initial contextualization within alchemical discourse (both appearing to conspire against any sense of authenticity or genuine sources), as if to re-emphasize this search for a compulsive reminiscence, a proliferation of DNA-like spirals are encoded within the novel's textual architecture, straddling the divide between city and desert. Thus Evelyn, hot in pursuit, is drawn by Leilah's 'small, cold hand up [a] spiralling staircase, up, up, up' (PNE, 25), a scene later augmented in Tristessa's Glass Palace as Zero, his dog and Evelyn chase Tristessa up another spiral staircase (PNE, 120). But this is a scene put into reverse at Beulah, where we are required to 'Descend lower. You have not reached the end of the maze, yet' (PNE, 49) as 'The corridor wound round and round in descending spirals' (PNE, 56). For Beulah sends origins into full reverse 'thrust': 'what's become of the slut of Harlem, my girl of bile and ebony! She can never have objectively existed, all the time mostly the projection of the lusts and greed and self-loathing of a young man called Evelyn, who does not exist, either' (PNE, 175). This becomes the one structural thread linking this bastardized monster's journey with the variety of mothers whose name is evoked here, even if only to be banished from sight. For the mother that Evelyn cries out to as he lies, foetus-like, 'in a blind room seamless as an egg' (PNE, 51) at Beulah, is not only absent but about to be eradicated, replaced by the clinical care of a technological womb.

Yet what better motif than Haraway's cyborg to explore the nature (and culture) of gender relations and their textual exploration through fantasy fiction? That 'All of New Eve's experience came through two channels of sensation, her own fleshly ones and his mental ones' (PNE, 77–8) demonstrates that Eve/lyn's androgyny renders him/her a cyborg. But in addition (and again in the true spirit of Haraway's creation) s/he is also a typical manifestation of the postmodern subject and his/her problematic position regarding the so-called 'natural' world. As Haraway tells us, 'organisms are not born; they are made in world-changing techno-scientific practices by particular collective actors in particular times and places. In the belly of the local/global monster ... often called the postmodern world, global technology appears to denature everything, to make everything a malleable matter of strategic decisions and mobile production and reproductive processes.'[78] This is clearly the case surrounding New Eve's (re-)creation. In similar vein, Haraway's cyborg is a 'monstrous and illegitimate' creature whose anatomy is 'a hybrid of machine and organism'. And yet the victim status often inflicted on such 'monsters' conceals the fact that their contemporary cyborg double (which Haraway embraces as a prototype for new readings of female identity) is a creature who takes '*pleasure* in the confusion of boundaries' and *demands* the type of 'pleasurably tight coupling' denied its nineteenth-century counterpart in particular.[79] At first sight *The Passion of New Eve* seems centrally preoccupied with finding a role for precisely the type of cybernetic 'hopeful monsters' that Haraway and others seem to advocate. But questions remain as to whether Eve/lyn does transcend his gendered origins or, indeed, whether his/her existence as cyborg is genuinely liberatory. As is made clear, his/her femininity is fleshly while his/her masculinity remains cerebral. This reinforces, rather than invalidates, standard gender assumptions. In addition, though Evelyn becomes biologically female, his gender orientation remains masculine throughout, as his/her reference to Leilah as a 'gorgeous piece of flesh and acquiescence' (PNE, 172) towards the end of the text illustrates. Indeed Carter requires this inbuilt cultural tension, using it to play with (though certainly not along with) such binary oppositions.

According to many feminist theorists, society's phallocentrism derives from a foundational binary power structure within which the prioritization of masculine traits is privileged at the expense of the feminine. In their appropriately named *The Newly Born Woman*, Hélène Cixous and Catherine Clément illustrate this by listing several actual or metaphorical manifestations of this polarity under the heading 'Where is she?'.[80] A number of these binary couplings are directly applicable to *The Passion of New Eve*, but the most important is the pairing of the sun (masculine) with the moon (feminine). William Blake explicitly foregrounds this in his own poem about Beulah[81] and Carter metaphoricalizes it in her architectural creation of Beulah as a subterranean shrine. In addition, just as Cixous and Clément set these principles up in an ongoing struggle for dominance whereby one must succeed at the expense of the other, so Beulah (literally and in its architectural symbolism) permits entry to its depths only at the expense of the castrated phallus. And yet a closer look challenges such binary divides, for Beulah is a place of fusion, not one of separation. Or, as P.H. Butter explains, Beulah is:

> a state of being in which the contraries (male and female etc.) are in harmony, 'married'. For the eternals entry into Beulah is a descent, into a 'land of shadows' . . . a realm where shines only the moon, a reflection of the sun of eternity . . . the divine voice is heard in the songs of Beulah . . . So the daughters are muses, channels of inspiration.[82]

There are, of course, many very superficial parallels between this passage and Carter's version of Beulah; but on a deeper level David Punter claims that the major intertextual connection derives from Carter's Beulah being a place where 'extremes meet' in the form of the juxtaposition of technology and what Punter refers to as 'magic'.[83] However, while it is certainly the case that the cybernetic aspects of such confrontations can be summed up in Evelyn's description of the room as having the 'look of a science fiction chapel' (PNE,50), Punter's inattention to the specific connotations of the term 'Beulah' with regard to gender evades an important issue of relevance to the cyborg. For it is not at Tristessa's palace, with Zero's wives looking on, that Eve/lyn is married, but here at Beulah with Mother as high priestess and her daughters in attendance. In this narrative integration of the sacred and the secular, Eve/lyn embodies the ultimate marriage whereby 'a man will . . . be united to his wife, and they will become one flesh'.[84] This 'one flesh' is Carter's own cyborg: a complex combination of masculine and feminine, goddess and whore, secular and sacred and spirit and flesh.

Carter's usage of the mythological and the futurist also allows her to situate the cybernetic as a complex interaction between the temporal and the spatial. As David Howarth argues, 'temporality is equated with dislocation or event, whereas space, or better spatialization, is the moment of the representation or inscription of dislocation.'[85] This complicated reversal takes on meaning when placed in the context of *The Passion of New Eve*. Set against a backdrop of Judeo-Christian tradition, Eve's sacrilegious birth dislocates the established temporal sequencing of the biblical narrative and redefines him/her as space/hole by attributing him with that orifice out of which humanity emerges over and over again. This space functions to denounce the power of chronology and, in the process, symbolizes precisely that 'moment of the . . . inscription of dislocation'. This is a birthing which, like Haraway and Baudrillard's treatment of the body, invokes the mother's power only ultimately to denounce her potency. In this sense, far from being irrelevant, the mother exists as a central site of loss or, as Mother herself puts it, 'the wound that does not heal' (PNE, 64). No wonder, then, that Eve/lyn becomes a 'perfect stranger' to him/herself (PNE, 38), for s/he is not only, as is frequently emphasized, perfection through artifice, but also perfect-*ed*, finished and complete without genealogy.

In conclusion, one can imagine few novels more clearly encapsulating Baudrillard's belief that 'the soul is over with and now it is an ideally naturalized body which absorbs its energy'.[86] As Carter herself argues, 'Mother goddesses are just as silly a notion as father gods' and, in that sense, it is perhaps important to avoid the inevitable oversimplifications of ideological consolation.[87] A goddess of the flesh is far too close for comfort to received patriarchal associations of women's bodies with the passive status of the sacred vessel or temple. *The Passion of New Eve* remains a dark, sinister, perhaps even a dangerous book in terms of the nihilistic (anti-)ideologies with which it plays. In that regard Carter, like Haraway, leaves us with intriguing but worrying deconstructions of gender. The message implied by Carroll a century before still interweaves itself within the workings of this text. It is not only that the female body remains the locus for fantastic reconstructions of monstrosity and the grotesque, but that, as in the *Alice* texts, there seem to be very few alternatives on offer. As both narratives equally suggest: 'A return to origins, the pastoral, or "the garden" is no longer possible.'[88] In the end, this may well be the ultimate despair located at the centre of all current theories of fantasy and the fantastic.

## Notes

1 Lewis Carroll, *The Annotated Alice: Alice's Adventures in Wonderland and Through the Looking Glass*, edited by Martin Gardner (Harmondsworth: Penguin, 1970). Angela Carter, *The Passion of New Eve* (London: Virago, 1982). Subsequent quotations are referenced within the main body of the text, the abbreviations W (Wonderland), LG (Looking Glass) and PNE being used respectively.

2 Eve/lyn and Tristessa being androgynously gendered, I use the pronoun form 'him/herself' with reference to both. In addition, Evelyn's retained masculine orientation even after castration means that at no stage do I consider it appropriate to name him with the decisively feminine form Eve. Instead, the split form Eve/lyn is used.

3 Ann Donovan, 'Alice and Dorothy: Reflections From Two Worlds', in Joseph O'Beirbe Milner and Lucy Floyd Morcock Milner (eds), *Webs and Wardrobes: Humanist and Religious World Views in Children's Literature* (Lanham, MD: University Press of America, 1987), pp. 25–31 (p. 28).

4 Martin Gardner, 'Introduction', *The Annotated Alice* , pp. 7–16, (p. 10).

5 Gardner, 'Introduction', p. 9.

6 Sarah Gilead, 'Magic Abjured: Closure in Children's Fantasy Fiction', *PMLA*, Vol. 10 (1991), pp. 277–93 (p. 288 – my emphasis).

7 Mark Conroy, 'A Tale of Two Alices in Wonderland', *Literature and Psychology*, Vol. 37 (1991), pp. 29–44, (p. 31).

8 Jane Flax, *Thinking Fragments: Psychoanalysis, Feminism, and Postmodernism in the Contemporary West* (Berkeley: University of California Press, 1990), pp. 70–1.

9 It is perhaps worth noting here that Alice's initial encounter with the Queen actually mirrors this textual ending when Alice, chopping off the end of the Queen's 'sentence' with the word 'Nonsense', is saved because 'she is only a child' (W, 109).

10 Irving Massey, *The Gaping Pig: Literature and Metamorphosis* (London: University of California Press, 1976), p. 68.

11 U.C. Knoepflmacher, 'Avenging Alice: Christina Rossetti and Lewis Carroll', *Nineteenth Century Literature*, Vol. 14 (1986), pp. 299–328 (pp. 308–9).

12 John Batchelor, 'Dodgson, Carroll, and the Emancipation of Alice', in Gillian Avery and

Julia Briggs (eds), *Children and Their Books: A Celebration of the Work of Iona and Peter Opie* (Oxford: Clarendon Press, 1989), pp. 181–99 (p. 182).

13 This is an initiation trick played upon an unsuspecting 'victim' (usually a newcomer). The latter, having agreed to play '52 card pick-up', then finds the full pack of playing cards thrown up into the air and thus scattered all over the floor. Whereas it is traditional for this 'new player' to be left to pick up all 52 herself, however, Alice abandons the game altogether, refusing to play by conventional rules.

14 Batchelor, 'Dodgson', p. 184.

15 Allon White, 'Pigs and Pierrots: The Politics of Transgression in Modern Fiction', *Raritan*, Vol. 2 (1981), pp. 51–70 (p. 56).

16 Donald Rackin, *Alice's Adventures in Wonderland and Through the Looking Glass: Nonsense, Sense and Meaning* (New York: Twayne, 1991), p. 8.

17 William Empson, *Some Versions of Pastoral* (Harmondsworth: Penguin, 1995), p. 230.

18 Rackin, *Alice's Adventures*, pp. 3 and 9.

19 Empson, *Versions*, p. 204. Rackin, *Alice's Adventures*, p. 66.

20 Rackin, *Alice's Adventures*, p. 73.

21 Nina Auerbach, 'Alice and Wonderland: A Curious Child', *Victorian Studies*, Vol. 17 (1973), pp. 31–47, (p. 31). Rackin, *Alice's Adventures*, p. 74.

22 Gilead, 'Magic', p. 278.

23 This is a phrase adopted by Calvin R. Petersen in 'Time and Stress: *Alice in Wonderland*', *Journal of the History of Ideas*, Vol. 46 (1985), pp. 427–33 (p. 427).

24 As argued by Carole Scott, 'Limits of Otherworlds: Rules of the Game in Alice's Adventures and the Jungle Books', in S.R. Gannon and R.A. Thompson (eds), *Work and Play in Children's Literature: Selected Papers from the 1990s International Conference of the Children's Literature Association* (San Diego: San Diego State University Press, 1990), pp. 20–4 (p. 23).

25 Beverly Lyon Clark, 'Lewis Carroll's *Alice* Books: The Wonder of Wonderland', in Perry Nodelman (ed.), *Touchstones: Reflections on the Best in Children's Literature, Vol. 1* (West Lafayette: Children's Literature Association, 1985), pp. 44–52 (p. 45).

26 Anita Moss, 'Sacred and Secular Visions of Imagination and Reality in Nineteenth Century British Fantasy for Children', in Joseph O'Beirbe Milner and Lucy Floyd Morcock Milner (eds), *Webs and Wardrobes: Humanist and Religious World Views in Children's Literature* (Lanham, MD: University Press of America, 1987), pp. 65–78 (p. 72).

27 According to Iain Chambers this is the founding principle against which postmodernism strives. See Iain Chambers, *Border Dialogues: Journeys Into Postmodernism* (London: Routledge, 1990), pp. 22–3.

28 See the Book of Genesis 3:15.

29 Batchelor, 'Dodgson', p. 182 – original emphasis.

30 Luce Irigaray, *This Sex Which Is Not One*, trans. Catherine Porter and Carolyn Burke (Ithaca, NY: Cornell University Press, 1985), p. 24.

31 Batchelor, 'Dodgson', p. 181.

32 Auerbach, 'Curious', p. 46.

33 According to Irigaray, such paradigms form the basis of all patriarchal relations. See *This Sex*, p. 33.

34 Sandra Gilbert and Susan Gubar, *The Madwoman in the Attic: The Woman Writer and the Nineteenth Century Literary Imagination* (New Haven: Yale University Press, 1984), p. 12.

35 Gilbert and Gubar, *Madwoman*, p. 3.

36 Gardner, 'Introduction', p. 8.

37 Knoeplmacher, 'Avenging', pp. 305 and 309–10.

38 As argued by Irigaray, *This Sex*, p. 26 – original emphasis.

39 Knoeplmacher, 'Avenging', p. 314.

40 As argued by Jean Baudrillard, *America* (London: Verso, 1988), p. 125.

41 Angela Carter, *The Magic Toyshop* (London: Virago, 1981), p. 1.

42 Chambers, *Border*, p. 88.

43 Chambers, *Border*, p. 54.
44 As argued by Istvan Csicsery-Ronay, Jr., 'The SF of Theory: Baudrillard and Haraway', *Science Fiction Studies*, Vol. 18 (1991), pp. 387–404 (p. 401).
45 Chambers, *Border*, p. 71.
46 Mikhail Bakhtin, *Rabelais And His World*, trans. Hélène Iswolsky (Bloomington: Indiana University Press, 1984), p. 345.
47 This is a stance adopted by Donna Haraway in 'The Promises of Monsters: A Regenerative Politics For Inappropriate/d Others', in Lawrence Grossberg, Cary Nelson, Paula Treichler (eds), *Cultural Studies* (New York: Routledge, 1992), pp. 295–337 (p. 326).
48 This being Baudrillard's phrase. See *America*, p. 7.
49 Book of Romans 8:13.
50 Marcel Tetel, 'Carnival And Beyond', *L'Esprit Créature*, Vol. 21 (1981), pp. 88–104 (p. 88).
51 Angela Carter, *Omnibus: A Profile of Angela Carter*, screened BBC1, 15 September 1992.
52 Baudrillard, *America*, p. 56 – original emphasis.
53 This is a reading of cinema favoured by Baudrillard. *America*, p. 35.
54 Jean Baudrillard, *Simulations* (New York: Semiotext(e), 1983), p. 9.
55 For a fuller discussion of this see Jenny Turner, 'Travels in Cyber-reality', *Guardian*, 18 March, 1995, pp. 28–34 (p. 34).
56 Bakhtin, *Rabelais*, p. 320.
57 As argued by Baudrillard, *America*, pp. 72 and 37 respectively.
58 Baudrillard, *America*, p. 30.
59 Scott Bukatman, 'The Cybernetic (City) State: Terminal Space Becomes Phenomenal', *Journal of the Fantastic in the Arts*, Vol. 2 (1989), pp. 43–63 (p. 58).
60 Alan Dundes, 'Wet and Dry: The Evil Eye: An Essay in Semitic and Indo-European Worldview', in Venetia J. Newall (ed.), *Folklore Studies in the Twentieth Century: Proceedings of the Centenary Conference of the Folklore Society* (Woodbridge: D.S. Brewer, 1980), pp. 37–48 (p. 37).
61 Dundes, 'Wet and Dry', pp. 40 and 48.
62 Dundes, 'Wet and Dry', p. 37.
63 Baudrillard, *America*, p. 63.
64 Baudrillard, *America*, pp. 36–7.
65 For a fuller discussion of this see Chambers, *Border*, p. 103.
66 Istvan Csicsery-Ronay, Jr., 'Cyberpunk and Neuromanticism', in Larry McCaffery (ed.), *Storming the Reality Studio* (Durham, NC: Duke University Press, 1991), pp. 182–93 (p. 189).
67 Donna Haraway, 'The Promises of Monsters: A Regenerative Politics for Inappropriate/d Others', in Grossberg et al. (eds), *Cultural Studies* (New York: Routledge, 1992), pp. 295–337 (p. 327).
68 Baudrillard, *America*, pp. 28–9 and 96.
69 Carter's definition of surrealism is taken from John Haffenden (ed.), *Novelists In Interview* (London: Methuen, 1985), p. 92. The definition of the hyperreal is Raman Selden and Peter Widdowson's. See *A Reader's Guide to Contemporary Literary Theory* (Hemel Hempstead: Harvester Wheatsheaf, 1993), p. 180.
70 Baudrillard, *America*, pp. 9, 28 and 32.
71 Bukatman, 'Cybernetic', p. 50.
72 Baudrillard, *America*, p. 76.
73 Haraway, 'Promises', pp. 297–8.
74 For a fuller discussion of this see Haraway, 'Promises', p. 299.
75 As argued by Csicsery-Ronay, Jr., 'SF', p. 388.
76 Rackin, *Alice's Adventures*, p. 103.
77 Tetel, 'Carnival', p. 94.
78 Haraway, 'Promises', p. 297.
79 Donna J. Haraway, 'A Cyborg Manifesto: Science, Technology, and Socialist-Feminism in

the Late Twentieth Century' in *Simians, Cyborgs and Women: The Reinvention of Nature* (London: Free Association Books, 1991), pp. 149–81 (pp. 149–54 *passim*).

80 Hélène Cixous and Catherine Clément, *The Newly Born Woman*, trans. Betsy Wing (Manchester: Manchester University Press, 1987), pp. 63–4.

81 William Blake, 'Milton', in P.H. Butter (ed.), *William Blake: Selected Poems* (London: J.M. Dent, 1982), pp. 143–63.

82 P.H. Butter, *Blake*, p. 244n.

83 David Punter, *The Hidden Script: Writing and the Unconscious* (London: Routledge & Kegan Paul, 1985), p. 40.

84 As stated in the Book of Genesis 2:24.

85 David Howarth, 'Reflections on the Politics of Space and Time', *Angelaki*, Vol. 1 (1993), pp. 43–56 (p. 47).

86 Jean Baudrillard, 'The Automation of the Robot', in McCaffery (ed.), *Storming the Reality Studio*, pp. 178–81 (p. 180).

87 Angela Carter, *The Sadeian Woman: An Exercise in Cultural History* (London: Virago, 1979), p. 5.

88 As argued by Anne Balsamo, 'Reading Cyborgs Writing Feminism', *Communication*, Vol. 10 (1988), pp. 331–44 (p. 342).

# Afterword: But What of Utopia?

I began this book by situating my reading of fantasy and the fantastic in the rather utopian terms of play, space and corporeal identity. And yet it appears to conclude with the observation that utopia has become obsolete, evoking that archetypal utopian motif of the garden only in order to reassert its inaccessibility. To some extent this seems at odds with the overall ideological stance taken by Haraway and Kristeva, two of the most innovatory contemporary theorists of the body, both of whom have proved central to the concerns of this book. Thus, while I argue for the absence of utopia, they employ their corporeal redefinitions in conjunction with a broadly positive philosophical impulse, searching for new explorations and redefinitions of socio-cultural dynamics. Evidence that this must have at least some application to the utopic is present in Haraway's assertive belief in the possibility of 'weaving something other than a shroud for the day after the apocalypse'.[1]

In Chapter 1, I referred to Khana's reference to the utopian as 'not, finally, any one place or time, but the capacity to see afresh'.[2] That 'seeing afresh' is a piece of hopeful horizon-searching which appears to open up possibilities rather than close down alternatives. But this is unusual in utopian terms. As it is conventionally theorised utopia must remain anathema to the spirit of this project, being among the most rigid (and rigidly reductive) of generically bound forms. Indeed, what initially seems to be Khana's innovatory stance quickly capitulates to unqualified restraint. For in furthering this image as 'an enlarged, even tranformed vision', her use of the past tense immediately locks it up in a box. Not merely perfect, but perfect-ed, any conflicting voices are 'shut up' in the process. But Haraway's perspective on utopianism is radically distinct from this. Rather than offering us visions of perfection, she qualifies and complicates her optimism by infecting it with a large dose of dangerous ambiguity. However creative her tapestry, it is undoubtedly a warped one, wefted through as it is with the discourse of apocalypse. What, we might argue, is utopian about that? In order to comprehend this, we should remember Haraway's continual challenge to oversimplified binary oppositions, it being these that divorce utopia from fear and from loss. After all, without these there can be no desire for bliss. This not only makes her anti-utopian utopia more interesting, it also renders it far more ideologically credible.

This alignment of utopia with Haraway's work seems to imply the perspective of a particular historical moment. For in its exploration of the multiple and cataclysmic meeting point(s) between technology, global/environmental warfare and contemporary gender ideologies Haraway's work is very much a product of contemporary thinking. But it is important to remember that my confrontation with utopia in its absence emerges most forcefully out of a comparative reading of nineteenth- and twentieth-century texts. In these terms we are not so much dealing with a moment in time as an ongoing narrative (and thus spatial) dynamic. For the garden always returns us to a space beyond time and, as the final chapter of Carter's novel reminds us, there are no genuinely linear or finite options: 'We start from our conclusions. I arrived on that continent by air and left it by water; earth and fire I leave behind me ... Ocean, ocean, mother of mysteries, bear me to the place of birth' (PNE, 191). Once again, then, more interesting possibilities emerge through combining Haraway's ideas with those of Kristeva. For Carter's New Eve motif clearly depicts the garden as a substitute space for that originary mother who is never accessible except in phantasy. At this point, instead of utopia, we find ourselves located within a melancholic dynamic, one that might even motivate our fascination for such narrative forms. Much of the theoretical ground this book has covered functions to render this paradigm explicit. So we journey from Proppian lack through to Freud's uncanny obsessions, Bakhtin's grotesque forms, and the cynical closures of cyborg philosophies in an ongoing search for that ideal (which is) elsewhere. Despite its apparently pessimistic manifestations, this impulse is far more in tune with the utopian than we might at first presume possible. Thus, in Kristevan terms, though melancholia derives from the unassuagable sense of unconscious mourning that accompanies our position within the symbolic, it refuses to capitulate to despair or morbidity. On the contrary, as John Lechte informs us, 'it is a question of ... coming into the realm of the symbolic and developing our imaginary capacities and thereby producing a language for – *and thus against* – our sadness.'[3] The specific application this has to fantastic forms derives from their shared identification with the trajectory of the 'beyond'. Melancholy, in seemingly projecting towards a fantasy rooted beyond the parameters of the symbolic, propels itself (like Eve/lyn) towards an endlessly receding horizon. What it searches for at that always liminal place is the unattainable, infinitely desirable and uncontainable other. This has always been the space and place of utopia.

But this is no finite and fully resolved reading. In a book about boundary demarcations the site of utopia must remain one of contestation and allow for the inclusion of competing (even dissenting) voices. This returns us to Cixous and Clément's version of *The Newly Born Woman*. Likewise situating border dialogues at the heart of what impels us towards the discourse of narrative creativity, their interpretation of the writing process is based upon negotiations with and within that unknown territory we always associate with *sf*. So it becomes a point of 'crossing, entry, exit, sojourn, of the other that I am and am not . . . that tears, worries me, alters me . . . the unknown'.[4] Again, the first part of this assertion articulates the 'beyond' in both its outer and inner/inter-subjective spaces. But in addition, despite Cixous frequently being criticized for her 'utopian' (in this sense meaning negatively unrealistic) philosophical outlook,[5] her words here are resistant to this. The transformative possibilities encapsulated in these words require, rather like Haraway's, a violent deconstruction of the unified self. The true significance of such corporeal metamorphoses only emerges in the second part of their statement, 'tears' and 'worries' clearly functioning as bodily puns. So the former simultaneously signals ripping and crying, while the latter connotes fretting and gnawing. The resulting destabilization opens up this horizon, not just to a disruption of the boundaries of the self (those alter*ations* we have already situated at the heart of the interface between phantasy and fantasy), but also to a genuinely interrogative sense of alter*cation* within and beyond the boundaries of the text.

In freeing up the utopian to the boundary negotiations of textual dynamics we resituate the ideological defamiliarizations of fantasy and the fantastic in terms of genuinely transformative shape-shifting interrogations. As we have seen, for Barthes, this lack of textual resolution enables a flirtatious pleasuring of and in the mother's body which always takes place between the(se) sheets. Taking a melancholic projection may restrain our pleasure to narrative forepleasure but the positive aspect of this is that we will be left with a state of ongoing desire, perpetuating our endless, but always hopeful returns. I have defined phantasy as an 'intangible' source of fears and desires, endlessly beckoning and endlessly evasive. The utopia remains similarly beyond our grasp and beyond articulation, but it continues to proffer glimpses of an enticing and forbidding unknown of which we could otherwise only dream.

## Notes

1 Donna Haraway, *Simians, Cyborgs and Women: The Reinvention of Nature* (London: Free Association Books, 1991), p. 158.

2 Lee Cullen Khana, 'Change and Art in Women's Worlds: Doris Lessing's "Canopus in Argos: Archives"' in Ruby Rohrlich and Elaine Hoffman Baruch (eds), *Women in Search of Utopia: Mavericks and Mythmakers* (New York: Schoken, 1984), pp. 270–6 (p. 273).

3 John Lechte, 'Art, Love, and Melancholy in the Work of Julia Kristeva', in John Fletcher and Andrew Benjamin (eds), *Abjection, Melancholia and Love: The Work of Julia Kristeva* (London: Routledge, 1990), 24–41 (p. 38 – my emphasis).
4 Hélène Cixous and Catherine Clément, *La Jeune Née* (Paris: Union Générale d'Editions, 1975), p.158. This passaged cited and translated by Pierre Salesne in 'Hélène Cixous' *Ou l'art de l'innocence*: The Path to You', in Susan Sellers (ed), *Writing Differences: Readings From the Seminar of Hélène Cixous* (Milton Keynes: Open University Press, 1988), pp. 113–26 (p. 124). This translation is used here because of Salesne's specific choice of terminology.
5 See, for example, chapter 6, 'Hélène Cixous: An Imaginary Utopia', in Toril Moi, *Sexual/Textual Politics* (London: Methuen, 1985), pp. 102–26.

# Bibliography

## Primary Texts

BANKS, IAIN *The Bridge* (London: Abacus, 1990).

CARROLL, LEWIS *The Annotated Alice: Alice's Adventures in Wonderland and Through the Looking Glass*, ed. Martin Gardner (Harmondsworth: Penguin, 1970).

CARTER, ANGELA *The Passion of New Eve* (London: Virago, 1982).

LESSING, DORIS *Briefing For A Descent Into Hell* (London: Granada, 1972).

PERKINS GILMAN, CHARLOTTE *The Yellow Wallpaper* (London: Virago, 1981).

STEVENSON, R.L. *The Strange Case of Dr Jekyll and Mr Hyde and Other Stories* (Harmondsworth: Penguin, 1979).

## Secondary Texts

ABRAHAMS, ROGER 'Play' in Venetia J. Newall (ed.) *Folklore Studies in the Twentieth Century: Proceedings of the Centenary Conference of the Folklore Society* (Woodbridge: D.S. Brewer, 1980), 120–5.

AMIS, KINGSLEY *The Golden Age of Science Fiction* (London: Hutchinson, 1981).

ANDERSON, LINDA (ed.) *Plotting Change: Contemporary Women's Fiction* (London: Edward Arnold, 1990).

ARMITT, LUCIE (ed.) *Where No Man Has Gone Before: Women and Science Fiction* (London: Routledge, 1991).

ARMITT, LUCIE 'Space, Time and Female Genealogies: A Kristevan Reading of Feminist Science Fiction' in Sarah Sceats and Gail Cunningham (eds) *Image and Power: Women in Fiction in the Twentieth Century* (London: Longman, 1996), 51–61.

ATTEBURY, BRIAN *The Fantasy Tradition in American Literature* (Bloomington: Indiana University Press, 1980).

AUERBACH, NINA 'Alice and Wonderland: A Curious Child', *Victorian Studies*, Vol. 17, No.1 (September 1973), 31–47.

AVERY, GILLIAN and JULIA BRIGGS (eds) *Children and Their Books: A Celebration of the Work of Iona and Peter Opie* (Oxford: Clarendon Press, 1989).

BACHELARD, GASTON *The Poetics of Space*, trans. Maria Jolas (Boston: Beacon Press, 1994).

BAKHTIN, MIKHAIL *Rabelais and His World*, trans. Hélène Iswolsky (Bloomington: Indiana University Press, 1984).

BALSAMO, ANNE 'Reading Cyborgs Writing Feminism', *Communication*, Vol. 10 (1988), 331–44.

BAMMER, ANGELIKA *Partial Visions: Feminism and Utopianism in the 1970s* (New York: Routledge, 1991).

BARTHES, ROLAND *Mythologies*, trans. Annette Lavers (London: Paladin, 1973).

BARTHES, ROLAND *The Pleasure of the Text*, trans. Richard Miller (Oxford: Basil Blackwell, 1990).

BATAILLE, GEORGES *Eroticism*, trans. Mary Dalwood (London: Marion Boyars, 1987).

BATCHELOR, JOHN 'Dodgson, Carroll, and the Emancipation of Alice' in Gillian Avery and Julia Briggs (eds) *Children and Their Books: A Celebration of the Work of Iona and Peter Opie* (Oxford: Clarendon Press, 1989), 181–99.

BAUDRILLARD, JEAN *Simulations* (New York: Semiotext(e), 1983).

BAUDRILLARD, JEAN *America* (London: Verso, 1988).

BAUDRILLARD, JEAN 'The Automation of the Robot' in Larry McCaffery (ed.) *Storming the Reality Studio* (Durham, NC: Duke University Press, 1991), 178–81.

BENJAMIN, JESSICA 'A Desire of One's Own: Psychoanalytic Feminism and Intersubjective Space' in Teresa de Lauretis (ed.) *Feminist Studies/Critical Studies* (London: Macmillan, 1986), 78–101.

BERLAND, JODY 'Angels Dancing: Cultural Technologies and the Production of Space' in Lawrence Grossberg et al. (eds) *Cultural Studies* (New York: Routledge, 1992), 38–55.

BERSANI, LEO *A Future for Astyanax: Character and Desire in Literature*, (London: Marion Boyars, 1978).

BETTELHEIM, BRUNO *The Uses of Enchantment: The Meaning and Importance of Fairy Tales* (Harmondsworth: Penguin, 1991).

BLAKE, CHARLIE 'In the Shadow of Cybernetic Minorities: Life, Death and Delirium in the Capitalist Imaginary', *Angelaki*, Vol. 1, No. 1 (1993), 128–37.

BOOTHBY, RICHARD *Death and Desire: Psychoanalytic Theory in Lacan's Return to Freud* (New York: Routledge, 1991).

BOUCHARD, DONALD F. (ed.) *Michel Foucault: Language, Counter-Memory, Practice: Selected Essays and Interviews* (Ithaca, NY: Cornell University Press, 1977).

BRANHAM, ROBERT J. 'Fantasy and Ineffability: Fiction at the Limits of Language', *Extrapolation*, Vol. 24 (Spring 1983), 66–79.

BRISTOL, MICHAEL D. *Carnival and Theatre: Plebeian Culture and the Structure of Authority in Renaissance England* (New York: Routledge, 1989).

BROOKE-ROSE, CHRISTINE *A Rhetoric of the Unreal: Studies in Narrative and Structure, Especially of the Fantastic* (Cambridge: Cambridge University Press, 1981).

BUKATMAN, SCOTT 'The Cybernetic (City) State: Terminal Space Becomes Phenomenal', *Journal of the Fantastic in the Arts* Vol. 2 (Summer 1989), 43–63.

BURGIN, VICTOR, JAMES DONALD and CORA KAPLAN (eds) *Formations of Fantasy* (London: Routledge, 1989).

BURGIN, VICTOR 'Fantasy' in Elizabeth Wright (ed.) *Feminism and Psychoanalysis: A Critical Dictionary* (Oxford: Basil Blackwell, 1992), 84–8.

CARROL, NOEL *The Philosophy of Horror or, Paradoxes of the Heart* (New York: Routledge, 1990).

CARTER, ANGELA *The Sadeian Woman: An Exercise in Cultural History* (London: Virago, 1979).

CARTER, ANGELA (ed.) *The Virago Book of Fairy Tales* (London: Virago, 1991).

CARTER, ANGELA (ed.) *The Second Virago Book of Fairy Tales* (London: Virago, 1993).

CHAMBERS, IAIN *Border Dialogues: Journeys into Postmodernism* (London: Routledge, 1990).

CIXOUS, HÉLÈNE 'Fiction and Its Phantoms: A Reading of Freud's *Das Unheimliche* (The "Uncanny")', *New Literary History*, Vol. 7 (1976), 525–48.

CIXOUS, HÉLÈNE and CATHERINE CLÉMENT *The Newly Born Woman*, trans. Betsy Wing (Manchester: Manchester University Press, 1987).

CLARK, BEVERLY LYON 'Lewis Carroll's *Alice* Books: The Wonder of Wonderland' in Perry Nodelman (ed.) *Touchstones: Reflections on the Best in Children's Literature, Vol. 1* (West Lafayette: Children's Literature Association, 1985), 44–52.

CONROY, MARK 'A Tale of Two Alices in Wonderland', *Literature and Psychology*, Vol. 37, Part 3 (1991), 29–44.

CORNWELL, NEIL *The Literary Fantastic: From Gothic to Postmodernism* (London: Harvester Wheatsheaf, 1990).

COYLE, WILLIAM (ed.) *Aspects of Fantasy: Selected Essays from the Second International Conference on the Fantastic in Literature and Film* (Westport, Conn.: Greenwood, 1986).

CSICSERY-RONAY, JR., ISTVAN 'Cyberpunk and Neuromanticism' in Larry McCaffery (ed.) *Storming the Reality Studio* (Durham, NC: Duke University Press, 1991), 182–93.

CSICSERY-RONAY, JR., ISTVAN 'The SF of Theory', *Science Fiction Studies*, Vol. 18, Part 3 (1991), 387–404.

CULLER, JONATHAN *Saussure* (London: Fontana, 1976).

DALY, MARY *Gyn/Ecology: The Metaethics of Radical Feminism* (London: Women's Press, 1979).

DAVIS, MADELEINE and DAVID WALLBRIDGE *Boundary And Space: An Introduction to the Work of D.W. Winnicott* (New York: Brunner/Mazel, 1987).

DÉGH, LINDA 'Grimm's *Household Tales* and Its Place in the Household: The Social Relevance of a Controversial Classic', *Western Folklore*, Vol. 38 (1979), 83–103.

DELAMOTTE, EUGENIA C. 'Male and Female Mysteries in *The Yellow Wallpaper*', *Legacy*, Vol. 5, No. 1 (Spring 1988), 3–14.

DICKSON, ALBERT (ed.) *The Penguin Freud Library, Vol. 14, Art and Literature* (Harmondsworth: Penguin, 1990).

DICKSTEIN, MORRIS 'The Aesthetics of Fright' in Barry Keith Grant (ed.) *Planks of Reason: Essays on the Horror Film* (Metuchen: Scarecrow, 1984), 65–78.

DIDION, JOAN '*Briefing For A Descent Into Hell*' in Claire Sprague and Virginia Tiger (eds) *Critical Essays on Doris Lessing* (Boston: G.K. Hall, 1986), 192–6.

DOANE, MARY ANN 'Veiling Over Desire: Close-ups of the Woman' in Richard Felstein and Judith Roof (eds) *Feminism and Psychoanalysis* (Ithaca, NY: Cornell University Press, 1989), 105–41.

DONOVAN, ANN 'Alice and Dorothy: Reflections From Two Worlds' in Joseph O'Beirbe Milner and Lucy Floyd Morcock Milner (eds) *Webs and Wardrobes: Humanist and Religious World Views in Children's Literature* (Lanham, MD: University Press of America, 1987), 25–31.

DUNDES, ALAN 'Wet and Dry: The Evil Eye: An Essay in Semitic and Indo-European Worldview' in Venetia J. Newall (ed.) *Folklore Studies in the Twentieth Century: Proceedings of the Centenary Conference of the Folklore Society* (Woodbridge: D.S. Brewer, 1980), 37–48.

DUPLESSIS, RACHEL BLAU 'The Feminist Apologues of Lessing, Piercy and Russ', *Frontiers*, Vol. 4, No. 1, 1979.

EASTHOPE, ANTONY *Poetry and Phantasy* (Cambridge: Cambridge University Press, 1989).

EDELSTEIN, MARILYN 'Toward a Feminist Postmodern Poléthique: Kristeva on Ethics and Politics' in Kelly Oliver (ed.) *Ethics, Politics, and Difference in Julia Kristeva's Writing* (New York: Routledge, 1993), 196–214.

ELLIS, KATE FERGUSON *The Contested Castle: Gothic Novels and the Subversion of Domestic Ideology* (Urbana: University of Illinois Press, 1989).

EMPSON, WILLIAM *Some Versions of Pastoral* (Harmondsworth: Penguin, 1995).

FELSTEIN, RICHARD and JUDITH ROOF (eds) *Feminism and Psychoanalysis* (Ithaca, NY: Cornell University Press, 1989).

FELSTEIN, RICHARD 'Reader, Text and Ambiguous Referentiality in *The*

*Yellow Wallpaper*' in Catherine Golden (ed.) *The Captive Imagination: A Casebook on The Yellow Wallpaper* (New York: Feminist Press, City University of New York, 1992), 306–17.

FETTERLEY, JUDITH From 'Reading about Reading: "A Jury of Her Peers", "The Murders in the Rue Morgue" and "The Yellow Wallpaper"' in Catherine Golden (ed.) *The Captive Imagination: A Casebook on the Yellow Wallpaper* (New York: Feminist Press, City University of New York, 1992), 253–75.

FIEDLER, LESLIE *Freaks: Myths and Images of the Secret Self* (New York: Simon & Schuster, 1978).

FISCH, HAROLD *A Remembered Future: A Study of Literary Mythology* (Bloomington: Indiana University Press, 1984).

FISHBURN, KATHERINE 'Doris Lessing's *Briefing For A Descent Into Hell*: Science Fiction or Psycho-Drama?', *Science Fiction Studies*, Vol. 15, Part 1 (March 1988), 48–60.

FLAX, JANE *Thinking Fragments: Psychoanalysis, Feminism, and Postmodernism in the Contemporary West* (Berkeley: University of California Press, 1990).

FLEENOR, JULIANN E. (ed.) *The Female Gothic* (Montreal: Eden, 1983).

FLETCHER, JOHN and ANDREW BENJAMIN (eds) *Abjection, Melancholia and Love in the Work of Julia Kristeva* (London: Routledge, 1990).

FLORENCE, PENNY 'The Liberation of Utopia or Is Science Fiction the Ideal Contemporary Women's Form' in Linda Anderson (ed.) *Plotting Change: Contemporary Women's Fiction* (London: Edward Arnold, 1990), 64–83.

FOUCAULT, MICHEL 'A Preface to Transgression', trans. Donald F. Bouchard and Sherry Simon, in Donald F. Bouchard (ed.) *Michel Foucault: Language, Counter-Memory, Practice: Selected Essays and Interviews* (Ithaca, NY: Cornell University Press, 1977), 29–52.

FREUD, SIGMUND 'Creative Writers and Day-Dreaming', trans I.F. Grant, in Albert Dickson (ed.) *The Penguin Freud Library, Vol. 14, Art and Literature* (Harmondsworth: Penguin, 1990), 129–41.

FREUD, SIGMUND 'Delusions and Dreams in Jensen's "*Gradiva*"', trans. James Strachey, in Albert Dickson (ed.) *The Penguin Freud Library, Vol. 14, Art and Literature* (Harmondsworth: Penguin, 1990), 27–118.

FREUD, SIGMUND 'The "Uncanny"', trans. Alix Strachey, in Albert Dickson (ed.) *The Penguin Freud Library, Vol. 14, Art and Literature* (Harmondsworth: Penguin, 1990), 335–76.

FREUD, SIGMUND 'On Narcissism: An Introduction', trans. C.M. Baines, in Angela Richards (ed.) *The Penguin Freud Library, Vol. 11, On Metapsychology* (Harmondsworth: Penguin, 1991), 59–97.

FREUND, ELIZABETH *The Return of the Reader: Reader-Response Criticism* (London: Methuen, 1987).

GANNON, S.R. and R.A. THOMPSON (eds) *Work and Play in Children's Literature: Selected Papers from the 1990 International Conference of the*

*Children's Literature Association* (San Diego: San Diego State University Press, 1990).

GARRET, PETER K. 'Cries and Voices: Reading Jekyll and Hyde' in William Veeder and Gordon Hirsch (eds) *Dr Jekyll and Mr Hyde After One Hundred Years* (Chicago: University of Chicago Press, 1988), 63–7.

GILBERT, SANDRA and SUSAN GUBAR *The Madwoman in the Attic: The Woman Writer and the Nineteenth Century Literary Imagination* (New Haven: Yale University Press, 1984).

GILEAD, SARAH 'Magic Abjured: Closure in Children's Fantasy Fiction', *PMLA*, Vol. 10, Part 6 (2) (March 1991), 277–93.

GILES, DENNIS 'Conditions of Pleasure in Horror Cinema' in *Planks of Reason: Essays on the Horror Film* ed. Barry Keith Grant (Metuchen, NJ: Scarecrow, 1984), 38–52.

GOLDEN, CATHERINE (ed.) *The Captive Imagination: A Casebook on the Yellow Wallpaper* (New York: Feminist Press, City University of New York, 1992).

GOLDEN, CATHERINE 'The Writing of *The Yellow Wallpaper*: A Double Palimpsest' in Catherine Golden (ed.) *The Captive Imagination: A Casebook on the Yellow Wallpaper* (New York: Feminist Press, City University of New York, 1992), 296–305.

GRACE, GEORGE W. *The Linguistic Construction of Reality* (London: Croom Helm, 1987).

GRAHAM, KENNETH W. (ed.) *Gothic Fictions: Prohibition/Transgression* (New York: AMS, 1989).

GRANT, BARRY KEITH (ed.) *Planks of Reason: Essays on the Horror Film* (Metuchen, NJ: Scarecrow, 1984).

GRIFFITHS, JOHN *Three Tomorrows: American, British and Soviet Science Fiction* (London: Macmillan, 1980).

GRIXTI, JOSEPH *The Terrors of Uncertainty: The Cultural Contexts of Horror Fiction* (London: Routledge, 1989).

GROSS, ELIZABETH 'The Body of Signification' in John Fletcher and Andrew Benjamin (eds) *Abjection, Melancholia and Love in the Work of Julia Kristeva* (London: Routledge, 1990), 80–103.

GROSSBERG, LAWRENCE, CARY NELSON and PAULA TREICHLER (eds) *Cultural Studies* (New York: Routledge, 1992).

GUBAR, SUSAN '"The Blank Page" and the Issues of Female Creativity' in Elaine Showalter (ed.) *The New Feminist Criticism* (London: Virago, 1986), 292–313.

HAFFENDEN, JOHN (ed.) *Novelists In Interview* (London: Methuen, 1985).

HANEY-PERITZ, JANICE 'Monumental Feminism and Literature's Ancestral House: Another Look at *The Yellow Wallpaper*', *Women's Studies*, Vol. 12, No. 2 (1986), 113–28.

HARAWAY, DONNA J. *Simians, Cyborgs and Women: The Reinvention of Nature* (London: Free Association Books, 1991).

HARAWAY, DONNA 'The Promises of Monsters: A Regenerative Politics for

Inappropriate/d Others' in Lawrence Grossberg et al. (eds) *Cultural Studies* (New York: Routledge, 1992), 295–337.

HARLAND, RICHARD *Superstructuralism: The Philosophy of Structuralism and Post-Structuralism* (London: Methuen, 1987).

HEATH, STEPHEN '*Psychopathia Sexualis*: Stevenson's *Strange Case*', *Critical Quarterly*, Vol. 28, Nos 1 and 2 (Spring/Summer 1986), 93–108.

HIRSCH, GORDON '*Frankenstein*, Detective Fiction and *Jekyll and Hyde*' in William Veeder and Gordon Hirsch (eds) *Dr Jekyll and Mr Hyde After One Hundred Years* (Chicago: University of Chicago Press, 1988), 223–41.

HOGLE, JERROLD E. 'The Struggle for a Dichotomy: Abjection in Jekyll and His Interpreters' in William Veeder and Gordon Hirsch (eds) *Dr Jekyll and Mr Hyde After One Hundred Years* (Chicago: University of Chicago Press, 1988), 161–202.

HOLLAND, NORMAN N. *The Dynamics of Literary Response* (New York: Oxford University Press, 1968).

HOLLAND, NORMAN N. and LEONA F. SHERMAN 'Gothic Possibilities' in Elizabeth A. Flynn and Patrocinio P. Schweickart (eds) *Gender and Reading: Essays on Readers, Texts and Contexts* (Baltimore: John Hopkins University Press, 1988), 215–33.

HOLLINGER, VERONICA 'Cybernetic Deconstructions: Cyberpunk and Postmodernism' in Larry McCaffery (ed.) *Storming the Reality Studio* (Durham, NC: Duke University Press, 1991), 203–18.

HOWARTH, DAVID 'Reflections on the Politics of Space and Time', *Angelaki*, Vol. 1, No.1 (1993), 43–56.

HUME, KATHRYN *Fantasy and Mimesis: Responses to Reality in Western Literature* (New York: Methuen, 1984).

HUSS, ROY and T.J. ROSS (eds) *Focus on the Horror Film* (Englewood Cliffs, NJ: Prentice Hall, 1972).

IRIGARAY, LUCE *This Sex Which Is Not One*, trans. Catherine Porter and Carolyn Burke (Ithaca, NY: Cornell University Press, 1985).

IRWIN, W.R. *The Game of the Impossible: A Rhetoric of Fantasy* (Urbana: University of Illinois Press, 1976).

IRWIN, W.R. 'From Fancy to Fantasy: Coleridge and Beyond' in Roger C. Schlobin (ed.) *The Aesthetics of Fantasy Literature and Art* (Brighton: Harvester Wheatsheaf, 1982), 36–55.

JACKSON, ROSEMARY *Fantasy: The Literature of Subversion* (London: Methuen, 1981).

JAMESON, FREDERIC 'Postmodernism, or the Cultural Logic of Late Capitalism' in Larry McCaffery (ed.) *Storming the Reality Studio* (Durham, NC: Duke University Press, 1991), 219–28.

JAY, KARLA and JOANNE GLASGOW (eds) *Lesbian Texts and Contexts: Radical Revisions* (New York: New York University Press, 1990).

JONES, STEVEN SWANN *The Fairy Tale: The Magic Mirror of Imagination* (New York: Twayne, 1995).

KAHANE, CLARE 'Gothic Mirrors and Feminine Identity' in *Centennial Review*, Vol. 24 (1980), 43–64.

KAYSER, WOLFGANG *The Grotesque in Art and Literature* (New York: Columbia University Press, 1981).

KELLOGG, STUART (ed.) *Essays on Gay Literature* (New York: Harrington Park Press, 1985).

KENNARD, JEAN E. *Number and Nightmare: Forms of Fantasy in Contemporary Fiction* (Hamden: Archen, 1975).

KHANA, LEE CULLEN 'Change and Art in Women's Worlds: Doris Lessing's "Canopus in Argos: Archives"' in Ruby Rohrlich and Elaine Hoffman Baruch (eds) *Women in Search of Utopia: Mavericks and Mythmakers* (New York: Schoken Books, 1984), 270–6.

KINCAID, JAMES R. *Child-Loving: The Erotic Child and Victorian Culture* (New York: Routledge, 1992).

KING, JEANETTE *Doris Lessing* (London: Edward Arnold, 1989).

KNOEPFLMACHER, U.C. 'Avenging Alice: Christina Rossetti and Lewis Carroll', *Nineteenth Century Literature*, Vol. 14, Part 3 (December 1986), 299–328.

KOLODNY, ANNETTE 'A Map for Rereading: Or, Gender and the Interpretation of Literary Texts' in Catherine Golden (ed.) *The Captive Imagination: A Casebook on The Yellow Wallpaper* (New York: Feminist Press, City University of New York, 1992), 151–65.

KRISTEVA, JULIA 'Revolution in Poetic Language', trans. Margaret Waller, in Toril Moi (ed.) *The Kristeva Reader* (Oxford: Basil Blackwell, 1986), 89–136.

KRISTEVA, JULIA 'The System and the Speaking Subject', trans. Seán Hand, in Toril Moi (ed.) *The Kristeva Reader* (Oxford: Basil Blackwell, 1986), 24–33.

KRISTEVA, JULIA 'On The Melancholic Imaginary', trans. Louise Burchill, in Shlomith Rimmon-Kenan (ed.) *Discourse in Psychoanalysis and Literature* (London: Methuen, 1987).

KRISTEVA, JULIA 'Women's Time', trans. Alice Jardine and Harry Blake, in Toril Moi (ed.) *The Kristeva Reader* (Oxford: Basil Blackwell, 1986), 187–213.

KRISTEVA, JULIA *Strangers To Ourselves*, trans. Leon S. Roudiez (Hemel Hempstead: Harvester Wheatsheaf, 1991).

LAPLANCHE, JEAN and JEAN-BERTRAND PONTALIS 'Fantasy and the Origins of Sexuality' in Victor Burgin et al (eds) *Formations of Fantasy* (London: Routledge, 1989), 5–34.

LAURETIS, TERESA DE (ed.) *Feminist Studies/Critical Studies* (London: Macmillan, 1986).

LECHTE, JOHN 'Art, Love, and Melancholy in the Work of Julia Kristeva' in John Fletcher and Andrew Benjamin (eds) *Abjection, Melancholia and Love: The Work of Julia Kristeva* (London: Routledge, 1990), 24–41.

LEFEBVRE, HENRI *The Production of Space* (Oxford: Basil Blackwell, 1991).

LEWIS, C.S. *Of This And Other Worlds* (London: William Collins, 1982).

LEWIS, MARY ELLEN 'Some Continuities Between Oral and Written Literature' in Venetia J. Newall (ed.) *Folklore Studies in the Twentieth Century: Proceedings of the Centenary Conference of the Folklore Society* (Woodbridge: D.S. Brewer, 1980), 272–6.

LUCKHURST, ROGER 'Border Policing: Postmodernism and Science Fiction' *Science Fiction Studies*, Vol. 18, Part 3 (1991), 358–66.

MADDEN, WILLIAM A. 'Framing the Alices', *PMLA*, Vol. 10, Part 3 (May, 1986), 362–73.

MALEKIN, PETER '"What Dreams May Come": Relativity and Perception in Doris Lessing's *Briefing For A Descent Into Hell*' in Donald E. Morse et al. (eds) *Celebrating the Fantastic: Selected Papers from the Tenth Anniversary International Conference on the Fantastic in the Arts* (Westport, Conn.: Greenwood, 1992), 73–9.

MANLOVE, C.N. (ed.) *The Impulse of Fantasy Literature* (London: Macmillan, 1983).

MASSEY, IRVING *The Gaping Pig: Literature and Metamorphosis* (London: University of California Press, 1976).

MCCAFFERY, LARRY (ed.) *Storming the Reality Studio* (Durham, NC: Duke University Press, 1991).

MEIGS, MARY 'Falling Between the Cracks' in Karla Jay and Joanne Glasgow (eds) *Lesbian Texts and Contexts: Radical Revisions* (New York: New York University Press, 1990), 28–38.

MILLER, NANCY K. (ed.) *The Poetics of Gender* (New York: Columbia University Press, 1986).

MILNER, JOSEPH O'BEIRBE and LUCY FLOYD MORCOCK MILNER (eds) *Webs and Wardrobes: Humanist and Religious World Views in Children's Literature* (Lanham, MD: University Press of America, 1987).

MOI, TORIL *Sexual/Textual Politics* (London: Methuen, 1985).

MOI, TORIL (ed.) *The Kristeva Reader* (Oxford: Basil Blackwell, 1986).

MORSE, DONALD E., MARSHALL B. TYMN and CSILLA BERTHA (eds) *Celebrating the Fantastic: Selected Papers from the Tenth Anniversary International Conference on the Fantastic in the Arts* (Westport, Conn.: Greenwood, 1992).

MOSS, ANITA 'Sacred and Secular Visions of Imagination and Reality in Nineteenth Century British Fantasy for Children' in Joseph O'Beirbe Milner and Lucy Floyd Morcock Milner (eds) *Webs and Wardrobes: Humanist and Religious World Views in Children's Literature* (Lanham, MD: University Press of America, 1987), 65–78.

NICHOLAISEN, W.F.H. 'Time in Folk-Narrative' in Venetia J. Newall (ed.) *Folklore Studies in the Twentieth Century: Proceedings of the Centenary Conference of the Folklore Society* (Woodbridge: D.S. Brewer, 1980), 314–17.

NEWALL, VENETIA J. (ed.) *Folklore Studies in the Twentieth Century: Proceedings of the Centenary Conference of the Folklore Society* (Woodbridge: D.S. Brewer, 1980).

NODELMAN, PERRY (ed.) *Touchstones: Reflections on the Best in Children's Literature, Vol. 1* (West Lafayette: Children's Literature Association, 1985).

OLIVER, KELLY (ed.) *Ethics, Politics, and Difference in Julia Kristeva's Writing* (New York: Routledge, 1993).

OPIE, IONA and PETER 'Certain Laws of Folklore' in Venetia J. Newall (ed.) *Folklore Studies in the Twentieth Century: Proceedings of the Centenary Conference of the Folklore Society* (Woodbridge: D.S. Brewer, 1980), 65–70.

PALUMBO, DONALD 'Sexuality and the Allure of the Fantastic in Literature' in Donald Palumbo (ed.) *Erotic Universe: Sexuality and Fantastic Literature* (Westport, Conn.: Greenwood, 1986), 1–17.

PARRINDER, PATRICK (ed.) *Science Fiction: A Critical Guide* (London: Longman, 1979).

PARRINDER, PATRICK *Science Fiction: Its Criticism and Teaching* (London: Methuen, 1980).

PARRINDER, PATRICK *The Failure of Theory: Essays on Criticism and Contemporary Fiction* (Brighton: Harvester, 1987).

PETERSEN, CALVIN R. 'Time and Stress: *Alice in Wonderland*', *Journal of the History of Ideas*, Vol. 46, Part 3 (July–September 1985), 427–33.

PETZOLD, DIETER 'Fantasy Fiction and Related Genres', *Modern Fiction Studies*, Vol. 32, No.1 (Spring 1986), 11–20.

PROBYN, ELSPETH 'Technologizing the Self: A Future Anterior for Cultural Studies' in Lawrence Grossberg et al. (eds) *Cultural Studies* (New York: Routledge, 1992), 501–11.

PROPP, VLADIMIR *Morphology of the Folktale*, trans. Laurence Scott (Austin: University of Texas Press, 1968).

PUNTER, DAVID *The Literature of Terror: A History of Gothic Fictions from 1765 to the Present Day* (London: Longman, 1980).

PUNTER, DAVID *The Hidden Script: Writing and the Unconscious* (London: Routledge & Kegan Paul, 1985).

RABKIN, ERIC S. (ed.) *Fantastic Worlds: Myths, Tales and Stories* (Oxford: Oxford University Press, 1979).

RACKIN, DONALD *Alice's Adventures in Wonderland and Through the Looking-Glass: Nonsense, Sense and Meaning* (New York: Twayne, 1991).

RANK, OTTO *The Double: A Psychoanalytic Study* (Chapel Hill: University of North Carolina Press, 1971).

RICHARDS, ANGELA (ed.) *The Penguin Freud Library, Vol. 11, On Metapsychology* (Harmondsworth: Penguin, 1991).

RIMMON-KENAN, SHLOMITH (ed.) *Discourse in Psychoanalysis and Literature* (London: Methuen, 1987).

ROHRLICH, RUBY and ELAINE HOFFMAN BARUCH (eds) *Women in Search of Utopia: Mavericks and Mythmakers* (New York: Schoken Books, 1984).

ROSE, JACQUELINE 'Julia Kristeva – Take Two' in Kelly Oliver (ed.) *Ethics, Politics, and Difference in Julia Kristeva's Writing* (New York: Routledge, 1993), 41–61.

ROSINSKY, NATALIE *Feminist Futures: Contemporary Women's Speculative Fiction* (Ann Arbor: UMI Research Press, 1984).

RUBENSTEIN, ROBERTA *The Novelistic Vision of Doris Lessing: Breaking the Forms of Consciousness* (Urbana: University of Illinois Press, 1979).

RUDDICK, NICHOLAS (ed.) *State of the Fantastic: Studies in the Theory and Practice of Fantastic Literature and Film* (Westport, Conn.: Greenwood, 1992).

RUSSELL, CLAIRE 'A Study of the Folk Symbolism of Kinship: The Tooth Image' in Venetia J. Newall (ed.) *Folklore Studies in the Twentieth Century: Proceedings of the Centenary Conference of the Folklore Society* (Woodbridge: D.S. Brewer, 1980), 366–70.

RUSSO, MARY *The Female Grotesque: Risk, Excess and Modernity* (New York: Routledge, 1994).

SALESNE, PIERRE 'Hélène Cixous' *Ou l'art de l'innocence*: The Path to You' in Susan Sellers (ed.) *Writing Differences: Readings From the Seminar of Hélène Cixous* (Milton Keynes: Open University Press, 1988), 113–26.

SANDERSON, STEWART 'Why Was It A de Soto?' in Venetia J. Newall (ed.) *Folklore Studies in the Twentieth Century: Proceedings of the Centenary Conference of the Folklore Society* (Woodbridge: D.S. Brewer, 1980), 371–9.

SCEATS, SARAH and GAIL CUNNINGHAM (eds) *Image and Power: Women in Fiction in the Twentieth Century* (London: Longman, 1996).

SCHLOBIN, ROGER C. (ed.) *The Aesthetics of Fantasy Literature and Art* (Brighton: Harvester Wheatsheaf, 1982).

SCHOLES, ROBERT *Structural Fabulation: An Essay on Fiction of the Future* (London: Notre Dame University Press, 1975).

SCHOLES, ROBERT and ERIC S. RABKIN *Science Fiction: History, Science, Vision* (Oxford: Oxford University Press, 1977).

SCOTT, CAROLE 'Limits of Otherworlds: Rules of the Game in Alice's Adventures and the Jungle Books' in S.R. Gannon and R.A. Thompson (eds) *Work and Play in Children's Literature: Selected Papers from the 1990 International Conference of the Children's Literature Association* (San Diego: San Diego State University Press, 1990), 20–4.

SELDEN, RAMAN and PETER WIDDOWSON *A Reader's Guide to Contemporary Literary Theory* (Hemel Hempstead: Harvester Wheatsheaf, 1993).

SELLERS, SUSAN (ed.) *Writing Differences: Readings From the Seminar of Hélène Cixous* (Milton Keynes: Open University Press, 1988).

SHOWALTER, ELAINE (ed.) *The New Feminist Criticism* (London: Virago, 1986).

SHOWALTER, ELAINE *Sexual Anarchy: Gender and Culture at the Fin de Siècle* (London: Bloomsbury, 1991).

SHUMAKER, CONRAD '"Too Terribly Good to be Printed": Charlotte Gilman's *The Yellow Wallpaper*', *American Literature*, Vol. 57, No. 4 (1985), 588–99.

SKURA, MEREDITH ANNE *The Literary Use of the Psychoanalytic Process* (New Haven: Yale University Press, 1981).

SPENCER, KATHLEEN 'Naturalizing the Fantastic: Narrative Technique in the Novels of Charles Williams', *Extrapolation*, Vol. 28, No. 1 (1987), 62–74.

SPENCER, KATHLEEN, L 'Purity and Danger: *Dracula*, the Urban Gothic and the Late Victorian Degeneracy Crisis', *ELH*, No. 1 (Spring 1992), 197–225.

SPRAGUE, CLAIRE and VIRGINIA TIGER (eds) *Critical Essays on Doris Lessing* (Boston: G.K. Hall, 1986).

SPRAGUE, CLAIRE *Rereading Doris Lessing: Narrative Patterns of Doubling and Repetition* (Chapel Hill: University of North Carolina Press, 1987).

SPRENGNETHER, MADELON '(M)other Eve: Some Revisions of the Fall in Fiction by Contemporary Women Writers' in Richard Felstein and Judith Roof (eds) *Feminism and Psychoanalysis* (Ithaca, NY: Cornell University Press, 1989), 298–322.

STALLYBRASS, PETER and ALLON WHITE *The Politics and Poetics of Transgression* (London: Methuen, 1986).

SULEIMAN, SUSAN RUBIN 'Pornography, Transgression and the Avant-Garde: Bataille's *Story of the Eye*' in *The Poetics of Gender* ed. Nancy K. Miller (New York: Columbia University Press, 1986), 117–36.

SUVIN, DARKO *Metamorphoses of Science Fiction* (New Haven: Yale University Press, 1979).

SWINFEN, ANN *In Defence of Fantasy: A Study of the Genre in English and American Literature Since 1945* (London: Routledge & Kegan Paul, 1984).

TATAR, MARIA *Off With Their Heads!: Fairytales and the Culture of Childhood* (Princeton: Princeton University Press, 1992).

TETEL, MARCEL 'Carnival and Beyond', *L'Esprit Créature*, Vol. 21, Part 1 (1981), 88–104.

THOMAS, R.R. 'The Strange Voices in the *Strange Case*: Dr Jekyll, Mr Hyde and the Voices of Modern Fiction' in William Veeder and Gordon Hirsch (eds) *Dr Jekyll and Mr Hyde After One Hundred Years* (Chicago: University of Chicago Press, 1988), 73–90.

TODOROV, TZVETAN *The Fantastic: A Structural Approach to a Literary Genre*, trans. Richard Howard (Ithaca, NY: Cornell University Press, 1975).

TOLKIEN, J.R.R. 'Tree and Leaf' in *The Tolkien Reader* (New York: Ballantine, 1966), 1–84.

TURNER, JENNY 'Travels in Cyber-reality', *Guardian Weekend*, 18 March 1995, 28–34.

TWITCHELL, JAMES B. *Dreadful Pleasures: An Anthology of Modern Horror* (New York: Oxford University Press, 1985).

TYMN, MARSHALL B. *Horror Literature: An Historical Survey and Critical Guide to the Best of Horror* (New York: R.R. Bowker, 1981).

VASBINDER, SAMUEL H. 'Aspects of Fantasy in Literary Myths About Lost Civilizations' in Roger C. Schlobin (ed.) *The Aesthetics of Fantasy Literature and Art* (Brighton: Harvester Wheatsheaf, 1982), 192–210.

VEEDER, WILLIAM 'Children of the Night: Stevenson and Patriarchy' in William Veeder and Gordon Hirsch (eds) *Dr Jekyll and Mr Hyde After One Hundred Years* (Chicago: University of Chicago Press, 1988), 108–55.

VEEDER, WILLIAM and GORDON HIRSCH (eds) *Dr Jekyll and Mr Hyde After One Hundred Years* (Chicago: University of Chicago Press, 1988).

VEEDER, WILLIAM 'Who Is Jane? The Intricate Feminism of Charlotte Perkins Gilman', *Arizona Quarterly*, Vol. 44, No. 3 (Autumn 1988), 40–79.

WAELTI-WALTERS, JENNIFER *Fairy Tales and the Female Imagination* (Montreal: Eden Press, 1982).

WHITE, ALLON 'Pigs and Pierrots: The Politics of Transgression in Modern Fiction', *Raritan*, Vol. 2, Part 2 (Fall 1981), 51–70.

WHITTAKER, RUTH *Doris Lessing* (London: Macmillan, 1988).

WINNICOTT, CLARE, RAY SHEPHERD, MADELEINE DAVIS (eds) *D.W. Winnicott: Psycho-Analytic Explorations* (London: Karnac Books, 1989).

WISEMAN, MARY BITTNER *The Ecstasies of Roland Barthes* (London: Routledge, 1989).

WOLMARK, JENNY *Aliens and Others: Science Fiction, Feminism and Postmodernism* (Hemel Hempstead: Harvester Wheatsheaf, 1993).

WRIGHT, ELIZABETH (ed.) *Feminism and Psychoanalysis: A Critical Dictionary* (Oxford: Basil Blackwell, 1992).

YATES, ROBERT 'A Wee Hard Kernel of Cynicism: Iain Banks Talks of Tories and Space Ships', *Observer*, 20 August 1995, 16.

ZIJDERVELD, ANTON C. *Reality in a Looking-Glass: Rationality Through an Analysis of Traditional Folly* (London: Routledge & Kegan Paul, 1982).

ZIPES, JACK *Fairy Tales and the Art of Subversion: The Classical Genre for Children and the Process of Civilization* (New York: Routledge, 1991).

# Index